ON THE EDGE

ON THE EDGE

Collected Long Poems

KENNETH KOCH

ALFRED A. KNOPF   NEW YORK   2007

THIS IS A BORZOI BOOK
PUBLISHED BY ALFRED A. KNOPF

Copyright © 2007 by the Kenneth Koch Literary Estate

All rights reserved. Published in the United States by Alfred A. Knopf,
a division of Random House, Inc., New York, and
in Canada by Random House of Canada, Limited, Toronto.

www.aaknopf.com

Knopf, Borzoi Books, and the colophon are registered trademarks of
Random House, Inc.

All of the poems in this book originally appeared in the following:
Ko was originally published by Grove Press in 1959.
When the Sun Tries to Go On was originally published by Black Sparrow Press in 1969.
The Duplications was originally published by Random House in 1977.
"Impressions of Africa" and "On the Edge" are from *On the Edge*,
originally published by Viking Penguin, Inc. in 1986.
"Seasons on Earth" is from *Seasons on Earth*, originally published by
Penguin Books, Inc. in 1987.

Library of Congress Cataloging-in-Publication Data
Koch, Kenneth, 1925–2002.
On the edge : collected long poems / by Kenneth Koch.—1st ed.
p. cm.
"This Is a Borzoi Book"—T.p. verso.
ISBN 978-0-307-26284-4
1. Title.
PS3521.O27O49 2007
811'.54—dc22
2007024041

Manufactured in the United States of America
First Edition

CONTENTS

A NOTE ON THE TEXT

On the Edge: Collected Long Poems presents Kenneth Koch's six longer poems in the order of their composition, dating from 1953 to 1987.

During Koch's lifetime, these poems appeared (mainly) as separate volumes and therefore were not included in *The Collected Poems*, which gathers his ten books of shorter poems.

On the Edge is the companion volume to *The Collected Poems* (2005). Together they serve as the definitive editions of Kenneth Koch's published poetic work.

When the Sun Tries to Go On

And, with a shout, collecting coat hangers
Dour rebus, conch, hip,
Ham, the autumn day, oh how genuine!
Literary frog, catch-all boxer, O
Real! The magistrate, say "group," bower, undies
Disk, poop, *Timon of Athens.* When
The bugle shimmies, how glove towns!
It's Merrimac, bends, and pure gymnasium
Impy keels! The earth desks, madmen
Impose a shy (oops) broken tube's child—
Land! why are your bandleaders troops
Of is? Honk, can the mailed rose
Gesticulate? Arm the paper arm!
Bind up the chow in its lintel of sniff.
Rush the pilgrims, destroy tobacco, pool
The dirty beautiful jingling pyjamas, at
Last beside the stove-drum-preventing oyster,
The "Caesar" of tower dins, the cold's "I'm
A dear." O bed, at which I used to sneer at.
Bringing cloth. O song, "Dusted Hoops!" He gave
A dish of. The bear, that sound of pins. O French
Ice cream! balconies of deserted snuff! The hills are
Very underwear, and near "to be"
An angel is shouting, "Wilder baskets!"

For, yes! he helped me collect our bathers
At the white Europe of an unchanged door
Sea, the pun of "chair"
Lowing the flight-seducing moderate
Can. Treat. Hat-waitress city of water
The in-person tunes, drum flossy childhood
Banana-ing the change-murals off winter
Shy. Hay when when shy. Sick murals. Each
In call tone returns his famous cigarette
In labels the Easter cow stubbed man
Is winter the water treats its gusts, we

Love, up! sigh there is a daw truth, the
Manner singing, "Doe, O flight of pets
And hen of the angel!" black sobs to your poets.
Soda, as Wednesday of the east
Vanishing "Rob him
Of the potato's fast guarantee, court
Of Copernican season planes! O bland
Holly!" The breathing semblance of batteries
To five youth-artists . . . "Is it this inspired
That he runs the tree of bather? Watchman?
Glue." It is, fashion, they have up timidity
South, and the lain thorn, too. A lover's decency
In, bank! We: four: "Paint was everyone's top!"

Bomb, thank you for writing to me.
Oat sad, it was a day of cursing blue
Fish, they reunited so the umpire to finish
The exhaustion of the Packard and tarantula
Parallel excursion. O black black black black back,
Under the tea, how a lid's munificent rotation
Is that, he cries, "The daffodil, tire, say-so,"
O manufacture-clams building! Some days are
A fox of coolness and crime. Blot! Blot!
The wind, daisy, O "Call me up, I am
Listing beneath the telephone bat, some
Drum, death and resurrection," what hay ballpark
To forward the punch-mints! O hat theory
Of the definite babies and series of spring
Fearing the cow of day admonished tears
That sigh, "Blue check. The tan of free councils
Cloaks the earth is hen blond, oh want
The dye-bakers' coke and hilly plaza, too
Sunny, bee when halls key tuba plaza corroboration
Mat nickels." O tell us the correction, bay
Ex-table, my cocoa-million dollars! Next
To. O dare, dare-Pullman car! The best way

4

You howling confetti, is "Easter tray,
As moat-line, promise." How teach the larks!

And, dame! Kong swimming with my bets,
Aladdin, business, out Chanukah of May bust
Sit rumors of ethereal business coo-hill-green
Diamonds, moderns modesty. "There sit
The true the two hens of out-we-do maiden
Monastery belongs to (as! of!) can tin up off cities
Ware fizzle dazzle clothes belong (hand) the hearse
Walls bee bleed, pond ancient youth!" Who're
The den from coffee hanky *hofbrau*, at
Hint-magistrate. O bursar, off
Dollar rainwear, the itch; majesty summer that
Cough lady climate. Magisterial dandy. Apes. Ducks.
"Wanting, Satan, to mark glow-Virginia
A stair, this doe, Virginia. The sea cots
Magisterial lent 'who're' dodos. Aga Khan!
Mutt! the saint of perfect 'more oh' limpidity
Sand, 'bower,' hot, lens, O jetties
And sun rows, calming the Endymion, fair, peaches'
Aspirin" hare, "lewd 'ain't him' summer hat hit
Dulls." They are bottles looser than, pow! hair
Open-necked Kokoschka, leaf, deers, and.
Ashes. Lights. Who bouquet of till stomach
Llama-periwinkle, engine! as under the
Lore "happy mew" inventive "haven't" stalls sprint.

"O goddess handkerchief quartette and the pyramids
How uncommon is your silence amid the pimples
Of today where a skirt pencils your dismay
To the blankets of seemly wind, log-rolling
Foolishly the polka dots of this purged atmosphere
From everywhere, darling time limits! she-planes, and
Pear-planes! O closet of devoted airplanes
How dismissed the reciprocating Congo has to seem

Amid these pans! Ha ha they are the pyramid
Of my strings' dorothy weak hell of youth
Mango, cob, district, lode, shimmy, charmed banks
On a bin of streets." Is Moscow walk,
O lacks? I noticed you on an
Unbearably fast Pullman train, you
Muttered, "India," and bicycles parked in snow
Near the pancake's face, graceless perimeter
Of Count "Blotter," and Prince "Dit-
To," O "O pray"-rhyming cow manufacturer,
Began to wear, science and youth, oh
A pin's aspect, *The Merchant of Venice*. O sods
Of the blameless Atlantic! O murder of the tools
The cosmopolitan lint. Now. Rose bastardy
Millions and millions. She lends me the
Militia of. Bent cow pastures cough grape lights.

A horse is waiting for the submarine's
Feathery balcony. The hollow castle, like a boat
Filled with silliness, is more sand than flag, its
Loose earl phones, "I am dedicating this stanza to you
Marching prince of hacienda quoits. In each bank
An October of pitiful sand is going to be hidden,
Like the midafternoon quietude of the elephant
Who wishes to be indentured, the foolish cosmos
Of the conch for a "soon patter" 's ear life, lad
Of penny, ear, and dock roses, and went to
Ran, sheep, kindness! O black kindness of the hot
Bugle sea-pal ditch-mite hem-location of
Pre-glove. Each birthday momentous peach stanza
Its bother. Llama llama llama llama llama, D,
A, B, O, F, C. Guns
Of pill will! Lint! Where it shows sane
Cat air bench, yas, dash, hoop, *Hamlet*
Of dirty cow-epigram refills, O why are we here?
Bench, dirt, majesty, science, flu, pier,

Sin of "at"s, boo, billboard's ragged canto
Ocean, bitch! "Lousy mineral that makes me shy
Of steering hot flags, mud, who, tin, blue
E calm April hat sky." Hour of. The. Hour
Bong! spins of denying catechisms, Persian pins!

In the St. Patrick's Day parade
I saw a pillow there. It had financial
Dogs! the earthworks did film its plaza! O cross
Head of the pennies' infant rubber sweet
Unglazed pyramidal announcing shaggy deserted melodies
Of "Kismet!" For who now talks of fate? O backs
Of the leaf resisters, blond south of tea
Remembering the bouncy fox Oh night at now he
The office Indian, bingo! What bashful brute
Hints, Oh they are sobbing, kings
Of everything, from aspirin to shoes, and that's
Because, locks of rhubarb with tin
Joys, town of the hateful bust, "Is," ant
Monitor like a sentence's Chinese
Terse cloud. "Weight, honk of deceiving bats, O shelves
Of the earth's tiniest bridges, the memory of short
Faces, are there still linens in your places
Crossword palaces blankets or bent crowds
Of rats, like a billion speeding prescriptions
For gout! O mass of closed bores! Knock
Knock." "The memory of finance is bare, like
A rock substituting for pencils in
A Midsummer Night's Dream." The crow
Flies, but. Harbor. Gold. I am straightening the lilies!

The hill passes for college life. Oh! My
Silver socks in this state of frost. The bed
As of course. The bin of cleavage hat low forest
Adze. A Canada of deceiving forest
Whose hail is the bench of golf links likes

The bad Egypt of a. Howdy, house! Gorilla.
Youth. Fable. Detective. Fur fur fur fur, fur
Midnight. Oh he shot out him like China vast detective
Yelp coop. Dance. Dance a. Bitter California
Of hen-walls, feet, and. Orchard. Ocean.
Oh speed the bench, the district has climates of thyme,
Banquets of fortune, stiff dictators of pep!
Yo-yo, that hen-weaving uniforms, O cloudburst!
"Him, nog, bad, evil, dump, soup, clogs
Stichomythia of brocaded hogs. Show me the yell-planets
Of calked mud and disintegrated satisfy show-people uppers
Of dynamo-isty troglodyte fanny
Mill hock, Jutes, and yell-fanciers
Of many scientific clue-desisters matches prints
On lonely flotsam hoops beside the maggot dusk
Of parachuting dampness, figurative
As lost mints,—howl, sea! The barrow of fulgurating
Plinths are unupbraided by the fat
Kittens of uniform lightning." Sheets mortify!

Is there nothing that gives that "in" a clue,
No moth or beautiful "sock" flower? Wigs, O
Tables of plastered asters, mastery
Of the wig-and-dog show, "But there's no breast here
Of limp or smoky factories, like a cot
Of seasonal folks, the benedicts' brightest, hate!
Lethal. Haps. Ocean bitter song phone cows
Delvage fog's." I see the cancer in your poetry,
Sunflower! O the hair-raising cuckoos in a flake
Of snow, they are bending the rifles in Caucasia now
While while. "The underwear finishes snow
Lately, of outstanding Finland. Earth. Wire. Mottos.
The fish are as warm as painted suggestions
For finishing. Hill. Hip." Oboe! Rebus!
Preposterous rhinoceros of a pilgrim's happiness
At being chef! O tan, bonfire of time's worsted ships!

Your feet in marriage! "We" is being offered as a
"Chicken coop." "Well" is a "bare
Night," "too" is a "cashier's first blossom
Crossing the soft marine Atlantic as the bosom
Of *cheval* and deepest classicism
Wants the cold and bay-leafed sitting room
Of room" and the "day" is "neck of east
Living beyond," "shower" is "blank peanut, the calm sheep's force."

Blanch tepee rose agora wheelbarrow filled when
Lace temerity ex-"gyp the blond
Stair toe sky's morose tea" clouds, lover
From the sixth Caspian, tombs, and straw, "O store
Of lambs, dream of pads, my! Bucharest of
Decaying lamps' ridged colonic soul ands tear
Pleaser, that locating Solomon, there is *Much Ado
About Nothing*,—sandwich of cars, hag! as we or
Limited true hot people lemons, Shasta is too
Faster the, sip! yo-yo! holly! wheat! man ho high he
Blimp on top of Canada demon, nineteenth, lace, and
Scoptophilia of deserting pins, "I forgot he was dead!
They passed me on the way to my own funeral
Of top hats' tree don Samara cocoa Western heart and
'Paper' phlogiston maps of 'pea'-steep yo-yo banners
Of 'grew' badly, the socks' man-apes, difference
Sea canyon." Hats! hacks! heads! Is buzz. An
Cow-oyster, dollars! alimony of disease-art-lemons, O
Poo, the knack of name's plate's poodle, "Ends" is
Sang, "House! mate of jim-jam corralling puce
Teak!" Out! Badder, yell-place nick and socker-
Glow, each is and, joyous handlike knickers
Cuckoo. "How could you have gone, bitter
Roistering hint glove task phone 'ache' factory hoop device?"

Spot, "kee," sun. My hand of devoted hands
Babel sick, yowl earnest "bee"-boat, seven, connote

"Yoo-hoo" of a gray, bad "bat" disk "bat" boat key
Helen, Sue, loss, sea "hoe" "doe look"
Of candour. Yards! unbalanced "Percy" yachts dew
"Harold," Otto, change "curve" troop boat "tree"
Ben, the middle of. Oh stop, dancing, "Sidney," black
Tripes! Hollow pigeons. "Loma," itching porch and meadows'
"Chinese characters from block, land odd dress, wolves'
Hill." "Bob" at sharpens "this" canoe, Betty
I'll "Molly" hick tables' dumb morrow, "fit" Cajun-
Money, South hat A.D. Maria Theresa, honds
Of blue "gal," hurting the sable boats ump George
Of receding pets "Fairy Story" act is "then" "Chloe"
S bottle E honor house banknote with stiff looks!
O blinding treason, tee-clouds "It is better to give
Banjo receive" pop, gardens! "Herb," doe, us, in, ace
"Cass Horse." Peace! pans! jonquils
Of a body's discrete jungles, nert of the duped torture journal,
"Orange Nights," where a coma's weak cigars
Sped the ice drink saving hoop, "Calm city climates
Of porch-limiting beach" a bonanza of falsefaces, to "we
On the earth, holiday of canoeing rockets
Bang." College the yo-yos. Leaf! Ape! Eldorado millions!

The worried Chelsea "runs not our dance, fee
Lymbariums," Norway my Chelsea, blunder-
Kensingtons. Ah, certain lamb of Sheba
And darkly papers, his, career-dancing cocoa
Matchsticks' genteel
Disintegrating plaza of bound, round,
Choosable tins, diamond
As the choice of carfare, hungry
Jewish flanks, tanks of chaste liquids
Sent by the Pope, O dirty youth movements
Of the wild cursing salad
Of sidewalks' bending
Few romantic ears, Sheba O hens' bonanza

Of Cuban cash registers! What bad religions,
Bowls of hat, and touring columbarium religions
Syntaxes the parachuting mysteries.
Of. Bag. Tellurium. She. Bounced. Across.
The stairs! O kremlin of distinguished blotters!
I was touching your cosine, thou best of the kittens'
Tub airy Andes oar-pardoned rooms. Despotism
Piano kimono. Calm men, an "airy frightened cars
Of peaceful me 'how is fair?' Perspiration at big clouds.
Hold the play me, again beyond the clam,
Winter. Shame. Cow. Sen." "My railroad turns blue

At the faulty whistles of your ocean, eep! mighty steamship
Of *Child Life* magazine. By the sun of bar May India clues
I fled an midnight's how droopy Silesian clock bear
Carved, sum! tea new possum Colors Change. The big beer
I drank, imagination, when, I felt. The sunrise. Other. My belt."
She puts his clothes into the conversation
As if a pearl fan-danced. She shouts, "Ice water!"
She heeds the fan-dancing of his conversation
As if police force. She shrugs off the angel
Of his interest, blossoms, grow! as though
Seamanship. There are black lintels of clouding clocks
Of banjo dust she marches against the wall.
She sacks the train of swaying logs of snow
In mint apartments, trying to be kind
As mastering easy music. There is a pound of shelves
Which she does not know where to put, therefore
Classical Greeks. As she has painted, every parcel,
So that it resembles a soldier. Shame! Wheel! Shoulder
Of needy clouds! She wanders through
Name, soda, grass day earthing
Nigh if landscape's "cold," "inch," "tough." She inner sun as
Quotes' daring bedroom, air sea
Land beau hop's "consistently" free. O "Crew of dynastic sweeps,
Mayn't we return to the filthy London of your childhood?"

In the submarine hats conversation, beds and.
Oboe den of heathen bonnet floats. Cry,
"Tube, he, S," coptic arrangement of
Pay, he give "Bernard" hill M.I. enemy
Flower. "Jane" pony, O "Russell"! That few hog wild
Saracen bakes gypsy frog "leader of counsel, who
Is brick." White hill hat fools the meadow hat
Fistula bog Greece, ad intention of begonia's
Nameless shoes. "Marsh." Eye crime your bistro,
Mad we am everything. The hot grip
Of clay rhubarb, in cozy suns, of driving birds
At pill alliances, and crazy suburbs. "Hoops
Fight me. Hot. Air. West. O lair, O tamest yak
In air beseeching clarifications' post office
Weak. Dray colossal, hip, emps one clip hasp
C-bars. O Romania!" Yes est.'s talkative brassieres
In wow-cameo flies. Dare. Toe climes
Two D, Florida lake bill-piano. Please, Bill. O
Walls of British enthusiasm. Hill-grown soup,
Time, axe, we are in. How Roman "Shirley
Who was going to place the freight-baked state
Of eight 'do-go-away's onto." Itchy sabbath
Ha, ha. I am fenced in by reluctance
Cuckoo commas, and daring "deceased fences."

Lucky the moaning caretaker, favorite the sea
And numb to dirt, exhaustion, face, each, flax,
Cologne, pitiful comic strips commingling gold
Fracas Endymion dimples with clocklike rhubarb
The cuckoo clock shouts, mad cuckoo clock
Bartender silence-creation "fills." There are.
Homily of shops "mock," dear house of yo-yos!
Horse "nay," a differing comet of yo-yos'
Balanced deserving cheese "giants" cuckoo clock
O matadors! defying and "oh," levels of sweetness's
Cheese. Blah. They are Harry, Susan, Lynn

Blotter. "Major" Blotter, with film of "Gordon"
Cuckoo clocks, the passageway to Easter. Motto:
"Cosine the defeated hips." O pazzling dizzling author
Of *Chow Face, a Nincompoop for Dogs!* "Murray,
Lyle, and Jean" Cuckoo clocks. O Madagascar
Mazda wintry tights. Sascha films
"Ellen's Back," "Eileen's Bock," "the"s, "so"s.
O sartorial "tree"-camps of demanding yo-yos'
Faces of "von Mirror" 's. Hobby. Natal. House.
"Wotan, leaf are my cuckoo clock. Show me, that imp
Cheese! He are forgotten satch bell of a glue bell,
Listener-bell." Train sigh in the "Andy" bell show-off,
Too "Yorick" "Bill." Ding dong ding dong there is the bell!

Stove! you cursing troopers of Egypt
Black, "heart"-egret, result "scowl-balcony"
Midnight, "What" bottles of, looms!
Intelligent valentines, "spent" 's, and "cap" 's!
Hoed youth, not beside. Mineral's little
"Agnes the lea, O terrible Hoo 'Kays' of frost's
My general'll coming down. So match, is
'Pet'-gown, whacking, miss, and four 'got
Ladles.' Danish." What short script "Ha Bessarabia
Ha Bessarabia." Taster of Northern Lights,
The cheerful disuse of Safety matches, the period
Of "Oh I hate the murdered streetcars'
Stove! the blanched pyramid, sounds nice, bee,
Kom Tom, hoodoo, banana class, array, likes who,
Plaza. Carolina of useful fetes O lovely soup the
Carved, gentleman, lonely, of raided springtime
Dance, cocoa-pain! Billonaire loading-guns, is
Bending myopia for glass steaks. Monster veal chops
And mint cuckoo consommé, glass bananas, glass
Oysters and peaceless bicycles, running
To, fats! the train, a glass arch remover, Ben
Loth, light rays, O shoes! 'Rather than kill

Be killed'-store of wavy nickels. Shore! See their
Little hands," the month of coat-Lambeth spare sea monsters!

"A copy of 'Chews' has ripped my cheers a pack"
"The somnolence of Genji" "Hopeful" "Engine-ski-mo
Modern" "German pea hospital" "O cloud binge"
"Country notice mother, 'll take the city
In marriage" "Baked snow" "Empirin tablets
There is a closet of every beneath" "Youthful
Marzipan" "Chow Frigidaire" Now, be uncommon
There is a package of
Red, white, and blue RATS! charging. Houseboat!
Film star! "The eating I mentioned to you
Last Thursday was totally unlimited by
Mediterranean comic billboards wordings'
Sailboats of misdirection, as if soap
'Mocks' the tea-tablets' December wrongdoing's
Bear." He was more British than an icebox. Out
The rats ripped him. Shovel. A pier
Of sudden "Flo" gladness. The minted peach-fly
Sounds, "O badger of repeated adzes,
Longtime, few, hat, het, boat, sand,
Lockers, knee, mistress of Aix, umpire with three shouts,
O blue tapeworm, sonnet of powerful indifference, nest
Of hallways of birthday sheep, soror, tie
On pretty benches lay my ore coaty head
Wind the banjo 'mock-hooped,' Andy dust 'Freemason.' "

Earthworks of genuine Pierre! Molly. Champak's. Egypt.
Esteban Vicente. Melodies'. Cow. Advance is chewing gum.
Saith Bill de Kooning, "I turned my yo-yo into a gun,
Bang Bank! Half of the war close pinstripes.
Timothy Tomato, Romulus Gun." "The magic of his
Couscous masterpiece," saith Pierre, "is apple blossoms'
Merchant marine gun." Ouch. The world is Ashbery
Tonight. "I am flooding you with catacombs,"

Saith Larry Rivers (more of him later on).
There is also some fools laying on their stomachs.
O show! merchant marine of Venice!
At lilac wears a beetle on its chest!
These modern masters chew up moths. How many drawers
Are in your chest? Moon Mullins' Moon Mullins
Put his feet in my Cincinnati apple blossoms. Many
Dry cigarettes have fallen into work's colors. The shop
Of geniuses has closed. Jane Freilicher
Might walk through this air like a French lilac,
Her maiden name is Niederhoffer, she tends the stove.
"O shouting shop, my basement's apple blossoms!"
There is a tiny drawer more hot than elbows,
Season. Number, favor, say. Old winter oh
Winter. The park is full of water veins and
Surly council members, or sad Creons. Sway, unsound airplanes!

O dog! knee-Decembers of an egg-
Sabbath, the dispensaries in a south of foods'
Mailed "bowwow" summer, peripheries. I I
That murders Carolina soup is
Stonding in the ho! of taken columns' dear
Shaken bell of fast! Mallarmé cologne's
Constantinople dove-winter. They say she travels
Like brick ontological ("bay" bay) parlor
Communist hill saber news ape, Otto, Tyrinth
And. What? sweethearts! ember district worm
Hair raising! In the submarine lost blankets
Of Commedia dell' Arte parachute loop Canada.
The dancers "took" in the forest of Egypt, yes the
Contenting Telemachus of dissenting "bough"
Sweethearts, sweet periods after summer's woe
Season red participles, O manager of Latin
Sights! the worst fevers. "O Soma, delirious hexagon!
How I have been shunted into the batter's box, rats,
On local music, shy motto, tear! sun-wafted tear!

'Brote,' brought, to Columbus!" Oh where is my origin's
Style-raising-disinterest-tack-St. Louis of
Charlemagne true day council of murdered persimmons'
"Eep"? Mother, we are dancing on the closet in
The sway defeat column comma mixed-up oxygen! "Beau!"

O the worst, owl! Car blankets the
Defeats' component lady other slim rose
Racing the bell four warmth May
Tie O banner constancies'
Sharp dens. Away! for you,
Bell! the southern mountains. "Am list" handkerchief
Yo-yo and butlers! "That science of plows
My Endymion, mind, shoes. The air
Rates gold, engine of sigh, cogs, rheumatic
Freight. My hat! His. Seven. Since. Birth of slot machines
Upon a gypsy cola." Vember. No Sept. Oct.
I am bathing the turf in airplanes,
Saith Cary Shivers. What no-man's-land of gout
Hens! "There is a sharp usk to the 'rows-
Me-out-to-his-face,' " O most twins! twins! twins!
"I folded with him shyly Madagascar,
Pots of myriads, pliable rents'
Birth airplanes, and he, he—" Sad crop of
Gentle newspapers, hog! Pleasing air of Chicago
Why, don't run toward me with the
Your handkerchief as Saturday reservations.
Oh now the train is plugging us our shirts'
Pianos', hem fractured dogs. Gold mustard!
"A day is 'what a season' is the temporal doughnut."

"But he lends wing to our murder case" ugh what
China of dancing joke books. Hairline here's the
And melody of hopey rats. Lilacs for your birthday
Sim. O are there sharecroppers of worded sweets'
Nonsense prizing Bibles of glowing beds'

Mild joy dance-incineration, rebus? O Rebus!
Coat of lobsters, flowers, menstruation, leave us
Empty out this dedicating Chaucerian passage they
Often, shower, often, weeds, "manage to cuss," said
"Sid," House of the Gifted Orphan. O bands
Of church, painters of false weeds, mommas of
Country appearance, hay's unclassified wall
Suit stock! Manners! God, General Pershing,
Itch, water, unclassified silver. But you. In.
The sands of, what—shifted bayou bombing like nets
"Samuel." Eat tea sets, love; bother. "Frank" Cuckooclock,
Welcome to the speech of hods. Oh, ow!
The silent merchant is invaded by desperate "send
Us-up-to-the-woodchuck-for-coat-she-enterprise-
Pin-clue-bock-hurt-Sven white elephant
Of pacing German Childs restaurants, at mint
Concerts to pick at sunrise 'a world's nose,' "
A daisy elephant, the merchant marine of sheds
And dancing nose, commonly "nose of sherbet and 'seems' weather.' "

The yo-yos of Paris knock together in this
In this. "We ran, shuffling, tobacco, sun, hat.
Borderline, pooly collar! Black
Lint! O China! where, poodle, savior, Negro, said,
'Happiest rose and dear buy rosin' " is,
Then they all came together again, in
Out-of-date, "kin," barefoot rose of aints
Shirtwaisted for several union. Where a pin
Montparnasse crutch, "the D.C. roses are
Fat!" Bush! Then I knew. The sixteenth
Bashful locker, the weary "Joanna"
Room Indian was my—palace of leading snow,
How there you are! with matrons
On Tokio seats' south-placated loop columbariums
Is farther gypsy. Oh notice! there are piers
Under, the, shy sweet Elaine, and along, last

Year, about this. . . . "Orchard five yards long!
O packed saviors of prickly heat! what from
'Keats' you O nut shoe bandboxing surface
Leopardskin fireproof rose magistrate, deaf
Queneau. O period of conceited shoplifting by
Sham tissue 'pay fear' that with stoves tulips,
'Meddy tears,' 'jan-quills,' and shooting Flauberts
Of 'we-fill' light, O Commonness Very of sheds!"

The yo-yo's mother is not from Paris. She dranks
"Peegs." Left you. I left you. In Russia
Blanket miller floaty. Bay day Canada mirror
Canada be to pare the floatsy rose "buy 'em"
Sudsy landslide marigold woowoo "looks like." This
At the bottom of twins. O. My paper glass
Is Sheridan Square. No, office. Daring Hoboken
Of twisted Studebakers. She fills
A Mediterranean heart with friendly costumes. Baa,
Mirrors the sheep. Nert. There is a carfare in my window
Why in after *is* blossoms. Oh. Brother of turning gold.
The cops began a workout. Cheerless silver
Matches. "A day of foreign roses the sheep
Love clowns the clouds and Major 'T Cigars'
Works and drinks." A maritime virgin sinks
Beyond the *Leslie C.* O bogs of Syrian dogs
Of marriageable playing togs, Count
Pat, there are Gemini in the faithful seminar
Of serenading teabags' windows' dynasty of hops,
Yes, bather, sermon, untire and so
I think I *can't* understand your bath, know
The Sabine film substitute outside chimpanzee meadows
Of health. That ship is hall of landslide's
Say, Dee, end Saranac ore, "what was," "tint," seas!

Mew. R. We're blood patents that weird pink
Tea—fro, runs "Silo, Bill; tea" Madam steer, shower

Of wear-me-out-in-the-feet-aspirin, satin
Trireme shoe statue might Himalayas its
Tramway scene box. Hill-dog, pay! Grab
The fennel bee of the hollow Macon Subway
New, cockroach of faded ilk, deceased rosemary
London, pens 'draped "golly," and, over
Pied sheep, damn upstairs I see sigh "No umpire
Shovels, Lambeth." Orange magic, sensibility
February amid the strawberries! Raspberries
Mutation moth of a deceptive hillbilly's
Luminous, snow, Cossack, waited, tree. Sense had
Shakes, ovary along, beach, true
Fringe of I May den chorine clockwise raspberries'
Hindrance loop of water Pindar-dependences'
Snowy Sam-a-top of wondrous Thrace
Of if of of of shy's blessings "whin" a cold
Houses of deserted aspirin, cell-less rosemary!
Cinder, hollow, China roseberry.
Rune shelves, a merest baby council-chamber
Motto: Sistine Chapel, "fair weather, fewer deserted
Anywhere comma rosaries, lime-tree ovaries
In quiet subway, hooray, 'Sue' of deceiving umpires."

Wear out Sue, and who is she, wear "Am I?"
To the shirt's dance, south of bells! And the
Myriad of con sister fan hensy. O dotes
Wear climate changes. Wear the Sistine granges!
O matador, the charming "a fear" of bells,
The masonite of deporting bills, goose affair,
Hen affair, shirtly, hoop, a client, balcony
In central "horse." Oh the sea of pipe
Criticism is a nest egg of hags'
Merchant marine shelf confusion. "District Ninety,
Howp, this is Commissioner Jimmy. Leap the darts."
Chancellor of my ballad's celluloid hearts,
Lump together! "And the bear wangled from the goose

A distant holiday, mirrors which are also shoved
High, daring hearts, and the plasma of cupidity, dire
Tin, shocking hooves." Mercenary strangers! she
Is Caspian and underwear, the sentences
Of "How pipe! how district October page nice
German loop! Gaga midgets' tornado as
Niece of. All your. January musicians of
Tan!" At summer he figures, "Tornado
Tomato, badgers of defeated licorice, some
White bloomers of breathing calamine, determined
Shoulderies of demented cobwebs, sea-high feet."

As Copenhagen, O remains of the "ear
Factory" tunes "Quiet Venice, door to seem the door
Able plaza toe, Sim, quiet orange Egypt,
O birth of the oranges, range of fells
'Coalmine'-quacking dirndls of 'thy shifting smack
Smearer than the "kill" of soup,' liberty to sigh
'Positive bracelets, of oranges, the rattlesnakes,
Forget my key, O den of deceased lemons, den
Opera quietly no-place Pullman car if lemons
Really.' " But he prints has hit is nowhere is
As defending Egypt rugs from under the moor or
"Solid beans of Stonehenge," the cow's
Mulatto imperialism, dancing "life invaded shirts,"
O merry chowdog of receding pills,
Why aren't you back at home? Emergency. His share
As bursted hens the decency "of" lemons, now
The "Blenheim" of conceited automobiles'
"Feet air" doors, a Sanscrit "lying at" his feet
Mirth filling the cat racial "doughnut" memory
Yes yes. How am I stupid dear strawberry
Mountain? Has the day "knucks" rarely
Money reason and show "sea" "hoop" cheery fountain
Of Moscow Saturdays, orchard "wain" my love
Is lemons, Norway, hamp, sure? Location bigs

The "three" soap stairs, and "my" tower sunbeams
Escaped of devoted Swedeland O sharing miss—
House "bather baby" pot, millionaire pages
Under a shouting lemons of disapproval
An military! shoes baby to take off
Lilac is courtroom cool Decimber house on
"Quaffed" judge-simplicity, Apollodorus'
Cuckoo top hat birthday landslides of
Of! Wills! O tubes of disastrous London by
North us, codpieces of benching cloud-
Blameless surf disk-formation as
Shooting the comet "Birthday" cement feet's
Doorway, "Santa," build of repeating tassel-
Commenced shirt yo-yos, unMarseilles! These say
Or after air is. "Rambling" "my pin" "the forest"
"How nigh he ware D (cooling) con Santa
Dim yay! yay!" Hopeless, bobbed air
Eighteenth "Sir Face Din" cows limb
Couscous ick's bowed maritime BABY
Sham "tree"-blamable, as midnight summertime
"Safely to film a cow with hair-beautiful-
Dense potters of shoe-breeze balcony out is
Baby to defy delicate; merchant, O talcum oranges
Of the sea-as, wholesale face at sighs wheat dove!"

"The church of spended babies is all right,"
The peanut telephones, merry peanut, "If."
Our, climate, promotion, Sundays, "If"
When the bursar's damp clubs. Shyest cups
In the spirit of sound effects, dandelion "If"
And "Stevie" asks somewhere sweet streetcar
Of street-sweet car as the valence of talcum
Moderation of cosine's talcum. "These
Lemons if, stereotyped. Buy now, in shame,
Thick quietness's first linguistic dove." Every-
Thing possessed. O donation Frank O'Hara to

Lightness. Donation, "Sea
Of quietness's dirty froth parachute with yellow
Disinterest buckaroo-plazas O shy pal
Of mirthy telephones, and gyroscopes! our bittersweet
Good-bye! The bun-sleeve hopes you with its heart!
Of plotted asters, O my faded shark! Den, feasible,
Quieter than the pinpricks in the onion
Saying 'Chicago! Chicago!,' ass from a million years
Ago!" How that dove is corduroys, and how
The ship walked through its sweetheart, "Custard
Of the Blenheim caves," he counts on screaming, first
Reason to year, up! the egg, changer the
Cosine of since, dank pool, cot, now the waves' growing tenderness!

There is a plinth I am hopping. You undress
The years, O waggons. There wind bottles
Off deceiving minnows. Frankness, deer, what sleds!
O Shalott of shaggy air, "Lumber-time," and
"Jeering, Jeering Notation." Now we are
Ours in the air! The murderess eats clams
In Norwegia, cement of our burning frankincense!
Cantata of American troubadours,
What north woods? "Outward the cuties of concrete
Pure she's-castanets, bowing toward the summery Irish
Stairway to gypsy phonetics." They murder my clouds
In your "fancy delectable conceit gyroscope
To 'tossed where we bled, ache, burning dinosaurs!' and
'Sheds of that blinding pace.' " My my-nurse,
Austria. "It was a season of candy dinosaurs;
I picked up my bottle and fell
Danger candy dinosaurs. You teach me German
Phonetics." They labeled beneath the church-road table.
That was Greece. It was the first Shasta.
He built an envelope. She watched him beneath her eyes.
"Those are lids that were his kind effects
O summery gypsy phonetics!" Now she drinks coffee.

The Irish have been murdered. For copying.
O the sailboats of her eyes, a Southern Cross!

"In growing Canadian fields of stupid iced tea
I wavered. Could I be the
Magic scoptophilia pilgrim of growing pirates'
Nest? Lackawanna Mary-go-home three million.
O January month of cloudy lightning
Future, lint of mountain hat-bag
And Ceylonic wheels, murder my postage stamp
For me!" There is a Bessarabia of guns
Pinpointing his deluded shoulder. Ouch! Tristan! Men
Calmly disturb the delicious pirate. Women
Find his grape shirts, orange
The distance is, filing, motto, pea, chariot's
Coercive May in line cuckoo clocks, that
Summer is here! "Embasket the gloated fibs,
Realize the cashier's desk, flub the sea
Of rotating pipes, hat-joyous arranger of thugs'
Repine, oh shop in the germ-surveying
Lulu-bards, plinth my hat-surveying figs'
Youth pot-parks, darling the arranges of sog-
Mittjoy is Germany weather, dank gods of
'People will knock glow home, match, symphony
And Constantinople of conceiving pods' dancing
For joy in the middle, loves' car-in-case
Sea, dirty roses of plowing space, mailman-songbook,

Earthenware, clockwork, hen-disinterested
Pittsburgh, shy mirror of hats, O
May! in the delicate burnoose of chocolate
Crayons, council chamber of tea, owls, blood,
Champagne, dear 'Old Sturbridge,'
The glass nude confined in a sailing blanket of
Hats' sun, with what curves I.
Heater, blondes of questionable space! Cow-

Fair of cheated, and nursemaid of sweet blondes!
Month of blondes! Bombs which mislead, chatter,
They *dire la malade n'est plus à deranger, ça, ça*
Alors, éteiente comme elle est, oh la la, morte, comme
La malade n'est plus bombs away sea of lurch
And cloud hill-her blondes the quiet sarsaparilla
Near a thug's twins. *The Merchant of Venice*, O
Landslide of decayed strings, shafter
Menner and gone. They talked at the
Dove, 'we' Danube, yare, mischievous yo-yos'
Plaque of recent parents the dirty cloud, mustard thrill,
'As' beach of china, a bird's cleanliness
With birds', chewing gum and (banjo of peels)
O Florida's pockmarked coast. Magic
Apes! other quiet climate inside my collar
Blondes me, hoop! knotting car fierce damped cuckoo clocks,

The stevedores banyan 'trees,' boughs, terebinth
Is longing for 'cleanliness, near or down the nights'
Rag of your night is we batters' terebinth
Of sorrowing sighs, 'Leaf, matching and cow,' the dense
Blotter, which tears, O bag! the rooms polka
Of feeding clowns', bitterness, 'ant'-terminations'
Sunrise. What is the use of disease
And this floor? O barristers in the
Europe of a blond dress, American chiefs'
Shower of bears, tears, bland
Modesty of the 'cokie's' cities' sherbet
Feathers of deknife, chowmiller and bath
Tundras, of devoted. Stare, China, at these uniform clouds.
The murdered potatoes are keeping the sun
From its sun, common marriage of simplicity with
Sulfurous. 'Ant's'-disease, is the sun. Sang 'Blondes
Of the breathing can.' Seldom 'you' buy
The sharecropper, O sea! 'Daniel of our
Lions' den,' church of dismayed lint, how tall

The periods are, Romulus and Remus of the
Joking casket! Tennis on fields of lint, 'The
Sun.' O lost back, the matadors of toothless cities!
That is 'worm-pretty.' Headless. Mayan
'Soon' of shore, the quietness of Silence Mare Show

Lamps is, monitor of a chapter-freed delphinium,
Delphos of the merry climate of 'What are rules?'
Reason, linen mead, air, ribs, oh the size of silence
Bearing shods! Let me, settee of defeated 'rows
Away, photo,' quit the Hernani and
'Tea'-deadening shower, Mazda, climate, quits,
Denver, rose 'like the black youth
Of copper, this summer's solid quince, and colleges
Of delighted silence, pin, carry me and use the
Pan complimenting your head-
Line of frozen knee-bullets' shirts'
Quietly delphinium and freedmen faces.' So,
Sorrow magic greens." The winter ends, as
A pig discovered America last night. O boys. Now.
Samuel. Ocean. Clever wisteria of logs. Hoe
Of tweet-tweet hens hat charming college-bunny
Nexus-filler, hooray-pillow, llama and
Dewy-faced limerick of charts. For pyjama.
Semantics of village, *joyaux*, buildings, "loops."
Rather. "Heaven" clutches his head. Sweet summerwear.
"Comma, I showed you different climate, whoopee
Step-the-soap stairs. Wow languorously lethal.
Tyrinth. Difficulty sweater. Parachute, nun, "Queen
Bath," oh, arrivals in the potatoes of. The city.

Sails! earth, "how perished laundry?" Bin. Clad.
Coconuts, binge, paratroopers, wheat,
Castles of dancing tattoos, even paratroopers
Of an orange's daily injustice. Malabar. Shredded Wheat.
Lemons what "few," kiln am "burr day
Umber" members deSouth, helmet, on "teached

Imagination, calm." O dirty shrapnel of conceding
Skates' first laugh "after" youth fields'
Lint queue of "sat"-bath, "after," shrapnel
New, cracks "after," bug retires. Sheeps' lackey! yo-yo!
Dock. Rays. Easel. Set Andes
Shirt-manufacturer decency of cold,
"Hens. May-nifty, motto. Donatello, sway now
Terminals," cups of French steam! April blotters
Miss you, Donatello yo-yo. O black literature! Back
India yo-yo home. Matches, wee. Colonel. Asleep.
In. Wee. Comical landslides of
Pretty legislature. Bent "lions' " Algiers, Illinois.
Conch of sashayed pill. White is appearance
Germany bathroom cow nutty ashamed personal
It's purple. Breaking into my heart like a
"Climb this blotter of permanent yellow lace,
Weary old *comédie*." Am burr lace. Desk. Pick
Up the yo-yo. After. Hebe. "Thanks," in this purple hour!

Bong! went the faery blotters; Ding Dong! the
Country of Easter! shore! each toes
The marriage bin, shouts of "Conch!" "Ruthie" "Lurks
Behind the 'pea' is basement's Illinois
Obtuse radio lithogram!" "Coptic!" and "Weak Beddoes
Less-us-the-shirt!" Ran behind me-Vishnu, all
Summer. Closet of how it seems! O bare necks
In October, closest apparent "film star" of the
Buffalo. Peter of Carolina's neatest snow-
Pier condescension. O haughty chapter how
Clear was as apparent cruelty, bonnet,
List, tackles the lace. Hump chariots the summer
Either desires. Ether, so tall
As ice, sees her cuckoo hooves at desire
Margin. Amour dodo cranberries. There
"Art," "blamelessly," cashes, D's, wed's hat's
HEADS! Joyous midnights, different clams!
Oh the word "flotation" 's cosined beaver rotation beneath

The "seelvery" dog-freight cars, mammoth
Stomach-quiz-raspberries we parent
Cuckoo Mary coast-disinterest verst of "cheese" diversed
Flags of the "comma stare" rewhipped
Georgia of teaching cash registers to "hat" side
Of pale "plates," the bitter "nurse" southing "ha"-green "stangs"
	forward!

O badgers, badges, bats, bags, bags is,
Black, blacks, rats is, as, is as, as, is,
Badgers as, is, is, bridges', bags, bags as is
Business of the fourteen (I noticed "Henry") badgers.
Dark plantation of these furious sidewalks! First
Lifted-up usual "Mamie"-hello, dockworker,
Pancake, silliness, feet-locker, lower-class,
Power-gasp, Kokomo, dithyramb kimono. Whang
Bang! collar, bleachers, parachute, delicacy,
Noun, Janice, dental work, siren, sirens, boulevard,
Tarragon, limp May, wine, decency, earth, mountain
Sidewalks, decency, earth, sidewalks' happy sirens,
"Match wrappers! Match wrappers!" Juno, Janice,
Meat hooks, Elaine, lilacs, parapsychological
Cocoa-distinction plasm, jowls of the seedy grocer,
Monday, disinterest, sea ramparts, banjos, groups
Of pineapply-flavored Jericho lemons. Sleep, sleep.
Merchant marine O thousandth freight in Venice,
Cutie, waters, envelope, chapter, thousandth,
Frigate, sleep-resisting billboards, if mountain
Choreograph, seventeen, resisted. Maldoror,
Shirt ads, of wintry face. Council of blackest
Dogs, sleep, is slain. Cutie. Is resisted.
Visit is. Disinterest. False solomon's seal. Go to sleep.

"I arise from dreams of thee, open-air bell
Ohm tiny match his hat duke wheat son
Wild, Peru. Genji of deciding cups'
Care-cup! noun, as ash, flossy hit"; we

Are the hips of everybody's son; nat-
Urally, leaves a sun, day, choked up, read or, is
Anybody! disturbs naturally "th' sweater
Empties the feet in Yarrow. Hal is musically
Very is, jay weird sight of tomorrow
Bannisters." Surge of banditti, oh,
Sweethearts. There is a seventeenth moon deciding
Wheat-ministry-triangle-deranged churchmouse.
End tea socialist clubhouse before you begin
Eating sweaters. The pears are dancing. What rain?
Manna isthmus, dose of climate, way
Orchard noun and in the Swanee sheep. "Baked
Hats! to arrive from seams of tree
Service, town. Anne in delighted orchids. O mashed
Lakes, biers, seventieth pyre of green
New Yorks, loam 'where beautiful
As Eden, voodoo shades in Charleston religion? "Sue"
Weak, daring, America,' " and the raided shocks
Hobo, mean, soporific knicks. Marjoram chinchilla. O sea
By quirk, calmness, shy, "Indeed-ape," bob the thousand!

Orchard of the deceiving ant, penthouse in
Mere cunctation of "we" browing air-patience
Toreador matches-siblings "Oliver" Bowlingballs
And "Mary" Isn't-working-the-dream-downward, come home, shake
Fiery sea aspirin, as "I'm using a the Lake Poets'
Win-bandit-flowers!" From Huey's casement
March, April, and solemnity, the cool sincerity babies
Up upon chair-car, flying through nameless England! Banjo
Of peace! monthhood! ooh, Soho! yak of the German clams!
Pack of "The Diamond Ships" ' bursars-maying-cards knee
High true she "Boston" domino! "Shirt can I wear, is
The cue ball's dirtiest Delibes." O monthly
Syntax of a florist's cones, "Charles" with the blink
Face, characters from Canada! Dizzy the Charleston
As pink merchants, green you are faded yoo-hoo!
The classroom, O pitch! these surface classicism

Plotting the tube's creation from conscious mattresses'
Series of dismaying springs. O logs, manner, and T-
Square. "The horrible ditch is ended. Now
Yo-yos air parachuting flamingos, job hunters
Have breached their blue home; nominally the cuckoo
Is such a chair-far hunter. Wintry the tables blue
Deer, in the tables of Z-dancing, 'Koko' are here,
Sew, too, shun the further 'ants-eat-people.' " "Loud and bill!"

Bandana of cavey sea-tins! pyjamas! ladder on
"Eek's" bugle call of shallow GLUE, PIER, SOLDIER, and
SPILLWORT dirtiest case of the marshmallow
Sin language, merchant marine of chows! Back, lurid
Leaf of the Chair FINANCE! O
Santa Claus can heaps behoove love cemetery
Gypsy. Market of playing Beans' Research, Baa
Lethal tagsheep. Erp. "Kill my shabby
Dog with careless BEANS. Or jellybeans
Will complicate four research-
Pilgrims in, lazier than the, GREEN
Rebus of opium. Oh, daze!" Why shirts came RED
As youth ex-Canadas, shallow doggest dream—
Lamp, "Sunday I boxed a COLITIS pinprick,
Shore!" Ugh-row of the lazy-towels-when,
GERMANY and CALIFORNIA again! The RIGHT
Beans hill know a banjo toga-conference
Disinterest. Sherman for president! Surface
Chow, O green! air, go away. BATTERS
Up! "She decides to become the climate
Of ARABIA, she bannisters two CALIFORNIA and
Diamonds. Sense-tea-wear bay dun off oof focus
And becomes WELL-BEING, the turtle
Of grace, knickers, and cactus. SHE has no colitis!"

O Barrymore, the choosing of a place
Beside the Russia of dirt's Coliseum. ADS

For nothing! chowdog chowdog as "this" hearing aid!
Manhattan, you are the author!
Blankets, chancellors, film-dogs, nurse-waves, banjo-
Stevedores so cashmere as red, O billboards the
Passage of "gorge" delicious-makeup season
Shasta of pirates' disinterest "tornados" and
"Shack of hued blimps!" O best
Bench, Bessarabia. They are watching the feet on
My eyes; the dust is resenting halva, "Marriage
Of Figure." Oyster had gherkins and his eyes
Were breathing like the Chesapeake and Ohio
Railroad. Dog pats him to slip, certain lilies
Of Canada blind HIM. God, what an awful night
To be the terrible illness of Southey's dog!
They are picking out some lanterns is Nephritite
Dirndl is connoted handkerchiefs. Why, Violet!
You here among the summers' dogs? "White?" "Why an
Heartache isk more total than bananas'
Windy" violets freeze! Say, there is a
Sharecropper of total blackness. Uncle Steven's
Hat! We never expected kin to blouse
Arabic, up! O "Ladislaus, the loss is gone to sleep!"

He: "The strawberries are putting." She: "Brilliant Egypt,
I wonder about the ladies' dancing carfare
That Percival said was 'baby us, brilliant oranges!'
They say for my sake she wore a silver kerchief!"
Bill! How Mordred to Arthur you my handy gear
Of fair sexiness, she thinks. He places: "Lock
In the baby of you fair oranges. Lock
In the baby. O doubts, mirlitons and foghorns!
They say he had appeared to be a bench,
But Canada toured him in her brilliant pockets
And he became her 'Solitude,' a large, furbished painting
That used no hands the way anciently oranges
Listed to the bugle call's left." Allah, frogslegs!

They are so tear-bitten! Water as lovable clues
Deceives-as lines there cuffs showering "purple
Scientists who tea their frost"; lobster,
Why haven't you been invited to the painting?
"I was too cross, and too yellow. They really
Aren't the two you sawed in half yesterday. Watch
My pins!" Lands! I saw a lobster leap the gas range,
A merchant of March. "She sold me two red kimonos,"
A dear thinks, "and yet, when I walked the Allahplaza
Remembering dirt kangaroos, I forget my name.
Is it 'Shorty,' or 'Polly,' or 'Julie'? Oh it may I am the nurse!"

O soul of all my life, ah solo flight
Beyond the Mexican blue! "It is predicted
Giraffe-gorilla-that-I-am-to-be-killed. Lethe
Corral me 'now' the burnoose other blue
Landslide!" Mud, tortoise, the Japanese fighters!
Good Bound-Face wrote "taxi" the hall December
Ladies'-club-youthful Frigidaire-men's-room red
Chanukah of a donated judge, to see
The Canadian pottery, "bee" was so characteristic-
Ally lacking in "these" persimmon-decorum of
Loud, that that. Oh many was the "hick of cancel worms!"
Her quiet wig was a parachute. Stones!
O the bad answers through a bin of petite ruins
Shines! "Magic. Earthface. Geranium. Bad-
En-Baden of pretty sharks, yo-yo-column pin
Buying teas. O the mastery of his fenestrated
Shark!" Yo-yo said: "Die, Patty, of disease
Blossoming larger than 'we're'-tarts barking silt
Now in the midst of raspberry-time, which gophers' exile
Is merely a hack window, jumped down in the back
Love believing blouse, song cheery velveteen,
Mocking rose of gifting satin. Beds. Some
Deerparks." Day lifted their skeletons.
They came to the blossoming veteran; and fancied beer.

And terebinth, lobster of this season. Mudlark!
Oh, barriers were shooting, the billionth
Coffee of "wonderfully" dizzy tea. "Man, or
Cosmopolite, lair is the bird of mints'
Island. Balcony cosine of the hays." Each
Forgets to mention "that frozen candy." Birthday.
I am so happy that I could split
Fire engines, to know that blue is here.
I wonder if lobsters have always known how it felt
To care for the midway at most candy
Beer. Either, yes, tomorrow, is evil, or
I ain't feel it. There was "wonderful" chow
Last night. We barefoot the enemy. Glad
I have like her gold, yet glad
That, and serious tomorrows at silver toes
Free Island. O Danube! mirth, at
Tennis, was "the lea." They "danced" with me.
"I gladdened this worried Catholic bishop
Summer!" Daring Wotan, the King Lear of my
Courtship! For he is bringing "chairs" in the
House. His barrister walks: "Fading rose,
Mummer of the shy weird golden fingers',
Eighteen, a deserved aspirin. College
Is nice!" In that month, youth carried each frigate!

Monsters label his hill: "Mantle Hill, Cuckoo,
Air, Moth. Their gorgeous Philippines
Is friends of Ireland. Ask 'Herbert,' lowdy,
The weak cosmopolis of raspberry sherbet." Some
Time ago I forget about all proportion. These are
Crumbs. They dance. Its sleeping state. "Wonderful chow"!
O marriage with coastlines of aspirin. I taste
Them, "howdy, airplanes." This nice reason
Their chair hat my finger, is "don't," summer! Gee whiz
Of curtains, has lariat of she Fig Newtons'
Really. Ha ha. Are you hysterical,

Lefty, now? With what reason does your hat
Come out into the sleepy bottom
Up the Canada river, the merchandise, "Alf," dossier
Is late church. When last night we separated water;
And May-time habit clutched at tennis. These yes-
Whites! O odge, pyjamas! Marriage of recent white
With bear shooters, the Mississippi. Gin of cares,
Plower. O Jeep! red white and blue
Tans, rooming is Santa's first beach, class
Of beaten Gulf Gas, murders! Constant
Constant mad mad. Hen! engine of rejoicing gin!
There is a big airplane running O my
Blimp, across the defeated Mexicos of aspirin!

Daylight, now, this wreath of hogs.
Oh, there's a burglar called Smoky.
The bugle call is managed thunderware, the babes
In arms have all been turned to Octobers, with
Baskets in their shoes. I know this "are":
Baskets, murder, ending shoes. Each taxiing lobster
Knows that baby, she is as delicious as an orange
Blimp. Night! Tanager! O tuxedo
May conceited lobster! guarantee is orange
As "Molly's in the rowboat." Guarantee
Me the badness of each sharing strawberry
Of notes. She as taking out her under "Where
Are logs, cannibals, and sheep? Is this the
Malice, good summer! of a yo-yo's streetcar?"
Oh I lay on their bed, in the beginning, at the
Baseball. Carry me, Mary Ann, carry me!
You may think each hair is phonograph
But Canada of delighted wrong. Borrow you are
Blue. Blue out came to meet the bar
Flotsam gypsy earthwear reading, can
Of German blossoms, dentists in Cincinnati
Fancy attitudes, cotton to defeating summer.

"Nancy, Georgia is now quiet. Pale win-
Ter duck, meet limbo. May, hen, oh, Mississippi!

Military 'where are?' youthless, inks
Well 'git' mad, O sharp! Not 'over-where'?" and
Either youthless syrup. They man could buy
Location-qualify to "hees" lemons Jan lay on
Oyster melon charge account Epidauros. Match
Us, we, first inks: giant, cuckoo, and red, but
Maced gold, O sweetness of deceded chemistry
Marry. O the sweetness of braided celery on
Tile badgers, "he is the funeral of any cat.
O courts! March was 'hen' whist 'yew' ear
Funeral, cat." "In the mission house through Mondays'
Mission powders of marvelous pink (Death air death
In the Deathhouse) (Leap!) missionary
Cuckoo, loves, ape, mortuary, defeat, is almshouse
'Mary' House, we days of long
Thirst, cuckoo clocks sandy as green
Germany mouse Northrop. Ivy, win, you, say.
The America of—cocoa, ash, bin, ivy." "Nude,
Bandits, mouse, rosemary" "Wintry is the silence" "Marshmallows"
A. Lurid chances, stop. Fishing carefare.
"Indian bench *malade*. Wheat. Amble south
Is amble." "He wears the sweetest bench
Of bandits American is the world." Dancing
Of of. Oh! Loud, ant, the snow, waitress

Canceled the youth of day knee's blue waters'
Ceramic foster gun. Shabby
Animal crowding Hun. Bleeding knickers,
Perfect "came to alone balance of five weaknesses'
Sharecropping the crow-doughnuts of hay-peanut"
Jan lay, the sea had, when, comedy Epidauros
Weakness, "perfect," change for these marshmallows'
Contour, gee, simplicity, American yo-yos! Sen-

Sens of peculiar mildness! The barrel is
An "country of embarrassment," to the charge un-dimes,
Not-waitress, enter the sea. You died of embarrassment
Winter, crazing pin of the marshmallows
Gone blue, magic at Easter; and the phones'
Welfare corset of genius again-society. "Nail me
To the pillow the Anna Dime of showering pillars
Severance mute alcohol." Major
Interest artist "Daniel" in the why be again
Their cots of snow O waist in the pink
Column! share of my east! savior
Of useless notes! Common way, the
Churches it aspirin, south un-day, blue manag-
Er charm that lakes to "Big Sea," un-Dane
This sleepiest one, dime land hokku kerchiefs
They. Green, the shirts of his table, lain down to be gory

Knees, un-, Lord, order, a, commanding Saracens
Carles li reis, nostre emperere magnes
O foolish Fords in Spain! *Set anz tuz pleins*
Tresqu'en la mer cunquist la tere altaigne
Bachelor, Hugo, and cockeyed Milton! win-
Ter arches, decency with eyebrows, gun-
Sight of brocaded fixtures, lockjaw in
"Youth Wins Each Private," lariat of mo-
Ronic; damp, who was your nurse? "My own." Stockings,
Whiskey, "Lay me. Bread limit that has tin sheep
Esteban Elsewhere, hoop! cold-blooded hymnal
Judge because the cuckoo leaps. Cockeyed mate
Wait till all "dear" Saracens "ant" in their tents.
Mix-up! Weevil-show-time! Hundreds
Of pages, holiday, tryout, fear, gold. Nan
Waxed "neat" to the Sarabandes, coma is Hans
Chalk. Pierre knocked on the cool weevil
For a British hour and a half as the nail files
Were old sixteen years old crucibles' marshmallow

Wheelbarrows' service yellow, O bonny balconies of
Hunk! Aegerian buildings mad in junk-
Red and the ponds of bell-ink coffee "of sweet true
Comedy, to say 'there,' " but Roland bleeds:
Pyrrhic, umbrella, my! hammock collars you. Cuss. Wheel.

Nine days to one you may the forest this
Europe qualify imaginary pastry notice
Summer hat curving to placard yellow
Dens of curving imaginary violets
To steep the order, "White illegal portholes,
Who dance is the sun, March wind, say Venice
In Sumeria, peculiar, loving potatoes, gone oyster
An, correspondence sweet, no out of blue
Andante, Shelley, these pastry follow
Their latest oyster. Can give each quiet blotter
So nude notice, end, tea, bareback rider,
All over town. Then sew, use the sea, mad
To begin where blotters the cigar-orator-
Hay-lobby. North anything off dream you've been
Ant, dear collies in yellow, barristers in green. These
Courses, wonder a white as no, be given, run
Who cranberries, yes, in backwoods blue
Till sigh, their challenge. Go, slim blockade,
Oats-dairy! We're not all back
Engining black, engines London, kiss, night,
Endow. Forthright is the sheeplike elbow
And the bins of a tern's resolution!" Weeping mixed
With "Golly, she alone kissed us!" and paper
Kenneths, thrown against the windows of outlifted airplanes!

Bay leaf! for you are burned by the midget sun. And
Marriage, to the cold, mint stables of anyone! Bay leaf!
Landslide! Marshmallow! Feces! Annoyance! Sew
These leopards into place. Bay leaf! Uncut faces!
Lumber! Wait! The curtain of the pyramids

Is lifting! Bay leaf! He is the pirate of underwear! And
She almost promises! The lark is their loosest hearts'
Greenhouse. They die when shirts. Some professor
Muter than Long Beach! O bad! dirty goods'
Limited sweet hearts! As now, she cereal-planes
Council chamber. Heatbox undie heart. O bound
Calico mirror of "ten sighs"! Certain
Nights I cannot sleep; the wind calls me, "Stewart,
Go out among the loganberries, preferably
Alone. The lake will lie there like a barber." I get
Up, and the stovepipe seems paler than Alaska!
Cold is the parachute, pea, fine the sun, merry
The purpling heart-commissioner, January,
Pencil, otter, Michigan. Orchestra beds!
I name you yet I know you, hopeless Jimmy!
What is the climate Monday pyramids
Bay leaf! etcetera. "Gonads have that clear pencil,"
She said; "the madmen have all retired. There
Is going to be April faster than next month when it's April!"

Showers, summer, handouts. Will the locusts
Be okay? Marjoram, chancellor of the pill creamery
Dollars you paid who to rest your house batty
Cemetery cloaca bended knee; evangel
Of the rosary batteries! What "perfect" yellows!
When Jimmy felt that orange chain he felt
The excitement of a parachute at sea! He linked
"Plaza" and "joyous parachutes." Nathan in his car
Honked. Uncle Parachute filled his camera
With joyous razor blades and "perfect cameras." Sleep
Walked carfare by the sea. A boat "pelvised"
Arcady, it was so green. "Oh, then,
Can't we marry velvet?" screamed Jimmy. Down went
The surf, in. Most often. He would have carried the yellows
Back into the cabinet of detective yellows. I bet
The rookies have never noticed anything. Sewn

In his car, loosely amid the raspberries. Shoe!
Lux soap might make you a swan. Surface, chimney,
Banjo. Hill, bicycle, aspen. Oh he shook socks
In wildness ridge, bounded off against his car,
Woke Nathan, fared through the wilderness of dogs
To surface, twined this bay leaf, and shunned airboats.
It would have been nice for you "that lemons"
Assume he is streetcars, O quiet half bench of wood.

Call, lean, boar. Swim. Is three
Birds. Win to. Sweet. Medallion-and-
Garage, tassel. Wheat. Lonely. Bag woods or
West-ear lemons. So, in no; and. Deep. Maharajahs.
Six. We will you us half lift is. "Oar-lemons
When" that movie is. Final. Aren't you liable
Touring-bee, us please? Shirt-India cars; and
"Either thou socks sue the sun, air-
Hole, tan surface, pear-clock, Gemini
Ands youth, purpler. Thee, bears as pure sacked
Reason sunlight 'Mary' tellurium maharajah:
Blanqui. Their shirts water as
Mist! Who cold dassn't-Mary, theatre. Henry,
Soda Gun? Ouch, dancers!" Sunlight is those
Little with. In. Cow next door; rabbits
Year, fail-tent. Next coat. And January, theatre
Calcium calculo California ban, yearns
Calcium theatre, oh. Oh. Endance shoe
Mans. Un. Bare decent dachshund was, pour
"Ain't" trimmer wick. "Angel can wintry
Cocoas repair," oat quiets him, clan-
Destine shirts! Sandal of derring-do
Harangue by these fields Blanqui
Of Mary, and sunlights in bomb!—green, endocrines we next dove

Barricade "um!" dare Z horse in
Who yellow legs. Andes wrench news hand me the

Curtains win freeze: location as Chelsea blue
Finance tree, hook, deprivation. "He blankest of rugs'
Dens, toe, and 'character nearest bells-hills'-
Dogs. The soldiers wander him rum. Danai-
Cringe-yellows. Shaggy Ghents!" Now,
April hinges wonder parachute toilet brainbeat
Limerick surfaces lilac pessimism leaway merchants
Toys ant Jane you were's active neon so
Peanuts away the nominative air-green Indian
Momentous shall I peculiar lilacs button canary
Ocean billets man cloak Sumerian lilac orange
Lane bannister sunrise Congo to sea
Bond mention sameness lilylike parachute. We
Foundation limousine the sea. Imagine that
Clothing! O beans, hinder climate red
Bandanas' come each oar para-seating doll-sweaters'
Coppering knee "Hippolitoid" "poiple" chaperones
Tree, songs ditch answers lemon. "Dear Phillips,"
Endymion quiet the merchant marine Saturday
Luna fan seed desk "Nursemaid ooh subway act dusk
Raspberry gee am cup ho-ho landslide
Mill, mano, risk, later" senators. Fenways, eagle and maids

Other "lingering" rabbits' youth lift fiery yellow
Nomination show-time assassin, "Sweet
Are my cares. My den is column, news,
Coliseum. Marriage are my bent
Gloves; and normalcy this Fenway muse as color
Sandy. Chow, and music's officer, see, hop
And dare musics' greatest lungs. Llama end
Hairpin balcony shoplifting color. Hi, blue
Bears! vote for me; I glow." Santa of So! O
Terebinth of teeny colors, an ocean's collars!
Mantelpiece! Unhonor quiet as the worm
Invents. Us, season of punjabs and death-
Mints' cogs, marriages with sheepdogs, beds, and

Stunts! Lintels, pow! are everywhere, care limns
Doped heads. Alcohol of frayed lintels! faro-
Delivery, O sleepy lungs' "placard" high, say, "Blue
Backs, General Win-Madison-Square-Garden April
Of querulous testicles!" Bench of the curving weight-
Lifters, solemnity of, hat, teething orange
Winter "May! hill!" sewily dear half nickel. And how
Pass chocolate, hens, pin day-suits, and water
Lariats! Soutine modesty China, ant! weightlifters
Balcony-minty. Canada, why: Easter say, "How stunty
Bear rose the, dean drums, 'an entirely fiendish wafer!' "

China there are benches on the chairdogs'
Color-wimple, "May I bent
These tedious ranches?" howl, Lulu! and I
Hairdogs' yes, I, when fine stooges am
A bare lea-snood, polish, rum, Andes, tiptop legs'
Mentioning gold dust to hay! Kinsey! Marxist College! "Ann"
Word! How! stables are we; end I yes
Dither; "she belongs to me fatter than a drugstore,"
Ben Jonson, shirtwaists, and pretty magazines'
Carolina, "Though mother is a new
Baby, Carolina, pigeons! Sherman for president! Molo-
Tov is diving tomb eye my tippy chaircar; lungs'
Dog airminds Atalanta's" Hill which first
I Monday Eskimo my inkbook; wheel hollow
Labor Alpine, this, dirty Angevine, sea, bear
Toy-poetry; "Make it a mistake
A your pyjamas, ace the. Lanterns on North
Can." "Youth Major servitude landslide
Cokes." Ha-ha the berry. Colors men. Inchings
Frogs and magazines. See at the cherry colors
Men, sun witty ham's cop rays, engine as
Sea, dogs. There they are, has, gold, in, hen.
Pardon me. Little matadors. Carcass's neat gold
College, he: yo-yo-terebinth, what little lungs!

America inch lover Santa cares ago
Bicycle; Me: Matchwrappers an ever rainthing ugly.
Wayne: Drag sheep away into maritime
Cupboards. Sarah: Mockery, colicky streetcar
Universe raspberry shirt pin lie sweaters'
Sweep, out, today youth over youth muttering, "Housetops'
'In movies'!" Are there lariats an defeating cans'
Choice rocky melancholy Jericho and-is-side pillow
Scene, seldom is Nevada, munificent, walk to cruelty
Angel. Eight art. Hoops pond links balance. Aaron: Mock
No. Otto: Gentle parmigiana, us key raindrops, crackling
Choochoo magician piano, red, balance. Lattice
Mirth—sandaled sheep. Ken: Doubled holiday, piano,
Miriam the mirror, Atlas, Liliom, Cambridge. What
Horses dune Marilyn key E sparkling? Hands
In cold as. Kent: Oar-shape, find the peary space
Mirth "hads" light at "time" the magician city
Nancy; truth masonite showers furniture. Anne
Endoplasm Cincinnati concert millionaire show
Their sweethearts every Ingres youth Jericho furniture, O
Canada, Havre knee nursemaid the tawdry wastebaskets is
Notepaper brassiere, O landslide
To "perfect" Greece! When I was totally, and "seize
Lemon," laudanum of preparing streetwalkers' sunrise clove-tan!

Scenic parachute. Column. Pear. Elevator
Sent hair swans. Bam the students. Pillow
Then Swedish underwear. Year-horse. Bogs
Season curfew than Atlantic merry Christmas howl
Inchings act students' dairy lazy us. Pegs!
Southern. O we "marshmallows" water its crazy-dairy-
Necessary students, interests yam then "Is some" shoe
Wait aw the scenic dairy in "Yes I am
'Tree' is 'melody spies' purple" oy their blues gen-
Uine great vanished cloud! Bins! clasp of the pre-
Liminaries too tinder pie rose, late, rosin, discovery
Banjo peanuts lyricism that rosin

Fails discover genius Mother's Day lank church
Of Country Pin! Banjelo, tangelo in
Meet—Hands! cloistered sharks! dairy
Farm of delayed face-dimmed "cosmopolitan
Asia fastest say wood Germany faculty defeated
Nuncio bled 'fanfaronade, gimp disky bees
Llama cow furnishing Delibes gamma raspberry
Jericho munificent function opera delphinium
Sheba!' " Axe! charity! kin-berries! lay-lows!
Opera bare your Chinese Polonius Ping-Pong
Slave Mycene Germany calendar reform
Savings bank endoplasm coconut sea hood foggy ankles

Easy to Coney Island, winter, and pep! O matcher
Of teasing matches, matador of "teethes," mangle-
Course of "seizing barricades," O colon, merit-
Eagle, bandager "Ozzy Carpet-Faces lilac mercy
Interest, ant, life," beaver, soon-you, bare
Agora in, moronic sukiyaki, O tenth
Summer! minus! Andes undie drifting shoe
Meritorium, sharethismatzo, end, Lulu
Born, scene, Canada, me, LeClos
Wolf! airwaves! sandwich, there are receding
Ox, maladive; merchant marine, selfless
"Solomon," fishes. Tarragon, Aragon, hula-newly
Endeared Ingres-shaped mint clods'
Jeer-storm-its heavenly mirrors, youthless ale! At
"Three Teeth." Amerigo! summer!
Bins! embarrassment! "Weir a cold half an angel
Den mid-altitude car reception decimation lie
Here, Z blue. Morrow angel Anza tune the
Morrow January-mirrored two!" Mentioned
Aspirin grin as lemons orange belt
Possibly do; chair coat midnight soap
Paris engine kimono eastern comma "their place
Tacit end alls you"-mate ear of, bat! summah west
Matchsticks Eden of is "Daniel" "urban hill!" Oy! Hail!

Yesterday an usual fainting pen bananas
Auto. Winter for my catching out flags not
Merry in my room! Denver! orbèd hags! O fan-
Shaped leaves' British Museum's stern
Aspidistra of brocaded Annamarie Lily Ann Ber-
Tha Leeway end America these day, O motto, modern
Ant fair impudent charm's gay beauty
Shellfishing doughnut-ankle's arm Mildred
Lois, and these, iceman, the tear-men, E
Soon, wave me, modern, blue-ascendance Cal-
Ifornia, day, mantle, sorrow, lands "Lindy
Maritime hunch knee baloney youth he's French!" I
Nearly fell auto this museum! Lair-bins,
O comicals! Majesty, their green and suitable hogs'
Ten guitars which mother I climate
Sun grateful Marie-bannister-soup craving their blue
Deer, the men who cocoa lilac
Hips of peace January mistral hemp Detroit
Of saving lurid nits, O mouth, curseway to the south
Might-Helen, syllabic (bet-chair) gin-telephone
Louder than the earthware thinks! "Charles? Telephone.
Teeny, sure to send Dale a sundial."
Central are the token seas. Tender Labrador of bees,
Paper antonyms. O the hill picks up, that is pink.

Weaver, the bandanakerchief, a hen's, nuts'
Shannon. Looms that take care of America! O
British guns in Glencannon! Palace of gloomy
Insincere physicians! Moron of every positions
Heaven is cutting the passive mirror too
Close to us! O Rembrandt in a bottle, sleeves
Of the joyous pituitary, maritime
Interests, coalescing "Mammy Slope-the-
Pink-up-into-them-," believers in wattles!
O bear cats! bear rugs! bundles of Shinto wristwatches!
Goateed shoe boxes! lariats of striated dust! mints

In comma formation, San Salvadors, mirrors in
Transition, senators, cosines, and nuts'
"Chair which he might dance balance blaze
Knee"! Oh! Ocean! demon of the dem-
Demonstrations, the sweet formations, wheat-hap-
Py neat-fornications, O savage! licorice as
Broadway! What number in my shoe! Faro! Lie
Down! Shave! Miracle! Borax in Neptember, flock-
Magine, genius-blessing, toss! cure-you! They
Are not mine! O anono, a May "thyme," a "nuss"!
Bravely I built you at Faro, jail-word-
Sin-ban-chill-sane-pollen-car saying, "Tweet
Ins!" Motionless air raid! bungalow of peaked clay!

No wonder! parachuting germ hay-mow squad and king
Every ant is king! minnesingers in gown-
Boxes, ladies, money; WE
Childhood sew, weak ladder peppermint Balkans
Every mild is king! banjos (aye) going
"Yessirree-streptococcus," Mercedes
Avenue, win D shy parachute of the oyster
In enamel youth plod hinge parachute
Down hair, motto! Boled parallelo-
Grams, weaver is not king! Jaded, though
Mild ands ant, blotter, yo-yo ship sate Jericho believer
Angevine "Sewn in his car,
Loosely, amid the raspberries,"—hokku! revolver!
"Winter comes among him, latest coffee
Peep, oil, April; Angevine, cop, noodle,
Hinge, birthday, Peter Pan: 'Say it is not so
That why bee weevil dinner landslide mite
Caretaker, blessing his handkerchief; whereupon
Laurel and Hardy.' " Certainly tomorrow is weapon
Pleonasm. Dancing, like kosher ice water
Lays. Rob the conceited strawberry, engine
Count on the deceitful oyster. Imagine the

Sea, that knights! Borrowed his fading isinglass
Ankles, cocktail shakers, churchgoing leaps, umpire, Virginia,

Biltmore, "Sue Group," matches, all go, "And
When we had almost turned to aspirin, the
Paris of three-feet germs," O notice-
S of green and limpid lemons to "an
Office, air-built, nine offer," Mary-chute Sen-
Sen battery milkshake oh are hottestblue
Lends, and weewee were to be seen (badger
Nexus of youth weed anvil-surly borax! Shah!)
Tour, acey rink, momma, YOU
Came, dancing whippet of tie-college, hoop! yo-yos!
Bather, bannister, sleepy sight, ant, mutts'
Quietness needling "are hoop chair" is
Encephalon, oyster, the weariness crying
Encephalon! matador of potassium phalanges, slim
Hobo, militant cheesecake, my real
Merchant of Venice, The Winter's Tale, Two
Gentlemen of Verona, Salome, labor of the defeated images
Or-Kenneth-strous baby for "magic location, thou
Lazy Boston in aspirin, sweetheart, earthway piano
En-soma lemons." Ore-parachutes! better than the Island Queen
As sting sighs, O mint, church, sail, Sun-
Day, whoops, in rocky Pittsburgh, sharpening pencils
Beside the leafy badger, notice how
Bare arms singing "Wheelbarrow," merchant marine, cry it. Lemons.

Ornithology, man "hid"s in glass! whoppers
Of Dean "A yes joke," rum deceiving by
Hay cooked balcony swart lemons in. O
Columbus! Can doing beery silver naturally "wheem"
Georgia of costing Sea Arabic,—outlines
More "entire empire" sweet asterisk yellow knee
Khan rabbit. Sofa, peanut, end girlhood, how
Lorgnette de-orange all, in white. Orchards

Of dental sonnets. Add ad ad. Hand orchestras
Hay-knee "ousand Meary Thousand"—Yale
Okay acorn is in in-orchestrous phalanges'
Podge! More! the caretaker is free with aspirin
Showplace America to-me; cost-Max! O backs
Wonderful, eagle angry's-light end, O! arrest
Oyster. We, after all, more pink bee, solder
Airy banner sea toy carpets, baseball
With hand seas; O wagons! Shave the
Lea angry ope behind orange "Lag, up from new
In, as, woe Jericho this difference wonder," acts
Silly; worried whom green-O lakest badger,
Nouns! Winter, Caribbean, curvy elope-grange-
Masthead: pigs! "Science tells me that you
Are a pig"; writer of handmade orchestras,
Bather, "end," willow a, church, fin, aid-fool's

Sigh photo dream cargo sit loop worm, hike! San-
Ta S weeping pigeons oar gore ninetieth
Working bended bow is "nineteen," axe our
"O mustard-wanton" streetcars O shyest red
Eight and April imaginings culver Lulu silver
Banana peanut savannah. Hollow buildings
Of "Die now, mother No-forks lethal
Ale-blue silver," color, moth, ah inch January
Flag-pinned; shy savannah-green forks "egg"!
O not! Bearing chute of dressed tomato's
Yoohoo coastline opera-eagles, jangle
Odd. Oyster favor disintegrating marriages
Table yellow, "Oh summer is hot for fools!"
There were British linens in the
Tepee emotion disintegration glamour garage
Nonsense magazine olive midnight cuckoo
Gyroscope titivate America gingery showplace
Shallow lime wit motion Santayana O cuckoos,
Gray, fearful, yum yum, happy, our gypsy pow-pow

Mayor, sty of distasted elephant-elevator
O shiver prunes, nightways, tea-deserved sob,
"Am I losing this mantle of scientific lemons
To Hobbes?" Idiot, ankle, bakery jobs
Kisses, and migraine gobs of *Hamlet*, a China of sentences.

Formed by the note-taking of mud-pushers, as
Formidable as violets. O fair field of the
Form of Hussars' climate of conceding harps'
Fork jujube aimless Louisiana, O wraps'
Forest of "Lee Herman jail." Salivate in
Focus, nineteen-ninety oh sunshine, back
French, livable, dairy, engine, choir-man, sea
How fair are airy strawberries' feeble
Monster anguish, oil! Oop-Oop the Janitor! Fire
"Summer," his contentious "lane." O sorrow-waiter
Of mines, and "Wifes of cotton! butter! water!
I am crazy in the lintel of your cups'
Parachute Madonnas! O misery of samples. Sea!
Marriage gee umbrella grapefruit, houses
Of rotationless cars' marrying season ere
Yew, O glassy oyster of deceiving green
Anciently Pyrrhic lousy able to
Junction pool incinerator theatre badgers,
Badgers, badgers. Eye! winter! goatee!
France! O culmination of the side step, Peru!"
Angel answer "den step" "con-feeble" orchard-motion O loops
Of "Wow, ethers of cream cheese!" De-
Grelotte the chive: "Ignorant summer madhouse,
Douce working Madonna—lilac, cuckoo, disintegrate!"

Oh there was a bear of ginger bugs! They lo-
Cated ox, ink-millionaire, duck-balcony, O Jan-
Uary the blimp of oyster-Pisa! Shine us, nicks
The pear-coop balcony. O coptic frogs! See
"That," silver ceilings, olives, Cho-Cho-San

Of smiling truck. O Bridget! Junky! Hackwork!
Sleepy-come tables, lustrous pouter, he, gin the
Lake opera satisfaction deserted hankies. "Yes I
Comma serum baloney cancer shoe
Buckle China deserted lemonade, for you
Of all youths. Bad luck! blue! Indians'
Safety devises, O grandmother Forest! Links! Foremen
Without shoes! Lilacs gigantize my my my
Earthest lilac lie lye delinquent, shoe, wax
Joking, about-miracles, gentle, able, goo-goo, golf!
Lime insurance! O barricade of loft miracles
In tune with: grills, pier-accountants, gnats, gorillas,
Morris dancing, spies, peas, llamas, and chairs filled with gorillas
Last night: Georgia of pleonastic squirrels'
Frigidaire! toy bloodhounds! O bough
Of crusade lanterns, how I love you!" I bit,
With my "ornithologeeth" mackerel hum baby, cuckoo
Copley Georgia dimple yo-yo Sheba
Networks. Act graceful, blue! "Day and here nitwits."

Shirt "and vivacious quiet feels you"
Barracuda up "Gee, knob" they (are)
Cow-fables in genius Gloucester. "Ye
Arch noodles," grapefruits
Give "fair" boscage to needly Rockport. O bands!
Roman's! lintels! steeples! sagas! bands
Of (white glue of day, earth, Japanese winter
Under mile-an-hour kimono, wheee!) shoeshine
Marriage of (shabby industries ape big south
Of boobs) lime ginger ale of lilacs (Poe
Jealousied fruitation bounds Andes coo rig
"Dynamee" poop deck "sun-marine" un-"Go, lazy jasmine"
Bike, water; happy boat nit, is as oh ooh ump
Ape lala newish, 'ray! Jewish Shasta
Of brocaded bumps, minerals with lifesavers'
"Attachable-andiverous-ology-lulu-cars" buying

"Yessy" space, orchards' changing mirrors, and eye
Of deceasingly grouped lemons. Look, jobs! So
Mary Janice silvery palace Edgar Poe
Fin giant, boat, chase, America; aorta of
Nixing lemon jobs. Waverly! and councils of jest-
Chalk, proving by entrance, oop giant palaces,
Lint) ha! to winter (shorter pear, then very blue,
Express-leaves, answerable) or bee, red yellow.

(Shower paybill ocean pin-bear agora Lulu
Gin-pear ice of gripes loganberries with sea
For Latin names archway and oyster polly
Knee fandancer peaceful showplace O blobs
Of paradise shining like sill-pill
In Orient Romany shining selling successful
And eagle bathroom night-Orient oak-cow and
Airplane of shirtwaisted barristers each
Mildly okaying solidity to boulders dam and
Advantageous going to sleep butlers louse
Hay nook contingent planetary
Inventory nunnery, harbor! O wax, "vax"!
Postulates of deceiving acid gramophones
Ixtapalapa yo-yo January naked cripple
Of telluric lemons O bond salesman
Streaming with held rugs bindery
Of paraded oh-ohs, eighteen me that
Lindbergh slumbering mailman-osis piracy luncheon at
Packhorse, giant trade unions Mayed, dove,
Gramercy thoughtless Lindbergh, O keyboards
Better than the city's navel, Shostakovich
Of drunken caps, "Gee Vizzikers," to
Town we heard them say, "Sizzle go fizzle bandana
O Santa, lay down the coping saw!" Boats! Good night, tea!

Commuter, joy, rabbit, air "even"
Khan dairy-shy "wheel" give me,

Stair ink dove. Pants of Rome. Rake
Bannisters of bee, star, fate mink pans
Georgia each terebinth agora, Thousand
Listen. Maldoror weewee hoop baby. Oblong
Sen-Sens. Leaf-brick. Hoping
Bay-sea pier-attitude are "glove"-pink
Shorthand nylon air-pilgrims to bin-dove
Noonal phlegms, achings badger rake! Ore
Din of hope lea "gas" mention shy
As in Shasta, dabble—cornice, mandrake
Seraphim. Oops! "Quiet be my double. North
Bandana cuckoo indentation hoop we; air is
Ulster wanter, a Jericho. O bills! And neigh
To me, janissarry, pilgrim dividing snow
Manges, town me shay sea dirt devising rains
Doughnut on high! Octember of the jeeping bear-
Mackerel, sunder! Inch of teas, peas, and pink
Layettes, O morn-a-phones! Jane! Jane!"
Dippy weave bay deem housey "erf!"
Giants, "ipes" remember Oberts Plossom
Gingerwearing tea fenestral stripes
Choochoo against against. Act is, matinee!

Ozone, ips, dismaying humps! Lockwater
Of gingerwear manteau! for I pierced
Bicycles, Manuel de Falla. George Ozone
Fell bike dead Hannah-master the shoe-ox,
Blips! Oh, Cajun, inch; house of the starry itch,
Master, jujube of beep-beep eagle classicism
Horary. "Light me hoo-hoo chaste
Agora delicious eagle bumpkin sobstory. Edge
Of the beebee adze. Germany shouts, 'Hello,
Baby, than-hortatory!' Orange midnight, cous-
Cous an 'border silly' yum yo-yo I
Plate ooh dada atch aitch itch eye knees higher
Than as is Wabash Wabash checkers-pyjamas."

50

Orchestras dimpled that month, climate!
O backbreak of the fig-poker, tablet mirror
Cool gin-jujube. Borrowing heck of the Stars'
Is-manifestos' Clarissa of coo-neck. Pie, die
I, bun, oak, love-way lemons breeze altar
Hip weary clove. "Mention the shopping parachute
To Billy Cathay, shaving about India
Quiet yes halva shoe-department geranium
China. Jonah models paregoric." Plagiarism
Of sunny stars! massacres of the little models
For "Bee, Arthur, talent-way loops ginger adopt where you."

And once again her stomach functions normally—
O parachutes and zeppelins, good morning!
He sassy fawns, we rally; ope, ope this
And mandarin Jill, hoop the girlish beach, loss
Quiet in, in, dinner function: "How
Alabama the finch, chair Otto us decency crumbs
Dinette happy normally. O good morrow,
Finch." Amos, the plaza leaped
Abnormally incinerator good mood. Water edge
Engines idea in lemon paper; he shoves
The water away; it is "their." A long
Wrist, Jeep monkey and "locust for good
Location, rioting red raspberries hove
To Alps of comic gin—Weight! mirrors! as
Phonograph as decency abnormalcy banana
Joyous screen penumbra group wait ah
Pill! Oh, how did you get here! Weave
The curvacious zeppelin." Mary
Me O now it knocks. Plaza? "Gypsy." Earliest as
The weekend of focally month lemons
Happy. Shy, shy, shy! Fiend, fiend, fiend! O arid
Lams, goof, pier of brocaded nuts! Fishering
The lamented dish, is a sofa, A. Goof,
"Dish-a" air, airy grandmother "soofa," "bahg"

Nymphs of Boston! Caruso of the pilly chafing dish!
Periods of pink, pyjamas, we: a noted weariness
America illness pyjamas; cow food, lemons
And gypsy raspberries! Oyster, Havana, the common sense
We olive eagle perforation choir gypsy
Sweetheart. And the tennis scones. Cow-raving
Island bad, mad, "oopal," shoes. Hay
The simian as day, bay, dermatologist
Eleanor, "she-food was dully sheep-food
Only as ear, waving pyjamas," grandmother
Of the screaming links! "Out! Up! Ear!"
Basement, "tea-pool," Ernestine jujube coliseum
"Arf-woofs"! Lady, cloak eve banana wool
Might eerie and "arf-woofs." Idle pin!
Wary Indes, speech of grandmother, or
Ore, ad, Dillinger as dim rotation agonies
Policy germ, taffeta, ink's cuticle. But his
"His" is "Is"; as is baseballs of weary fizz-
Lyre protector,—orchid of cow-faced pyjama-
Career-waving shove-malady on Cuckoo-hay
Links, bobs—of hit mirrors in yo-yo hare
Pursued leafy suitors. Oswald Mobile Bay
Easy blasphemous giant "is" root beer casket
Under gal Chinese wastebasket,—O brilliance!

How serious was serum, and the wave's "apric" therapy
Tonsilitis-ing cocoa-dandruff to soothe Labor Day
The Menshevik chilblains toot-toot gypsy lemons'
Cloak past you, evilly riding that bicycle
Rain, shops and. Houses of cruising furniture O dots,
And dandy, manned cuckoo by quitter-labels
Of shy-announce, April-beer, common-cuss, ware
Blue gypsy, O nincompoops, daisy, Aristotle!
Weary is the merchandising South Pole. Orchestra kale
Is near. "Genius of clowning and cussing bananas
Of daily 'blue' and seep, joy, joy sleep of teary

Purple, the Japanese movement of art stars'
Bangor of shipping 'can-knee?'s! Owl-orchestra
Of the shy dandy music shops' distinct
Diamond Avenue horse-porpoise flirtation, O beans
Of 'sody'-metropolis's weird-wee gigantic-blains
Of bundler-nurse! Oak buildings
And shy lanthorns, pilot of graves' damp horns
That chirrup, 'orchestreed' pill-more,
Unshabbiness! O loophole than loophole 'thass'
Eagle of silent bingo, groups! Bessarabia! this
Distinctly! apples!" Very nutly they shine
"Beaver" "Clue" "Pylon" "Imp" "Kentucky" and "Biltmore"
But of orange greens, lane violent raspberries.

She showed me his or her nurse, O ices!
No kiss or railroad station as bitter orchestras
Basing loop quiet tarragon-way-pats of blond
Madonna. O jinx of the shyest sphinx's
Axe-flotation career-numbers of backroom
Tinny notices' limbs of collusive
Plug-its-planets, opal! dime is dancing! And bakers
Follow his wilting literature. Actions!
Pins work, "follow" his sweepy limeade. O
Now-monsters! April castles is Falernian
Jowl, big lintel of teeny January
Bug railroad-station bicycles, bug! hi, bug!
Gypsy, bug, and "Am, yo-yo, blue, a bug,"
Cycles, orphan, often, a bug, "Yay, oh yes, a
Bug," hey! hey! Isn't ear a walk
Down wavy "ladder-somes," or passenger
Climates, white! red! Carolina! ancient bug
And a mottoed sail, dear faint aster orange
Monthly duple say quick-sail-as-unbottoms-
The aster rouge, in the closings
Of every literature. O continents of buttons
Where are we hiding? From? Ooop? Alpine bug,

"Gingeah," history, lilacs true little fiend
Of tyrant limns, bologna! This is that.

Dairy of true green bugs! "At all," eye
Weird conclusion orangey pink hammock whistle
China basing fair, elephant, tie-
Hanger, "it's music of the spillwort
Fooling 'Dumbness' Castle, O climates of the
Waving and catatonic arms of pantries of
Blooming ink of pantries of."
Pineapple donation cuckoo interrupted me:
"Shoe, house, bitterness, careless in shop
And gonad farm, what learned detective
Of colored submarines, quiet Dixieland
Of these shamrocks of blue, embarrassment of
Eating two cups when only one was
Served, the delayed parking meters under a lake
Of lion-parachutes, O collarbone that wins
The fairness test, gin, and cover for the furnace
Of kings' sighs, January, Easter, the bent climate
Of culver, leaf listings, O! tan!" Shy
Rain, and the beauty of the "dug-
Out mirror of that steery Mexico: class
Of blue air white unconscious, sea
Pasting in harassing loops of green
Dichotomy to 'hoo hoo' funnies." It cleansed
Uganda. One series of crazy gowns.

At all! at all! pink metal, and
Beer-crazy medal of keen "has his worst summer"
Ice junctions! "Tomorrow ivy Gogol jewelry,"
Hairy, true sea, landing phone, oyster, bag
Of disky rockets weeps away, hay!
Rackets is "timpistuous rizzberries," icings of love
To care some,—"inginns of timpistuous barracuties'
A-vailable injinns." O April of the terrified revolvers

Aiming their women at the shoe boxes
Of my hope! Legal, faraway, cokey-mutt forests
Of the limitless jail, him, Ann, in and
Is Andes-knees! cool, cool is rather bombastic
Or cuckoo deep-sea forests honey-monastic
Oh shine wherever! and the Georgias of classical honey
Country hoop! fizzle! majority limit
India-cakes-is-revolvers-cancer! "Tie paper giants
Hop yo-yo Norse ring. 'Eep' sheeps
Time Andes bassoon ever gracefully. The red where
The final oop! oop! of granite ginger motorcars
Of quite green. Cow, that my neighbors are sleep,
Ginger, parade, hoop, May." Ah! linden, where
Evil Edith eaten the enunciations of
Tea, thunder, and the bare parachute edge
Of "Lark, hoop-walker, teapot-they-go to" sleep!

Now it is May in the ape. O acids
Ceremonies of artificial end as so autorides! duchess
Bees Santy Gloria of "Do nice," broken addenda
Of "Hoping today piracy automobile
Idjit dampness, O bag! this dampness
Alacrity of the automobile" "For waving flags
O an incinerated bug" "Bag!" "Andes, why not win
'Her' " ale and now Waverly do so
Basement "Al Lemons": cot where eye believe
Panegyric sweepstakes custodian day-
Brought lyricism to these cuspidors. He wakes
At night, looking for the shadow-boxing
Cousins, April and armistice; but mystery
Enshrouds the answer and deep regeneration
Forest to the limping funnies, and blue
Is her daylight's agrarian following; for she
Lycanthropy-odalanalyzes the tippy rainboxes
At jesting match-drops; since weary ovals
Most happen here these climate of some days

I walk. Terrified, shire of bear-
And-cotta sodas, he ginger-deers the
South, a light, for mirror of some days; equal now
To a deep ship, Ferrara, flags—swearing,
"Bonny Asian sacerdotal dove,"

He leaps pinstripe flotsam balloon cab's
Killing people wintry, eep! loop! simplicity!
Anguish! "O Andes of a paper dove,
And little miracles of my simplicity
With painful aspirin and smiley railroad dove
Of 'sinsuality,' see the minute that April dove
Me, birthless, hoops, lilac, and closets, iron
Saviors. They gave an orchestra of milk
To the ships and their first grape dove
Ships. For weeping psychoanalysis! and paper beds!
O crossroads of silvery paper, how
Jericho and we nifty whiteness I bled
Superior wardrobes into the railroad: a dove
Of China's paper, shyness, and a wafery head. Which
Lincoln of the surface bananas! O pots
In Havana!" "He leaves me have a banner like a
Grapefruit." Shorthand! These islands are a pinprick
In the sea. And yet. "O cameo, O bope, obe opeep
My cherished Solomons!" Feenamint porphyry candy
The bed was soft. "And yet I left there
Like a silent weir, bonging the clavicle
Of 'meelions' of tea-barefoot frogs; or their lanterns.
Oscar, simple, silly, city, ocean be-
Hind 'Prologue to the Canterbury Tales,' in bed!"

Mouldy apples, quiet limericist, hay! hay! dove!
"*Dunciad* I flailing food awake.
O barracuda uprising sleep snake sweet
Cow nifty hurrah surprising dawn, itching *Iliad*!
Cinching banjo! Jinx pituitary rosemary

O grandfruit! jeepy in the lilac nursery blessed
Betweeny 'gold-foo' and 'hooray-lips' nursey,
Chancing upon this Aragon 'injinns'
Slime to leap awake mercy! Papery!
Oh how the orchardy ocean lilts! Ape! Perfidy!
I fought him. I gate his head. Nigel Green
Said, 'Bees are without mercy.' I
Then said, 'A bee may not be without mercy
In the lilac future category of curtains
Which fail like tins made of lime.' She awoke
To the summer. A blue ass bit her knee.
She turned her two salacious eyes upward
Toward monotheism. 'I am scraping the
Halibut.' 'Are you a Christian?' 'No.' 'Then
Why, why are you aiding and abetting this fish
To be the summer?' O passionate oysters
Of November horoscope, unmarried hair
Of the morning sea! This mourning is beyond me,
The land's light upon sin's ornate weirdness!

Toe, its bench, we lay down in Illinois,
Anxious pilgrims. O loops! How the sea made war
On its arid tramps—of ginger; but nowhere
Cobblestone mirror garage blue two sea
January and 'Meet the finch': lilac! actress!
O melted kinship, in April, lariat of the two
Trees, blossom that is attracted where
The hill suffers, and motions softly downward
(Beavers at lunch, and biers, this is jasmine
Of smiling tomatoes) go toward, and after
Sombrero, oh cast a the lazy and into wear
Out isle 'in smiling silk' janitors
Of tea-tea'd warfare, surface shirts, cot
And bear, O bays bees cuckoos as free
Everywhere! Cart him away. The eaves
Are as freezing with leaves; and the sky

Of love limericks loomy coastlines at Garbage
Point. Or are there other shamrocks?" In tin
Sales why oh air Wyatt nut linen unusual
Ha ha ape one times destiny. Leafs cockatoo lemons
Piece of. "Andes dam de-bear, hay! hut! sheer!
They say that Mirabeau went nuts in Sweden
Behind the shoe-filled sea, yet at Amalfi
Balanced (oh ho ho) a green pill on his saber!"

April of belonging merely to his blouse,
She yelps. Oy! Beans! the sea! Badger
Noticed us yippee sat down in his chair
Simply cemetery. "Each whiz!" Powerful flights
In sea willow ouch orchard ankle
Of drooping beagle; and then! ale ale-letter
"Zimplossitude." Ant, a "shrimp of coruscation he"
O air deep-kneed checkers in a Humber
Of Turkish sighs! Pans me the hare
Of "economics," O linens linens linens!
"There are very factories angry sea,"
Ankle doughnut behind too I dream "ink-
Parachute-whiskbr" oom! oh I nigh no dimple creation
Different lassitude. "Tea-jamas!" Mirror-boat! A dance
Begins to sea. O lariat! patiences that we seize
Margins in into our weird fights. Bag
Of enemies! there are limping morons near your boat. Let
No bun stir! And the antlike idiots were
There, eagle, matchstick, an inch, and the fairground
Of due nickels; latch; wins. Oar "cattle" coming off and
There bee were opp oop oop! W. C. Fields in
Tosca, the billboards, a cow facing a mop
With these words, "Top hat in the underground,
Booby!" Han! I she hails, the nicknacks of acid.

"In my loafers I went to jail to see my brother
Perish in his little loafers beside the iron fountain

The milkman refers to yesterday as the Electric
Chair. I forgot, however, to bring along my blotter; and
When the electric men began to slug my brother
With tan shoes they had, on I mirrored Oscar Winter
Yo-yo tell them, but asterisk! Ocean of near 'misery'!
Hint that I was saying he sits in the chair
Near a water, of ladies' faces; and, oh, pyjamas
Lifted unto my hindsight their ladder-lantern. He says,
'Don't tell them back at home which I miss
Them,' and, Lord, I most to half empire gymnasium tears
Maggot; but loverly I bonged the hackwork cigarette
To novel inch as civilian lemons. And when, Monday,
Or someday, I am flying near the
Baseball of leaping electric lemons! For pottery
Is my shoe. Now, which I wish to say, and
Good! is this I don't care, for the modern childhood
By the sea which your Noah's Ark promised me, and I say
'Blah' to their mint stables of jugular whiskey
And veins of green talcum! I want to whoosh
Down an armchair, inch of the summer sunlight,
And find my brother, the grayed one, still reading his newspaper
And using his toothbrush, *or* using his toothbrush. Good-bye!"

Porches of dismayed patchwork how good-bye
This summer sun is! and these novels, cockatoos
Like the banshee umpire, thatself, wimple remarked
"Coop, ork, new-chestra, tin, gingeah, India where
India is suppose to be." "Now I see the nylon sunrise
Coming up on Whim-Bole Bend. Anna lays her matchstick undies
To the sweet finger, to the sweet finger of the wind. Bare
Roommates choir where lady seabirds ank-
Le comma weary dollar. Ape, but he makes money!" A
Garden momentarily films George Montgomery and
Ina Claire, monosyllabic, clue of the red ragweeds.
Oh now I know you! ape, red, panic-car, Kismet
Of diseased, ant, hill, roadhouses, school-pigeon

Of the tippy as rainwater motorcar! Clark Gable and Ginger
Rogers fall beneath the wheels of this motorcar
Of cheeping staff officers. How the gray leaves chirp
At the stereocopter filled with flying
Character-studies limited only by the harp
With which they publish "Myrna Loy, a Grapefruit of My Lilies,"
In quarto, and with volumes of lollipops, to document
Everything! And the green robins chirrup
At the sun which fills the dominant
Sad cars with its bilge; and the lofty ladies
Who limp through the bottom of ponds, singing "Raise us!"

"O rainwater how hairless you are! and when winter
Accomplishes everything you are as mercenary as gin
Today, deceiving the pilots of enemy airplane
Is loophole, ant-lake, and churchy-wise. Eye,
Simple doughnut apartment remember
When sunny a sandy daisy ripping in the country
March winter labor delicious party in my eyes;
Green whirlpools laughed on my foolproof shins
And I clambered through an Airedale 'win-pyjamas'; he
Told him I they warranty métier. Show
Of a creeping bunch. Of limitless lilacs; and where
Are the goldenrods of Schenectady? Near you. In Orpheum,
Giant 'theayter,' O lake-country! Where are the beavers
Who sought you in wanting clothing, parachutes
And 'arid climates,' and one, day fought you with
A bacchic soda of genuine airs of piers? O pod! park
Of the rotationless beggars nearing coffee grounds
With their airs. Airy hairs. Little minute. 'Injinn.' Cigarette.
Barefeet I waited ere the barracuda
Bared its air-sweet tinder-bet of rain-settered
Air-confessioning, 'a thousand and one minutes!
O rainwater how hairless you are! The lands of business
And the weirdest summer, oh!' " Lady in comic pyjamas'
Lacerated sleeping foot's bicycle of Limping Classics!

Mirth-marshes! how often a baked fly
Has fell from the swimming goldenrod of a clip
Notching the youthful daisy
Magazine, and lotioned you till its daddy,
Some mockless cheerleader from Syracuse,
Has fell. He fell into your jeweled eye and found it!
How marvelous is baked caddy! Remember the swimmers
Who raggedly swore by that film about "Eagles"? O mocha,
Years is so dense! Ankle compare ginger-rod
Notation dense. The year on its weeds of fence
Angel, thou, mirthless as the blackbird. It's somewhere!
And the ankle basement trees causeway sanitation
Lyrically matters to, has been, and so, Samara,
Jay and Sarah, gypsy goldenrods! O mottoes, mottoes, tomorrow
Is famous! "I live here. I buy my gasoline
Around the corner. And so I want to ship
Three liveries and a half of giant clematis
To Norway, in heat-bill dancing jewelry. To find,
Tunbelly fish of romance—sand page of blond Indians. Who
Sleeps in the nowhere of fire-basket? Somewhere
That's an institute, and the records play
'Climbing through Montmartre as balloons,'
And no rugged apes play with the thrushes
Who hand them sliced baloney until, married, they play cards."

Now she knows I notice everything that she notices,
Even Hawaii, so she has stopped placing notices
Under her sweater! Banners! And ingots
Of the lightest lots placed nearest the sewers
Of her choice of my mottoes, and nearly
Has fainted, I boxed magistrate seamstress demons
Who ride into hot shops! O calcium in deserted rococo
Spades! winter wear! "Why for me
In binges another, candy, thus world of brown
Key if dust, motto of the care-foot sleeping and deserted
Cranky rickshaw, in which he placed his lemons

Overnight, saying, 'Leave these here until the morning
Boldface type singles. England railroad expands
Feet.' Face and the roaring doctor mountain
Each England campfire carfare doctor, hurrah
Lake-strips. Penny. O commander." Clark tubes' shack May means
Going a lemon from home, ah gingerwear! these horses
Plaza geranium eep-temptation. I know! They face
Klotch florist's tomorrow, and bingo! how lethal
Are short faces! yes! "We lie, people, in deserted bags
Around the harpoon of his tipsy poetry, the
'Beg' that whale nought 'leg' yo be contented. Marseilles
And October in the sailboats, cook are near." O hands! Cossacks in
Desperation France-ing his sybarite grape hoop-cats!

O whale of girls, burgooning
Late. Oh! my "knee is fair. There I limp
Weevils into the air," Roger, whip
The decayed easels, "And plenty
Horseradish, it is airpower, accident insurance,
Tea of papers, and rowdy lemons. White Pomona
Of the shrinking star-cuffs!" "We! Ay
Annoy north and building. Latent
Pyrrhus!" Hey Jane! Log cabin wake up whoop
Parachute tin peanut lake. "Air of a
Million, shine high upon, dreary lemon. Loom
Of pare, all niece, the flower of
Accident insurance rag boats and leaves engines
Pan, April—uncle-weary to ginger. But, *oui*!
Clothing, sing-worms, and fail! my joyous gasoline
And caney stars, O spillwort!" Ape. Ate. Ben-
Seeds was late, oop! he went to high school
In a, ork! yes a blimp, oh married to the knees
Of not having, Indian as sharks, the reefed money
To order O doughnut coconuts there, weird
As mated, alcohol, the "ginger," a synco-
Pation, "Anagrams! fish! pools! babe! hospital

Of the careful linguist-itch-hand-fields-youthful-
Kentucky!" Evenings, places, a, it is a

Romance! under fields! one sorghum powder keg
Of chafey golflinks marry to barracuda
Left-wing childhood Santa Claus pyramid lilac
Birthplace changing Eskimo! Snuffing those pears
"Lately I advanced hats Eskimo. O tears
Of my First Wild Wheel, a laboring thatchery
Of sea-high, grouped cuffs! navel
Of the business laboratory, day an orchid's
Way birth cardinal season-animals
Went beer fear notification jailbird machinery
Of bees like 'gone' whim 'flam' oh inter-'mooped'
Pathetic lucky badger sea! Meant Wormwood sea
Of E double interlocutress's silk stockings
Making never seem like yesterday! Oh hop
How been in the!" "Jane. Hoop moorishness an ridge
On lilac cubbies." "Orange orange am-I dimple,
Immersed the whole sea?" Joke! Wish! Paintbrushes, toe,
Alabaster! "Onto which grotto and a sea-brush lemons
Chair-face gin-ear-all's matting time and Inca of
Careful soda shutting chair-faces oyster shooting
Dane-way of mirrors loons ant, 'arf-woof'
Of British gleeb, the 'nembus' of 'son-away'
Curfews' and naily kerchiefs of demon curlews'
Map-opping 'para-kiffs' grandmother. Is hen."

Oh yes, the golf balls! "We were three golf balls
Yesterday until pilgrim milkman rhododendron
Pansy of navy gorilla, limpid shoe box
Ten mirrors away. O lake, rape! these
Are the bedroom of furnitures own
Aspirin these are the daffodil aspirin the
Daisy desert a microphone of golf balls
A 'microphone,' a big nimbus, a hoop with daisy

Rarefying the mixed-up Popeye air, oh save me
From 'Cuckoo aspirin' Margaret the hell is
Tin impy, lie! banana." O Lou
Air! jadey was the cindery gym. Manners
Did not save me British
Aspirin and lips lion tiger daisy O meres
Auto: "London I gave you daisy auto London;
Hit the believed sissy! Magistrate
And dippy 'legistrate,' Camargo
Silver ferris, 'lasp' the bundling wheel
Of silvery golf-bells." May! paper-ladder!
Sincerity! O basements of childish loans
To gangsters "eighteen century mint car" diz-
Zy lamp under it shoe fine Ken stars weep
Cemeteries bee "uselist" snow. Corpse-Alps'-
Zither maiden, see, "Tamarisk the ocean!"

Serenade the minting ocean! jump
"Bee" lilac fishes, oh, football, shortcomings'
Now on pink sand boat O
White goat, staircase, "Santy's eyes
Amid them blooming group," solvency
Barracuda, ape, shortcomings, Bloomsbury
Of a sheep's copper knickers, O mome,
Tin of raining Sen-Sens, no, no, no
More waves of petting football
Air-condition, solidarity. He weaves
A necklace for the sun-dry
Of masonite sewer-mind a beach of lilacs
Meditating weevils' cherries or "ots" miling
The silvery cave, the victory of lariats
Over knitting! Bandanas! "Opera programs
Lead me. Listen. The field lay there
Lilac shoe. Mistinguette's Schopenhauer's
Coolest, very, bugs! O bony tops
Of the scarab, chairs filled with rooming houses

In the 'mine are very idly act gunflower
Serum ladies.' Soon they will bear those boats
A wave, nexus." And the mere light
Health lateness is boxers O cam in "flodge"
Of the tear "Kish" sea, man or ear is weak.

And, as, they. Oy lifting the bear
Opera India sweet net, where gin time
Soothes field a hay-coop of missing cherries
Arthur closet balancing "ictionary" the true
Blackboard in's blossom, daiquiris of blue knives
Rompers as "dinner ware," the deceiving licorice
Clientele. Milkmen! Salesgirls! Strindberg
Of crazy ocean! bell thou
Lane—equal—box hats dance uppery
Sum the Alps, O may tent soap box
Seeds! Factories of knitted daisies'
Cold semper fidelis, cheesecake, billboard, a matchbox
In brief case, as, lazily for the beard that
Beard that beard. Oranges and earth-lazy cherries'
Seen cups, oh or all. And. Nina Castelli amid the
Sweeping shrubbery. "Bankrupt soma, how chaircar
The will is, are they hills, toe, serious,
Loma, April, orange, serenade. I listened to Tchaikovsky
Where cows of pink. O nickels! the breadline
Of sleeping chills, thou merchandise
Leaf, in the lilies, of a hairline, this, 'commentates'
A dear savannah, the belts of alone sake
Reeves ale up toward walk for me, O Guinevere
That untie somas, of a nary work. Oh do green ships!"

And Alaska. Is, as, but. O Samos, blue! Near
Ships dairy mural dairy ships. Lantern ships
An daisy hue, might some are green. Nina! April
Soho kneeways. Barracuda of shining "Mexican"
Strawberries, liberalism! O aged green darlings

Of the 'Mericas, hunch, zippy! O location, look
At the merry, donning, palmettos, fairways
Of that buffing colossus "Peep Peep"! O
Doe! Marriage in Mexico amid the missing lemons
Of a parachute shining into the Mirabeau
Of your tasty kiss up in the March stars! Socking
The papery mirrors the limpid summers the very sutures
Of a timely stars' nimbus! watercress, O bough
Airy middle of giant impure true parasol swimmers
Blue. Toy-nature! In the bilges of a fair
Sure audience! They played "April Tiger," "Dig
Please," and "Secret Anatomies, a Parachute with Lemons
April Breathe Look Who Is Summer." Pickpock-
Ets and a different season the bridge us myster-
Ious lollipops' gambit Toussaint lurid seagreen bananas'
Shapeless crony, in the pyramid that all is
Life or purple! O gems! and beers
Drank up to the knees our green car baseball
On cheeriest red. Porch, thimble, and steeple!

O paints if time! A bough. Drinks the cow.
Unfaded red lemons, Santa Claus, marine, ow
Passenger, a London of musical coastline
"Sarah-fuge," benches gone equaling wavy "nice"
Halls. Save the defeating bells! Bend
My mind's six loops! Ah, beavers in the hall
With a trireme, merry coconut Triton
In, fall! the parodies of cinch, a stream
In Denmark, a basin of cherished spools, limping
Lanes, of "When, Mary Ann, eyes lakes is India
Merchant porch summer lethal leafy swim 'white
Rebus among dare homes is blue' is air wombat is
Is is is," banshee caretaker, suture, green. Ho, conduits
Of the wavy breast-line, which cylinders
Hat youthful climate! merry-cross, of "beads"
Of "beads" of beads! O bear! Hand-silly melons,

Believer-wear! Shoe, shoe, shoe! I dare you
To limp along O the fair mountains of a lifty pansy
Air rift! the bugles show. I dare you to
Mints, oh is golden! the bear-shaped leaf-cow of buy
One-two-tree-pony, of "never sees one blue page chair"
Harpoon limerick O the bee-parrot, "the werewolf
In the newspaper paints an orchestra" so
Many merry autobahns, boxing spinster!

O meetings! with gold bargains angel blockhouses
And bins, uppy "care-loose" seed! Weak nameplates
Umpiring the seaworthy Southerner-
Lake-opera, the killed mason of a dairy stone. Line
Meads! O bear the deflected milkmen, hog, away!
In the bishoprics of lime. "I am pasting silver
On Dad's picture. Ernestine
Lies in the garden, imagining the linemen
Galloping toward her silver pastry. I am alone
In my belief that Sheba leaks. O sybilline
Cogwheels, Saturday! Dreams you are the lantern
As the is foetus's punch." O daisies win! "Whin
Warren walked in Warren Warren's warren
There was limmons on the sea boat rail. O pail
Of apples that give the bargain clues
To its leafy gold! Pin-binge!" Lusting a meadow the curtains
Sail fifth shirt rail, "O bikes' last
Touch, now musical cancer!" Sheeps the hog away. May
Down, its, there, icks, tunes, "Solve me this some where
Blue cradles with their puppies, and the tinnest light
Of the 'worrild,' a manager sun green and surprise
The lariat of speaking hogs." His life was red, but
Oh, hats hip "Lear" of day. "Now-tation"
Of the singing rifles, which share, "zebras."

Maids! oh, a Moscow motion picture
"Flimmed Alpine blue," genius of mothers' crass producers'
Flayed livelihood of screeching juice divided

Into mysteries, boat, lilac professors, to the
Lemon of knowledge, bean, bean, Atlantic
Ann, "Miss Historical Peach Tree of Nineteen-Forty-Three
Orchestra Idiots Nineteen-Fifty-Three O Green
April of Vanished Bananas." Shirts! made in pylon
"Chimeney" manufacturings' damned blue
Sheep-castles of deluded carfare, weaving nudge,
Weaving nudge, O bombs! Loops of lacy match-
Sticks' blossoms' faint head's child's weak last
Cry's hoop-tiny May-ville poop deck's "as
Langerhans musical bayou of sleepy lemons' shy
Rare shy rare's act's" act's axe! "If need
Be peach! Blossoms of merry showmanship in Stone-
Henge, bugles! Loops of "the caretakers' jangling cigar's
Loops' rung-demanding caretaker's sweetpea's
Pylons, amid the clamor of rug-maddened seats'
Paper of closest-knit words' blossoming rugs' fair
Blue railroad eagle nine-tenths then will look out the
Windiest rose of fair harp-maddened space's lifts-up's-
Sky which nominative sea's solo cinch-
Lousy-mats' tree-church's a billion edge-nursery!

"Anna, soda their brains." "Father, finish is certain." O basements
Of cardex, "muneeciple" rungs'
Badger, agent, elephants that silver money
Career number "is" most, and try to die
Annoy "the Badge," lawn there wind from at seat
Lives is-maybe acts, who, rose, love fell
"His aspirin." April of we moss
Whos, Andy us where wind maze opera's we
Golf links, say "Egbert. The Floating of
Hips Blossom. A Nightmare of Amorous Delays. Thought
Turns Green. In What Century Mazda As Famous
Pericles!" We is running through his
This rowboat "axe" everywhere a fashion is factory
Celery leaping rose, agua. Hatred! Parry
Chute O summer of green "Penmanship is

April's pants," lovers amid these penmanship
Iron stars and latest can't-we-go-hosiery-of-the
Face British lilies! O bough
Eep-ad baby "sooma" and junction thousand
Lists May sweet "cars a a a a pill, season
Clouds of in and O emollients care, foot, blue
Evils," panzer. "O Kenneth tea Arab baby easels
Felt *arrondissement* gypsy tables and limps of
Needles parachute peas by, Lincoln, accidents."

He, day, believes is dogs "ne'ertheless" a
By the fishes' cocoa of today's sea sent
Collar loneliness home babies papers labors
Neighbors eagles capons savers of lilied
Papers of carbon moose's ape-bottling wintry
Soma of "a rustic Jeeps" facility, dim-witted men
Lying intercarfare raspberry "cup, be aware"-artillery
Amidst ye someday raspberries O Gloucester
Of faded robbers, cattle-bakeries and lint
Phosphorous eateries, mags! "Wearily woke up
Green bowwow. Artillery." Shapeless militarists
Caped Bongo Brow. O gypsum
Penthouses sweeter than a rabbit's pillows
Of airy green "Knocks," bakery
Of distinguished sighs! "How came the locks
Lethal paper incinerator vicinity choochoo fractions
Cuckoo nuts paper Freilichers if lilac sea-bottlery
Towel dispensary?" There air is very weird
Ape bit summer green air care "poop deck O lovely
Poop deck!" Black cherubs "a" shins
Lesson. Boat. Backseats motion its
Yellow carry us. Din to the "stair" of teeth
Blue mezzo soprano of sweetest decay "Indians
Air, blood, out," as bee-axed crazy-bell wigs.

Weevils, him! A Sue Artillery. Angel. Lye
Dim apricot, comma common comma. Change.

Priest-ape. Bay-foot is and
Laxa-team en-merchandise hope Savannah nearly
Congo. And bounce! Labour Party football lovely
Air "right bread to dam is must we limpid
China fateballs." O pennies! rime
Shirting a, sea: clock, to bridge—at's lovely
Sick's is wall easy as lovely dam-flowers
Lay America easel bunch! Hate! Equal. Lions. "Hey,"
Is the fields' operatic major amnesty smearing Congo
Silver "bear." Lives. Bicycles
Limerick the shorty beach O cosmos
Of "Last winter," tower of pin-hitting
Lambs!" Maid! Tree Hoop! Three "hoopers'
Ladies' night foot out tear inch above children to
Shirts. Bin. O lovely green
Aspirin. A limps. We." Ham expostulates
Swimming the bells. Tree-punt! O music of the
Shamrocks' peanut amidst the doughnut
License plates the ear silk. "Putt
The sob!" Nara of "Lame, I boat." Meek. Lilies'
Paper milkmen-tie. Us! Pills! O Labrador
Peach-quiet mittens' tea sun of cleared ozone trees!

Majesty O a blue arf kneeling hoop
Satire "Peaches need, owl, off, woof, May-
Time, 'the sea' of embarrassed fresh asphalt
Pastry laughers Lincoln of believed
Santa misty sentence nice clam deer Eskimo green
Solid. Rooms!" if sublime "grapefruit each-terrace
Lamp mice cooling-system licorice bizarre labors
For distance mighting silver coaties of green
Lay appearance proffers death lilacs nigh
Air gum in the 'shoot southern!' of prance 'kra!' knee
Sabotage 'limities' of shooting 'barbycuties' malice
Tots' visit love poultry sea bashing huts in green
Agoraphobe, O pain, Stevenson, Washington! Ship,
Mummy, woof, barefoot, lobster. Suds of air-

Proof. Tin. Bee-license. O reachest of the bays'
Spearmint copper 'neximo' axe livelier is toys
As engine-Britains, leaf, an miss. Sew, eep! the sun"
Bells asking lyricism is-mop. Corpse! Uncle
Pins! "He is sweet to" imagine
Of tree highest lint nuts hooray substitute
Fair limb a fields as cigarettes. Shy
Bessarabia puzzler eagle by "We waste" cincture fezzed
Clouds of preachy lakewater altars eep bell
You-you clubs arrive, Gemini of the hat ear eye fall peach water

Deem rafter. Cemetery. "Leem" eel batty bone.
O boa. Of the Fez Theatre. Laps'
Tricycle of we motionless London of bees'
Pent lilies and hooray schoolhouses'
Musical today loop lantern is surprise "schoolhouses" '
Peanuts' ladies' aspirin lanterns
Of climbing clematis, a lake of conceived doves' "Go
Fine ear character waiter. Modern, lilies. Congo
Of the defeated railroads, revolver. Lacy coat of the
Chancellor's ink mirrors of. Insane celery." Ship.
"O bayou, boom, icicles sesame the contained robber
Of leaves in chairs, savanna!" Crane? oh heron! Able
Balance the trip knee, comedy. "In the heap
Of Maytime llamas I limped upon the knees of
An old charcoal. Lemons" for a pound of the
Oxford! September air! Bun of old leaves of
Care each musical "Hooray, unpin the gong," sylvan water
Ape shell-ladder! Egypts! Mezzanine of deciding cuffs'
Anagrams who tea-tray "sigh them" objects "pay-sign"
"Leaf-boat" "love-object" "base-ball" "land-slide"
"Tea-ball" "orchestra" "lethal bench." Sum, are, lakes
"May-nagers" "love-times," sweet
Counter ale pan-banned gypsy-bin fools cabana
Gentle hiatus of sarabande "roof" "wide" seam!

Ko, or A Season on Earth

Ora non più: ritorni un'altra volta
chi voluntier la bella istoria ascolta.

Orlando Furioso, END OF CANTO XVI

I

Meanwhile at the University of Japan
Ko had already begun his studies, which
While making him an educated man
Would also give him as he learned to pitch
And catch—for Ko was more than a mere fan,
But wished as a playing member to do a hitch
With some great team—something to think about
More interesting than merely Safe and Out.

Inyaga, his professor, when he first
Appeared to Ko, seemed fashioned like an ape,
Protruding jaw and tiny eyes that burst
From high strong cheekbones of chimpanzee shape,
But later it was his teaching that Ko cursed,
Of which the body merely was the drape:
Inyaga taught him baseball was a sin.
Ko cried out! Inyaga: "Stop that din

At once, or else you'll suffer!" Ko subsides,
But his resentment every day gets greater.
Meanwhile the Dodgers all had taken brides
As was arranged for them by Mr. Slater,
Their crafty manager, who thus provides
A human interest for the fans, who, later,
When they find out his trick, will make him pay;
But for the moment it is Slater's day.

He drives the players here and there, shouts out
"Champagne!" and wishes all the women well
He's marrying to his players. What about
The women? They're contented. At the bell
They call "the wedding" they respond with shout
And glee, of which there'd be too much to tell;
Instead, I leave this sportive celebration
And go to England, where the Coronation

Of Amaranth the First is taking place.
Here Huddel, with his family gathered round,
Watches the gay procession. Huddel's face
Is twisted and is the color of swampy ground.
His wife, as though much pounded with a mace,
Is crushed and bulky; his daughter's like a mound.
This little group has one malevolent eye
Intent on Amaranth as he passes by.

This latter, radiant with joy, though sad
At his late mother's death, has not a thought
For such as Huddel, but with gestures glad
And strong with youth, proceeding as he ought
In gold and silver, thinks there is no bad
That he can't cure. And then his eye is caught
By jewels shining at a certain distance,
And to the crown he loses all resistance.

Andrews was also at the Coronation,
Dressed in a gray fluff suit which made him bigger
Than usual, but did not see the consummation
Because he was distracted by a chigger
Inside his pants leg. In his consternation
He went to the stationer's to buy a digger
To get it out. Too bad! the place was closed,
As anyone, in truth, might have supposed,

Because of Coronation. On his way
Back to the ceremony Andrews met
An English girl, who, later in that day,
He was quite certain he would not forget,
For various reasons. But of this we may
Speak somewhat later. At the moment let
Us note that Andrews missed the part when Huddel
Got all the Coronation in a muddle.

This latter, mindful of what might have been
If he by nature had but found admission
Into the royal womb, with savage grin
Stared at the glittering blue-white apparition
Of the crown jewels, and past the hats of tin
Padded with blue of the bobbies, into the partition
He clawed his way, where there was no one present
But those of royal blood. "Get out, you peasant!

You imbecile! you nut! you Kerry Blue!
You pig!" all cried. Huddel, though, looked about,
Affirming, "I've as much right here as you.
England is a democracy." "How about
That?" Dukes and Earls exclaimed; "not true:
England, if you had read some you'd find out,
Is a constitutional monarchy, and leans
Mostly on its traditions, kings, and queens.

In a democracy there's no such thing
As royal fam—" But here they were interrupted
By the noises of Huddel's removal, who as if on wings
Was moving from bobby to bobby, by each intercepted
While passing from one to the other, as each of them flings
His burden away from the royal partition, corrupted
By such a foul presence and, finally, dropping it where
There was no Coronation, there was nothing but buildings and air.

Amaranth, since he knew what he had done,
Although convenient, was quite unethical,
Whispered to the Duke of Melbourne to send one
Of his most worthy Cavaliers of Senegal
To seek out Huddel and give him half a ton
Of pence, which might, the King thought, be much preferable
To looking at Huddel again, for Huddel was repulsive,
With face of green, and every movement convulsive.

Huddel's family, meanwhile, on the sidewalk lumped
At first, had followed their flying father and now
Approached him in the suburbs. As if humped
From too much weight, the Archbishop of Canterbury's bow
Indicates Coronation's somewhat slumped
To Amaranth and his courtiers. Oh then how
All changes as he raises the crown on high—
Amaranth trembles with joy, and he courses by

The applauding crowds, driven mad by the beautiful sight!
Ko meanwhile had improved himself at bat
And in the field, and in the dim daylight
Of dawn appeared in a fake Dodger hat
In Tampa after forty hours of flight.
He'd flown from dim Japan! and though he'd sat
So long awake, he went without delay
To where the Dodgers in spring training lay.

The Dodgers, each amused by his new mate,
Were not out on the field on time, of course,
And Ko stood swinging at an empty plate
A bat he'd brought along with him. What force
He gets into his swing! Soon at the gate
He heard the Dodgers voicing their remorse
At being up so early. Ko retired
Into a bullpen, which he much admired.

Slater was leader of his merry crew
And brought them on the diamond with a shout,
"If other players slept as much as you,
There'd be no major leagues, I have no doubt!
Fortunately, you're among the happy few
Who really know what baseball is about
And can afford to, wrapped in wifely charms,
Lie fifteen hours a day in Morpheus' arms!"

The players laughed, adopting their positions
Upon the field. They stole and ran and caught
And hit homeruns past where you pay admissions.
Their game, although a practice one, was fought
With ardor and avoidance of omissions—
"My mate is in the stands," each Dodger thought.
When everything was over, they discovered
Ko sleeping on a bench, by tarpaulin covered.

Exhausted by his trip of forty hours,
Ko had, in spite of everything, dropped off
To sleep the minute he sat down. Of flowers
He dreamed, created of some silver stuff
And set upon a screen, not exactly in bowers,
But in formation, as if on a graph.
The background was quite blue, and there appeared
A silver boatman there, who gondoliered

Some ladies dressed in robes of red and purple
Into a little house, shaped like a rectangle
And colored yellow, round which in a circle
Stood little black-limbed trees backed by a fleck-tangle
Of what apparently were leaves. A gurgle
Of water seemed to splash upon the check tangle
Of one of the ladies' gowns as she emerged
To shore, by boatman and companions urged,

Apparently, to watch her step. Her silky
Purple checked and splattered gown however
Seemed in the moonlight beautiful and milky
And one could almost quite believe that never
Had water splashed it. All was in a still key.
An enormous yellow hand then pulled a lever,
And Ko saw warriors dressed in red and white
Dancing across some paper, as if in flight.

Each had a black mustache, one stroke of ink
Per warrior, each had long white ink-drawn sleeves
And a red vest, a spear whose tip was pink,
And in the all-white background one perceives
Some bright green tufts of grass. With a great wink
One of the warriors looks at Ko, who leaves
His dream immediately with a cry:
"Oh am I still asleep? Who's passing by?"

"We are the Dodgers," sang that merry band;
"This is our field, our bullpen, our delight,
Our Tampa, our spring training, and our land!
But who are you, who in the dead of night
Of anxious dreams in middle day do stand
And question us? What was it caused your fright?"
The Dodgers then subsided into silence
Like ocean birds returning to their islands.

Ko, then, returning to full consciousness,
Explained to Mr. Slater and his hitters
How baseball had been all his happiness
Since when, a tiny toddler throwing spitters
At paper lanterns, he had made a mess
Of one upon the floor, which was all glitters,
And how, established thus his skill for throwing,
His skill at playing had been ever growing.

"Let's give the kid a chance!" cried Slater, moved
By Ko's intensity, his education,
And by his trans-Pacific flight. "We're grooved
To take another pitcher on. Tarnation!
If this kid's good, the saying will be proved
That there are stranger things in God's creation
Than any of us dreams of. Get a glove,"
He finished; and Ko looked at him with love.

Although their wives were waiting, yet the team
Went willingly out to the field again
To see the stranger pitch. As in a dream,
But not the ones he had, Ko counted ten,
Wound up, and threw the baseball with such steam
That it went through the backstop, lost till when
The field would be torn down, and lazy goats
Would ramble through it gnawing shreds of coats;

It dug into the grandstand, where it stayed.
The crowd went wild—the crowd was mostly team,
Plus several wives. The catcher, with his splayed
Brown weighty glove, first spellbound, with a scream
Fell in the dirt behind the plate and prayed;
And Slater's agitation was extreme.
"Put someone else behind the plate," he cried,
"So that this talent may be verified!"

Another catcher came. Ko raised his torso
In a high arc, then slumped it down again,
Then raised his arm and threw with such a force (Oh
It was beautiful to see) that when
The players' screams died down, they saw that, more so
Than the first, this second ball had pen-
Etrated through the enormous blocks of wood
And made the grandstand shiver where it stood.

Slater had fainted; and the golden sun
Sent down its last warm beams upon his visage
Which lay upon the field like something one
Has splattered golden paint all over (syzyg-
Ies of manager and player that stun
Them both!). With bottled soda, for its fizzage
All shaken up, and then released to spray
The unconscious manager, came shortstop Gray.

Ko meanwhile was preparing a third ball
With glove and gesture, seeing all in ruins
The grandstand, which he thought for sure would fall
With one or two more pitches. But De Bruins,
The first-base coach, ran out and stopped him, all
Emotionally shaken by these doings,
With "You have done enough for now." Ko paused,
Confused by what he'd heard, and as if lost.

But let us see how Andrews, where, in England,
He draws sweet breath of day, is now engaged,
Who, girl-encountering in that queen and king land,
Should by all odds be properly assuaged
By now, outside the window hear a wing land
Or in the corridor a stranger paged.
In fact, it's thus; the girl he lies beside
Has beautiful blonde hair and is blue-eyed.

Her skin is soft, her body white and rounded
Deliciously, her breasts two islands where
Two balneary paradises could be founded
In which all felt a bliss beyond compare;
Her waist is small, as if it had been pounded
By Venus' hammer; and with utmost care
Her legs seem to be sculpted. She's alive!
She touches Andrews. "Take me for a drive

Around the city of London, that I may
See you a bit in some other atmosphere
Than this close-breathing beddy one, that today
I can decide if I really love you, dear,
Or if this has been but a holiday
Enchantment, fleeting as the foam on beer."
Andrews says, "I don't have a car," but Doris
(For that's her name) says, "I've a little Morris.

It's parked outside. You'll recognize it. It's
Red, with a reddish-pink interior. In
The pocket of my coat, with combs and bits
Of paper, are the keys. Hand me that pin,
And you can go down first and get it," sits
In bed, so pretty all from chin to shin
That Andrews, putting on his gray fluff suit,
Rushes to cover her with kisses—the brute!

At last he exits, seeking for the car
In the refreshing air of springtime London;
Remembers, hearing horns blow from afar,
How he the Coronation did abandon;
Starts, but then stops; thinks, "That is how things are—
My abandon-Coronation was not wanton,
But of an accident the glad result,
For which I should not grieve but here exult."

"Oh, thank you, London skies," in exultation
Andrews began to chant, but then decided
It was not really fit that Coronation
Be slighted for a lovely girl who glided
Against him by mistake. With hesitation
He stayed his steps and, doing so, collided
With a fine gentleman propelled by dog
On leash, compelled to leap about like frog.

"Pardon me, Sir," to Andrews said this latter
(The gentleman attired in red), and Andrews
Said, "Certainly he'd not store up the matter
As source of grief and bitterness, nor hand use
Against a fellow being for such errata
Of human moving, since it was not a planned ruse
But obviously an accidental bump.
As such, it made in throat appear no lump."

The gentleman, amazed to hear such language
From a common pedestrian, asked the origins
Of gray-fluff-suited Andrews, who with anguish
Said that they were not known: "My father's sins,"
He sadly smiled. "Come, have a fried fish sandwich,"
The gentleman exclaimed, who was on pins
And needles to hear the rest of Andrews' tale;
But for the moment his ruse was destined to fail.

For at this moment Doris, to the door,
Dressed in a light green suit, came, saying, "What!
You haven't yet arrived at my sweet car?"
And then their vessel did another knot,
And Andrews knew he had not known before
That they were on the ocean. "What a spot,"
He sighed, "I'm in, for I'm supposed to be
Reporting to the Station after three."

In fact the boat they rode on was quite large,
So much so it was really understandable
That Andrews did not know it was a barge
On which a little building, which was landable,
Of light materials made, which came from Arg-
Entina, stood. Poor Andrews sighed; his mandible
Fell down a notch: "How could I not have seen,
From where we lay above, the water's sheen?

But, Doris, tell me, when did we put off?
We were attached to land when I came in.
And who's the elegant dog-walking toff
I ran into just now? What was that din
Of horns I heard I naturally enough
Thought Coronation noises? What has been
Your motive in estranging me from shore?
Oh why did you speak of a Morris just before?

How could there be a Morris on the sea?"
Doris began unbuttoning her jacket,
Under which she was naked, hurriedly,
And sighed, "If you would come around in back, it
Would help me to undress more speedily.
I think I really love you. What a racket
My heart is making!" Andrews, with a stare
Of wonder, rushed to her and lost his care.

While their big barge is moving down the Thames,
Let's turn to Indianapolis, where the Speedway
Is filled with customers, who with ahems
And haws are waiting for the sight they need way
Down upon the speedway and with stems
Of pencils write their choices down with greed. Way
Past the starting gate a little car
Is finally admitted 'neath the bar.

It's coming late, but nevertheless may win.
Its driver has a shock of brownish hair
And pretty yellow goggles and smooth chin
And doth a driver's padded garment wear . . .
Boom boom! the axles clash, the gears begin
To grind their way, and who is winning? Where?
A big red car that bears the number Three
Pulls out ahead, or so it seems to me.

No, no—there's one of blue that's shooting out
Ahead of Number Three. What sounds of grinding!
Clashing! crashing! smashing! dashing about!
Then silence . . . then a terrible sound of winding
Followed by an explosion and a shout—
A flash of flame, then smoke, oh smoke so blinding!
Why did we come here anyway? Let's go!
But something . . . something's happened down below.

The little yellow car that we saw enter
The Speedway late now courses all alone
Round and round about the Speedway's center,
While all the others lie in wreckage strown—
Their drivers, half alive, too weak to banter,
Stare at their ruined racing cars and moan.
Who is this driver who has won the race?
There's not a single whisker on his face!

Who is it? "Here is forty thousand dollars
And an invitation to come back next year."
"Show us your face!" a young spectator hollers,
And off the goggles come. . . . With shrieks of fear
The judges scatter, like so many collars
Rustled by winds in May, and there appear
A crowd of blue policemen on the track.
One pulls his pistol out; you hear its crack

And crash of windows in the judges' stand,
Where still the horrid spectacle stands smiling
At all below, above, and with his hand
Makes a large gesture, which, as fans go piling
Out all the gates, sets fire to the grand-
Stands, which burn like tinder. The beguiling
Great theatre of sports goes up in oranger
Flames than rum when lighted in a porringer.

"It's the end of everything," one of the judges said
Who had managed to get outside; "it's the end of the track
And the end of the race, and with so many persons dead
It's the end of the Speedway forever." And he hunched his back
And walked through the fallen leaves, where crusts of bread
Lay scattered for Indianapolis' pigeons. "Alack!"
Murmured a schoolboy who had escaped alive,
"Now I shall never be let to learn to drive

In preparation for being a Speedway racer!"
His mother took his hand, and they wandered from sight
Into an ice cream emporium called The Glacier.
Meanwhile, back at the track, what once was bright
Had now turned dark and smouldery like an embrasure,
And all you could see aside from the flames that night
Was the winning yellow car, which stood untouched
In the center of that red chaos, and unsmutched.

The demon, fiend, or hideously maladjusted
Cause of this chaos stood some blocks away
Staring at Indianapolis, which, he trusted,
Would never be the same. "It's a great day
When something burns, explodes, or just is busted!"
He cried, and, looking at the sky, which, gray
With evening, seemed entirely in accord
With what he'd said, flew back to his yellow Ford

And drove it toward St. Paul. In Boston meanwhile
An investigation of the Speedway disaster
Made many a citizen desist from bean while
Reading of its results, which ever faster
Led to the conclusion that in that machine, while
Everyone'd thought there was a driving master,
There really had been some supernatural essence
Who regarded human beings as an excrescence.

The Indianapolis police, in fear
Of horrible reprisals, had done nothing;
They could not forget the horrid demoniac leer
In the judges' stand, that had set their pink hearts pulsing
White Valentine lace immediate as the foam on beer
Which into their chests like a great card still cutting
Would give them, no, no peace, nor any comfort,
But bade them stand stock still in pained discomfort

Or else it would perturb them with its edges.
Though Indianapolis may remember long
Its great disaster, already upon its hedges
Birds sing the very next morning a gay song;
Boys run to school; and carpenters planing wedges
Enjoy the smell of sawdust. Life must go on
Even though what one loves the best's in ruins.
Meanwhile in Tampa Dodger coach De Bruins

Took down his hand from Ko's left arm and said,
"I mean, let's wait till Slater comes to life.
For joy—" "For joy?" said Ko. "—he's almost dead:
Sight of your speedball pierced him like a knife. . . ."
Slater bounced up and interrupted, red
With soda: "We've got to find the kid a wife!"
He wiped some cherry phosphate off his neck.
"He can't be our only bachelor—what the heck!"

"You see—" and Slater then explained to Ko
How all the Dodgers had been married. "Naturally
You wouldn't like to be the exception." "No,"
Ko said, "but I don't know a soul here, actually,
And I'm not sure I'm old enough." "Go, go,"
Laughed Slater, "go and ask the catcher will he
Help you to meet a girl—he knows them all;
He can be seen at every Tampa ball.

His wife, as it turns out, is a Tampa belle,
And thus he's finely suited for the role,
Because he knows the Tampa women well,
Of finding you, as weevil finds a boll,
A wife with whom in company to dwell,
And thus be on the Dodgers, off the dole."
The players all applauded Slater's sally
Into poetry, whose wit was up their alley.

Slater, encouraged, continued, "And if you
Should see a girl whom you would like to wow
So she will be responsive when you woo,
Not scratch your face and answer with meeouw,
And when you speak of moonlight, answer 'oooh,'
Nor drive you from the garden screaming 'ow,'
Just ask—" but here applause him interrupted,
Loud as of Satan's angel band corrupted.

Facing his cheering players, Slater smiled:
"Let me continue, if you will, my friends;
I shall be shortly done"; and with a wild
Gesture of enthusiasm took Ko's hands.
"I think you are right! you are still but a child
And should await the bride that Heaven sends,
Not seek her out because a wily Captain
Thinks it would make the fans somewhat distracted!"

The players sobbed with joy and disbelief,
All standing 'round. What into Slater's heart
Had come, white-wingèd? Never had their chief
Wavered an instant in the sturdy art
Of baseball managing—not love or grief
Had ever made him change in slightest part
What he had decided on as Dodger policy,
Whether it was to play them in the Colise-

Um of Rome, or else in water baseball
To place them on the Grand Canal in Venice
With gondolas for bases. Down each face ball
Of water after ball of water menac-
Ing to flood the field fell. In that place bawl
Forty Dodgers and a girl in tennis
Shorts, the wife of center fielder Hunter,
A so-so hitter but a famous bunter.

They weep at human kindness. Slater's face
Is, in that darkening field, transfixed with light.
To Ko it seemed an ordinary grace
That he was not obliged to choose at sight
A wife so soon; but every Dodger ace
Was well aware that on that breezy night
Something had come to change their dauntless leader,
Who had, till then, been remorseless as a parking meter.

"Play ball!" The spell was broken. It was next day
And they were still all there, surprised and hungry,
In uniforms of red and white, to play
At baseball quite unfit, with wives all angry
Parading in the stands, their faces gray
From waiting up all night, the while a dinghy
Knocked up against a dock, where all would like
To go and sleep, not too far from the dike.

Andrews (upon the Thames, as you recall)
With Doris in a soft and chilly nest
Is now attempting to unravel all
The things that puzzle him—among the rest,
Just who that man was who with light footfall
Had bumped against him when he'd gotten dressed
And gone to get the Morris. "Is it someone
Who owns this boat? His dress was quite uncommon."

"Oh that's my dad," said Doris, "whom you ought
To get to know. He's an important poet."
She leaned against pink pillows. Andrews caught
Her waist as if he were about to throw it,
But only squeezed it. "What's that noise? I thought
I heard a yelp!" "It's Dad—oh wouldn't you know it!
He would come by just now! Well, you and Pater
Should get along, with your poetic nature—"

The cabin door shot open, and a man
(Or was it human?) with a hairy large
Long sloping face, which was all colored tan
Except the blackish nose, came in the Arg-
Entina-purchased cabin with a can
Of worms he used to fish with from the barge
And woofed and barked and quite upset the room
By running 'round. Andrews, alarmed, cried, "Whom . . . ?"

Doris spoke smiling: "Dad's integrity
Makes him, unlike most poets, actualize
In everyday life the poem's unreality.
That dog you saw on deck with steel-gray eyes
Was but a creation of Dad's terrible musical potency.
Then seeing the dog there made him realize
That the dog was himself, since by himself created,
So in this poem it's incorporated!"

"But," Andrews asked, "what poem? where?" and "Ah!"
Breathed Doris, "don't you know that what you're seeing
Is an ACTION POEM?" "You mean he's Joseph Dah,"
Cried Andrews, "the creator of 'Otherness Being'?"
"The very same," sighed Doris. "That's my pa!"
And Joseph, as if by his barks agreeing,
Shook his tan head and frisked back out on deck.
He changed, then smiled: "It's a nice day, by heck!"

And then he dropped a line into the sea
That had a worm on it upon a hook
And was as calm as any man can be
Whose poems do not lie in any book
And so are dead to his posterity.
Back to the cabin he gave not a look;
He stood unmoving as a propped-up log,
And at his feet there was a little dog.

"He's back to human," Doris laughed. "Let's go
Out on the deck and join him," she half-whispered,
Turning about so Andrews could kiss her. "Though
It's likely that it's nicer here." A crisp bird
Call sounded. Doris sighed, "Oh do you know
You make me, Andrews, really want to lisp herd
On herd of fleecy warm and white-lined syllables
To tell my love. . . ." Looking for where the pillow was,

Andrews replied, "I also love you, Love."
Just then they heard a huge unpleasant buzz
And felt the flap of wings, while from above
A watermelon head with silver fuzz
Bent down, extending them a horseshoe glove. . . .
"Dad!" Doris screamed. "I am not what I was,"
Dah cried, "buzz bzzz!" and shut them in a coffin
He threw to the waves, which buffeted it often.

Meanwhile in Kansas there was taking place
A great upheaval. High school girls refused
To wear their clothes to school, and every place
In Kansas male observers were amused
To see the naked girls, who, lacking grace,
Were young, with bodies time had not abused,
And therefore made the wheatfields fresher areas
And streets and barns as well. No matter where he is

A man is cheered to see a naked girl—
Milking a cow or standing in a streetcar,
Opening a filing cabinet, brushing a curl
Back from her eyes while driving in a neat car
Through Wichita in summer—like the pearl
Inside the oyster, she makes it a complete car.
And there were many sermons on the subject,
And autoists, come in to have the hub checked

On their old car, would stand and pass the day
With talking of the various breasts and waists
They'd seen throughout the week, and in what way
They thought the thing, according to their tastes,
Was right or wrong, that these young girls should stray
Through Kansas without even stocking pastes
Upon their legs. Although officially negative,
As for a law, nobody wished to make it if

It were not absolutely necessary—
Unless, that is, the nakedness resulted
In crime and rape and sinking of the ferry
That spanned the Wichita, in youth insulted
And age dishonored, in a broad hysteri-
A, in other words, among the adulthood
Of Kansas caused by the unaccustomed vision
Of these young girls, brought on by the decision

Of the High School Girl Committee of Kansas City,
Kansas, in an attempt for something new
In good old Kansas where the girls are pretty
But life is dry, and there is not the dew
Of new ideas and excitement, witty
Conversation until has grown blue
What once was gray (the window) and one sees
New day resplendent, hears the humming bees,

And, flushed with pleasure, goes into the garden
Out the great concrete door, and sits upon
A bench 'mid red amid yellow flowers and arden-
Tly resumes one's colloquy with one
Or two or three friends; but, instead, lifeguardin'
In Kansas City's swimming pools, or done
With supper—mashed potatoes, iced tea, and potroast—
One stands about and looks at a green fencepost

And wishes one were ashes in a jar
Unless there's something doing at the dancehall
Or some new kind of frozen ice-cream bar
One has a yen to eat. As for romance, all
That one can do is get into one's car
And drive out 'mid the sunflowers, just perchance all
Giving off their pollen, which as a lover
Defeats one who from allergy does suffer

And makes him sneeze instead of kiss. "However,
Economic prosperity has blessed
The State of Kansas," cried the girls—"why never
A corresponding aesthetic interest
To make our lives worthwhile?" Then one wild, clever,
Ingenious, terrible girl came to the desk
And said how they, by taking off their clothes,
Could change the dried-out thistle to a rose,

Enchant the atmosphere, and bring to Kansas
A dream! The plan was instantly adopted,
With the results we've seen. From foreign lands as
Far as Tibet and Burma helicopted,
Entrained, en-autoed, or on feet or hands as
Fast as they could move, came hordes who opted
To trade their leisure for a sight so rare—
Girls walking through the Kansas cities bare

Of any vestments, many-colored statues
Which had the gifts of movement and of speech;
Blonde, brown, brunette—like different-colored matches
Their heads; their bodies, almanacs to teach
The riveter his trade, the famous mattress
Tycoon how far and at what points should reach
The springs, the poet how to shape his lines,
The woodsman what is lacking in the pines.

As for the natives, happy Kansans say:
"I wonder what is in East Wichita Hooks
I could have missed when I went there the day
Before yesterday at lunch hour with my books
Still in my briefcase from my office. They
Say where I work the girls with the best looks
Are in South Wichita Turnings. Well, tomorrow
A bike or motorcycle I shall borrow

And ride to see them. Oh what a wonderful Sunday
It's going to be! and after I have stared
My fill (if it's not possible in one day,
Then when I'm tired out), I will, prepared
For the whole weekend, take my lunch, which Monday
I started packing, out to where the Baird
Brothers Wichita Freight and Packing Company flings
Its concrete walls, and past some wooden things

To where, after you pass the first three lampposts,
You see a greenish gully, which, descending
You find the Little Wichita through damp posts,
Branches, and discarded clothing wending
Its way, and you can eat among the damp hosts
Of weeds and reeds and toads; and then, ascending
To Turnings once again, the girls I'll see
And take a dancing vision home with me

As the bicycle bumps along. Then to North Wichita
On Sunday evening for a glass of soda
(Kansas is 'dry' and if you are not rich at all
You cannot get a drink there) at the Groada
Bowling Alleys, where, without a stitch at all,
From the University which is down the road a
Little, the coeds' bowling team will be playing
The fully clothed team which from Smith College is straying."

These are the plans of a prince! Yet they are those
Of a plain Kansan, whom to such *bonheur*
The girls' decision brought. O lovely rose
Of girl, where is there any parallel *fleur*? . . .
But now the headlines blaringly expose
(Chiefly the *Times* and *France Observateur*):
AMARANTH PLANS TO VISIT KANSAS TO
SEE IF OLD ENGLAND'S GIRLS SHOULD UNDRESS TOO.

While Amaranth is packing up in state
For his great Kansas visit, and while Ko
And all the other Dodgers lie in great
Exhaustion on the field, and Andrews o-
Vercome by Dah and turned to ocean freight
With Doris moves to westward, and the snow
From the high Himalayas comes unstuck,
Let's pause a moment, like a dairy truck.

II

If like a dairy truck the opening canto
Came to a close, the second should begin
In a like manner. Past the *campo santo*,
The drugstore, and the county airport, in
Great haste the milkman rides, begins to pant, "Oh,
How shall I ever paint in time to win
The bottle picture contest, which, it's true,
Is sponsored by the Cincinnati Zoo,

A corollary of the summer opera
And much more modern. . . . What strange man is this?
You talk to him, and meanwhile I will pop a-
Round in the back and see what images
Upon the glass containers' sides in tempera
Or oil or watercolor he with bliss
Of inspiration that he might win fame
Has etched. Look here! they're lovely, all the same!

The first one is all red, all orange the second;
And here's a pink one, bearing on its front,
Outlined in blue, a manager who's beckoned
To a first-base coach whom he seems to want
To talk to. Turn the bottle on its back and
You see the coach, blue-uniformed, a runt,
Making a gesture toward the dugout cover.
And here on this one here there is a lover

Depicted in a coffin, which is violet,
And he is purple. There is at his side
A beautiful naked girl, who seems to smile at
Their strange predicament. About them wide-
Ly stretch the blue, blue waves. A yellow pilot
From a pink ship assaulted by the tide
On the other side of the bottle stares at the sea
As one who looks for something ardently.

Here is a king, done twice, both purple-ermined;
Here on this next, which is, I think, the sixth,
We see the manager again. With firm and
Orange-veinèd hand he stands and picks the
Red-uniformed young pitcher from the ferment
Of bodies on the bench. The pitcher licks the
Ends of his fingers. In an orange sky
Small clouds of white and pink go scudding by.

Here's one of two great lands that drift away
From one another. . . . Oh, how great is art
That brings us on a purple-rainy day
A world of sunshine, insights, horse and cart
Trotting downhill. . . . And these milk bottles, gay
With red and yellow, are but a small part
Of all the art there is! Here are some statues,
Just for example, seemingly of catchers

And pitchers, in that cemetery yard
We're passing on the right—for as we criticize
His painted bottles, he is riding hard,
The driver, and the beams of sun which hit his eyes
Go brightlier back to that great globe. His ard-
Ency is caused (which is the thing that lit his eyes)
By his desire to finish work as soon as
He can, so he can paint—for as the moon was

To blond Endymion, art was to him.
Besides, the bottle contest had a deadline
Of May the sixth, and oh the chance was slim
That he could paint them all by then: a leadmine
Was easier to empty than of Jim
(His name was Jim) the sea—of blue line, red line,
Green line, brown line, yellow ochre splotch—
That was his truest self. Of course, he'd botch

A number of the bottles by attempting
To put too much on any one, with yellows,
Oranges, and reds each other tempting;
Or else with far too many girls and fellows,
So that no air was left, thus life exempting.
When one was finished, he would take a bellows
To dry it off. . . . But, meanwhile, let us turn,
From earthly vehicles where gases burn,

Away! to mid-Atlantic, where, inside
A coffin Andrews with sweet Doris lay.
The sea! the sea! Oh, how be satisfied
With living absolutely any way
But this, clasped to a beauty, and from side
To side deflected by the gentle sway
Of great blue ocean, with a smell as fragrant
As fresh-picked roses! Not far off, the flagrant-

Ly guilty Joseph Dah, who had recovered
His human presence, scanned the rolling whitecaps
In search of them. "It's a good thing," he hovered
Between a laugh and tears, "they both are light chaps
And that the coffin has some air-holes, covered
By wax the sun will melt: then they'll see white gaps
And know that they can breathe. . . . But how shall I
Find them again between this sea, this sky?"

He spoke, and, as he did so, twirled a lariat
Into the air, all twisty, rough, and white,
Which, when he pulled it in, was choking a parrot,
Who when released said, "If I would, I might
Tell you of those you love. A horrible pirate
Shall take them on his ship and try all night
To bend fair Doris to his black desire;
Andrews, meanwhile, they'll roast above a fire.

When morning comes, the sky with clouds of blue
Will cleanse the sea of shades, and you shall see
A ship shaped like a large white wooden shoe
Flying the Merry Christmas. It shall free
Your loved ones from the pirates. . . ." "Who are you,"
Said Dah, "that you can know what is to be?"
The parrot laughed, and Dah forthwith became
A thing it is too terrible to name!

There was no parrot anymore, but there
Was something larger, greener, more intense,
More red and blue, more insufflate with air,
Whose squawks would split the most resistant sense,
And yet upon that deck there walked a pair
Of human legs, supporting the immense
Catastrophe! and pirates' bodies filled
The sunny sea lanes by blue breezes chilled.

In several seconds it was over, and
The poet in the sunlight, till turned pink
By its descending rays, stood head in hand,
Not knowing how to act or what to think. . . .
Meanwhile in Cincinnati in the grand-
Stand everyone is raising a big stink
Because the game's delayed. Attired in blue,
Slater calls to De Bruins, "Come here, you!

This game is opening game, and we've exhausted
Our pitching staff! and it's the second inning!
We trail by fifteen runs. . . . I fear we've lost it—
Already, Coach, the box-seat crowd is thinning. . . ."
Then Slater took a penny out and tossed it.
"It's heads!" De Bruins cried. "Oh, what a din in
My ears that crowd is making," Slater offered.
Then both went over to third-base coach Crawford.

"I'm going to call in Ko," said Slater. "Yes,
I know it's dangerous: he throws too hard,
And Cincinnati's thousands cannot guess
That soon their field will be an empty yard
Covered with grandstand fragments; but unless
His name is written on each trembling card
That's held in Cincinnati hands, these buggers
Will kill us all—I've never seen such sluggers!"

To Crawford and De Bruins he indicated
The row of mighty batsmen in the dugout—
Rizitznikov, whose mighty club was weighted
With steel; Valcowsky, who could pull the rug out
From under any pitcher, and, elated,
As easily as you can pull a plug out,
Could dash the fence to splinters. Both were dressed
In orange uniforms with a red vest,

A special privilege granted by the Redleg
Management to such great hitters. Gostoff,
Who made the centerfielders fall as dead, leg
Broken, all a-sprawling; Iznivrostov,
Who swung his club as though it were a lead leg
And hit the pill so hard that it was lost off
In Cincinnati's farther reaches; Bensky,
Who tripled every day; and dread Mischensky.

To these were added Broczd and Zagar Miktsin,
Of medium build, but deadly with the stick
That made the ball fly farther than a pigeon
That goes to seek its mate; so red, so thick,
So rising from their yellow shirts like pigskin,
These players' necks alone made pitchers sick,
Because they signified what strength they bore;
Over their yellow they blue jackets wore;

Their shoes were red, and on their caps was scrawled
"REDLEGS," which meant, "You haven't got a chance."
At this array of strength, Slater, appalled,
Although since Florida a very dance
Of contradictions in his mind was walled
On when and whether he'd use Ko, as France
Is close to Spain, at once decided "Yes!"
Ko, beckoned to, at heights of happiness,

Can scarcely feel the field, the mound, the ball
That's put into his hands: all seems imaginary—
The crowd, the stands, the shortstop, Slater, all;
And cannot speak, nay, no more than a badger, nary
A word, but, speechless, sees the batter fall,
The catcher, then the umpire, and like pageant airy
The infield boxes and their steel supports
At his first pitch, which as a gun reports

Made a great crash. And then, from 'neath the stands
Where Ko's pitch penetrated, he sees stagger
A gray-haired man, who often with his hands
Daubs at his head, where, as if by a dagger
Struck and then struck again, blood spurts and lands
Upon the diamond. "I am very bad hurt,"
He cries, and while the players gather round
From outfield, bullpen, dugout, base, and mound

He tells them all his story. "I am Higby,
The famous catcher. . . . Yes, I know that I
Supposedly am dead, stung by a big bee
Upon the heart, while chasing a foul fly
In 1936, but if you dig me
Up in the cemetery where I lie,
Supposedly, you'll find I am not there.
A country doctor, good at heart repair,

Chanced in to see me when I had been given
Completely up for lost, my face all covered
With a white sheet, on which a nurse had written
'THIS ONE TO CEMETERY—NOT RECOVERED,'
And, pulling back my sheet, said 'One can live in
That body still,' and, going forth, discovered
A body in the hall he substituted
For me, and took me where he'd instituted

A little clinic in the country, by
A rushing brook, with haystacks all around.
There, underneath a peaceful blue-white sky,
The doctor tended me till I was sound.
I scarcely even now could tell you why. . . .
But I awoke one day and heard the sound
Of sparrows in the meadow and of robins
And of the merry farmwife spinning bobbins,

And knew that I was well again. I leaped
From where I lay, to seek my uniform
There where it hung inside a cupboard steeped
In mothballs, with its gay cuneiform
Of stitching 'round the waist, and then I heaped
A stack of bills upon the desk, and, warm
With my new liberty, ran down the stairway
To thank my benefactors for the fair way

In which they'd treated me, planning, of course,
To go immediately back to baseball.
I found the doctor riding on a horse
About the farmyard. But I saw his face fall,
Which had been brightened at my new-found force,
When I informed him of my plans. O ace ball-
Players, listen to what happened then,
And sympathize, as you are thinking men.

The doctor had a daughter, just sixteen,
Who, unbeknownst to me, while I had writhed
Upon the sickbed, cared for me—O Jean,
I see you still, I hear your father's cry, 'The d-
Urned fool's not worth it, Jean!' I see the mean
Face of your mother, from whose heart I'd scythed
Her only crop of joy: for Jean had desperately
Fallen in love with me. Her parents successfully

Persuaded her to ask me not to go
Back into ball, but stay there on the farm—
Thus they'd not lose their daughter. But my *no*
Was final, absolute! I saw no harm
In hogs and hay, in teaching things to grow,
Then cutting and burning them to keep us warm
And killing and cooking them to make us fat;
I loved the farmer's life—it wasn't that,

But that there was no smell of leather mitts,
No baseball insides all flag-colored string,
No fences, no place where the manager sits
With nervous hands, no plate, no anything
That makes a man a hitter when he hits
And not a lousy rowdy. Though they wring
Their hands and oil their shotguns, I depart,
And Jean comes running after—oh, my heart . . . !"

The old man staggers; and they carry him
Out to the mound, where, supine, he resumes
His too-soon-ended tale: "Her Father, grim
With resolution, shot two times—two booms
I heard—but strikes his Jean though me he limn.
Insane with grief, he built a pair of tombs,
Put Jean in one, and in the other shut
Himself, to die when oxygen was not.

I vainly pounded on his tomb, insisting
That one death was enough, yet came no answer
From out that sepulchre, whose columns, twisting
As high as trees, held, trembling like a dancer,
The mother, clinging there, who in the misting
Of woody afternoons shrieked, 'Yours this cancer,
This death, this hell!' I fled, and wandered for
Five years, as one who's crazed, and five years more

I walked the seashore, and for six in addition
I stood on sidewalks staring at the curb;
Till, finally, by some inward strange volition,
I drifted toward this field. I plucked an herb
That grows outside; and from the strange position,
Perhaps, of bending, felt strange thoughts perturb
My thereto deadened mind. All became clear. . . .
I burrowed in and built a cottage here—"

He beckoned toward the grandstand now in part
Destroyed by Ko's first pitch—"where I could watch
Some games, at least, until my sick old heart
Should stop, which now I fear—" Then with a swatch
Of linen came the water boy with art
To dress and bind, and wound his bloody splotch
Three times about with it, and gave him water,
The man who'd loved the country doctor's daughter.

The crowd was meanwhile totally enraged
At the immense delay and at the ruins
The infield boxes were reduced to. Aged,
It seemed, by twenty years, Ko held De Bruins
And wept and seemed to faint. De Bruins gauged
What Ko was feeling, and he said, "You new ones
Are all alike. You think you hurt old Higby.
He does this every year. He wears a wig be-

Cause he has no hair at all beneath
The wig he wears because he has no hair."
Ko smiled for the first time: his sparkling teeth
Were like white stars in light night summer air.
"Is that the truth?" he said. As in a sheath
His slim young body fitted without compare
In his red baseball suit; his hair was black;
And he was wet with tears both front and back.

"No," said De Bruins, "I have never seen
Higby before," but oh, he spoke it softly.
"I said it but to comfort you. . . . I mean,
The old guy's going to be all right—young Croftly,
The water boy, has bound his head . . ." and mean-
While Slater shouted to them, "Is it awfully
Important that you talk? Let us continue
The game, dear Ko, for if you want to win, you

Have got to do it before one a.m."
Ko took the hill, his hands with rosin stained
All blue, which, mixed with tears, from rubbing them
Across his face, wet as if it had rained,
Stained his suit purple where he touched it—clem-
Ency, you make us change our hue!—while, pained
And anxious, he looked often at the bench
But saw no Higby, and his heart was wrenched.

Valcowsky now assumes his mighty stance;
Mischensky is on deck; Rizitznikov
Is in the hole, and one great foot he plants
Outside the dugout, cries, "Valcowsky, shove!"
Mischensky hitches up his yellow pants,
And then his azure jacket he doth doff,
Revealing horrid muscles, twist on twist,
That writhe with every movement of his wrist.

Ko looked again for the old catcher, whom
At last he saw come out, in layers of bandages,
From inside Dodger dugout dressing room
Where he'd been washed and given cake and sandwiches
And dressed up in a Dodger-pink costume;
And of his taping one of the advantages
Was that one eye was free, so he could wink.
He winked at Ko, who felt his heart then sink

No more, but rise as to a small plateau
Where there is housing, water, and some women.
Distracted by the change, Ko pitched one low.
The next he threw as straight as a persimmon—
Valcowsky whacked it for a mighty blow
That would have hit the lights and made it dim in
The park if there had been lights on: the fence
Watched it fly over with indifference.

"O Ko," cried Slater, rushing from the bench,
"Why did you throw so softly those two pitches?"
"To be a good man, that is the essenti-
Al thing," Ko murmured. Slater plucked his stitches.
"You haven't gone and fallen for some wench,
Have you?" he queried. Ko looked at the niches
Far, far up in the grandstand. "No," he said.
It was because he'd hurt the old man's head,

But how could he explain it all to Slater—
He might not understand. . . . "Play ball!" there shrieked
An umpire. Ko glanced in, a calm spectator,
At dread Mischensky, and the heads that peeked
From out behind him—catcher's, umpire's. Later
He would repair the damage that he'd wreaked
Inside the catcher's cottage, Ko reflected.
He saw its roof-curve by steel beams deflected,

And windows broken, flowerpots disarrayed. . . .
Ball one! ball two! ball three! ball four! Mischensky
Trots down to first, a regular parade
Of easy floating pitches, in no tense key
Pitched, but gently tossed at the steep grade
Of the catcher's house's roof. Like an immense tree,
Up at the plate's Rizitznikov, for branches
His mighty arms. Poor Slater paces, anxious,

Along the third-base coaching box. "I have
No pitchers left!" he cries, while on Rizitznikov's
Left shoulder a canary lands who's rav-
Ished by the tree-like sturdiness and hits it off, 's
Contented, and he sings. Ko sees a dav-
Enport inside the cottage with some bits hit off, 's
Confused, with that and the canary, and thinks
He's in the country: all the Dodger pinks,

Blurred by his tears, seem bushes filled with roses;
The noises of the crowd, wind in the trees.
Then something slips, and his wet eye discloses
A real tree at the plate, with barky knees;
He drops the ball and on the ground disposes
His limbs for sleep. The Dodger Band, which sees
The situation clearly, marches out
And plays "Als Liebes Hingen" and "Turn About,"

And "La Celeste Empire" and "Ogni Volta
Tu Sei Nelle Braccia Mie," all with brass
For the most part. Their leader, Edward Bolta,
Is celebrated in baseball music as
A sizer up of problems that no dolt a-
Ccurately could see, and has great class,
As well, just purely as a fine musician
Who always gives a faithful, clear rendition.

There's nothing nicer than a concert where
You sit outside and are surprised by greatness,
And it is spring, and through the fragrant air
The notes come floating to you, saying, "Lateness
Is sad, but how can you quite quite despair
When there is so much love, so much first-rateness,
So many silver buds that bloom together;
And death, whose blue stains violet the weather,

Which naturally is pink, is but a foundling
Whom we can take or leave as we desire."
You feel you are a sunlit rose, a crowned king,
When Edward Bolta's brasses blow entire
And wantonly all C, the way a clown'd fling
His goods away into a blazing fire.
They made a fire themselves, those brasses, glaring
In the pink sun, with forty thousand staring.

The umpires, though the crowd was, were not quite
Distracted by the Dodgers' trick, which was
To stall till pitcher Ko appeared all right
And could resume his chores, pick up the fuzz-
Y rosin bag and throw in measured flight
The baseball once again, which if he does
Not, Dodgers automatically lose,
Having no other pitchers they can use,

And thus are subject to the humiliation
Of being licked by Cincinnati in
Less than two innings, and in consternation
Must seek in Cincinnati's bars the gin
And lemonade of April consolation,
Come back to quarters with a fearful din,
With their foul breath infect the squalid air,
And lose the respect of children everywhere. . . .

Thus reasoned home-plate umpire Otto Spiesenreiher,
A native Cincinnatian whose home
O'erlooked the dim Ohio, from the Diesenspeier
Family purchased, with the original loam,
Included, that was under it, through the Tiesensgeier
Firm in 1930, across the foam
From economically depressed Kentucky
Where you could sin, and win, if you were lucky.

Said Spiesenreiher, "This game has got to start
Again. Get those musicians off the field."
But Slater cried, "What this crowd wants is art,
Just for a while, and that our band can yield."
Sighed Spiesenreiher, "Crowd's desires apart,
This is a baseball game," and he revealed
To Slater bats amid baseballs on the grass.
But Slater: "Ours is music of grand class;

They may not ever play so well in future.
It's an aesthetic moment. Be content."
Howled Spiesenreiher, "I am going to boot your
Damned musicians off the field and dent
Their golden brasses. They shall all be mute, your
Brasses, Slater!" Slater: "God has sent
You down to show me error of my ways,
O Spiesenreiher, but hold while Bolta plays

'Sempre lo Stesso Giuoco, C'è l'Amore.' "
Already you could hear the first sweet strains
Of oboes, then a viola d'amore,
That all young lovers' dark replies contains
When at masked balls asked, "A chi il tuo cuore?"
Then violins, those gay orchestral brains,
And oh the mighty triumph of the brasses,
Like summer's sand strewed o'er November's grasses!

"How did you like it, Spiesenreiher?" moaned
The Dodger manager, when he could speak.
"Ineffably lovely," Spiesenreiher intoned;
"I hate to make them stop. I feel quite weak. . . ."
'Twas scarce the music's doing! The umpire groaned
And fell upon the turf; Slater looked meek
And worried, but he knew there was no harm:
He'd stuck a needle in the umpire's arm

All full of drowsy syrup, while he'd stood
Entranced by Bolta's strains. "My band, play on,"
Called Slater; "we've for sure another good
Five minutes till another blue-capped prawn
Comes up and tries to stop us. If you could,
I'd like to hear 'I Kissed You Until Dawn.'. . ."
And Spiesenreiher was carried off the diamond,
And Bolta carried out his new assignment.

A second umpire came to Slater now,
Den-di-Bem Rèckta, who, with speedy gait,
Ran in from second: "Slater, holy cow!
You've held the game up thirty minutes. Wait
Till baseball's High Commissioner, who now
Thinks highly of you, hears of this. Our great
Commissioner will crush you 'neath his heel!"
Slater said, "Den-di-Bem, if that's how you feel,

Have a banana," and saying so he picked
A yellow, appealing one out from a basket
He carried on his arm. "Am I being tricked?"
Thought Rèckta, but it was too late to ask it,
For he'd already eaten some. He clicked
His teeth together, clug!, and like a casket
Fell all at once to earth. Slater yelled, "Water!"
And Bolta's band played on, as they'd been taught to. . . .

Meanwhile, in London, Huddel and his family
Were going to a big display entitled
The Dog in Britain, they and their dog Ammily,
A small and pleasant not at all a bite-all d-
Og, not big enough to halfway dam a lee,
And very like a spaniel, Sir, despite all d-
Ifferences which we, if we were purists,
Would have to take into account; but, tourists

In Recognition as we are, suffice it
To say that Ammily's spaniel mostly, while
One sees a bulldog ear that's not so nice, it
Seems a shame, poor Ammily! but his style
Is mostly spaniel, though you'd wish to splice it
With terrier if you wanted to compile
A family tree—O tree which blooms so greenly
In those who live, and in the dead rots meanly!

So Huddel and his family enter in
Victoria and Albert Hall in which
The Exhibition is. . . . Here's Rin Tin Tin
In plaster statuary with his bitch
To welcome you. Blue-padded hats of tin
Reveal some bobbies, which makes Huddel twitch:
He hopes these guardians of the British nation
Do not remember him from Coronation.

Here on the right's a Sealyham, with eyes
Of baby blue, and down the row a piece
Is a Chihuahua bluer than the skies;
There is a smell of dogs, a warmth, a peace
That Huddel senses; on the left's a prize
Fox terrier, to regard whom's a release:
He is so neatly formed, as in a sweater
Of white round sound small bones! And here's a setter

With blue-pink eyes, aristocratic dog—
All smooth and flowing, charming, upright, oh!
And here's a bulldog, surly as a hog,
With black-white maps which on his back do grow.
And here beneath a window dank with fog
Is a large scottie wearing a green bow.
Huddel, with I do not know what intention,
Unties the scottie's bonds, and the convention

Of dog-admirers breaks out in hysteria. . . .
"The scottie's loose!" So goes the cry, which from
Row to row rings out, and with a very e-
Laborate system to which they had come
Through years of practice, after a trial perio-
D of last year and the year before, they drum
On panels, which makes nets fall down and blocks
All exit-rows more savagely than locks.

So many patrons wind up in a net;
Though they're released, of course, when it is seen
They're not the scottie, and are after let
Out of the hall. Meanwhile, with bow of green
Trailing behind him, scottie sets free set-
Ters, spaniels, bulldogs—biting their bonds clean
Through! Meanwhile, some jazz musicians who
Sense something's wrong (Americans, passing through)

Begin to, with their saxophones and trombones
And clarinets, blow "Baby, Don't You Know
A Man Is Just a Child," a tune to bomb bones
And dogflesh too, with middle section slow
And start and ending fast that make the palm bones
Of everyone contract, his face to glow.
There in the English April fog they stood
Outside the dog show, sounding very good.

Just what the purpose of their jazz maneuver
Was it was hard to see at first, in light of
The fact that canines rarely in the groove are
And scarce could be calmed down by the mere sight of
These six strange creatures blowing, creatures who've a
Style most undog, more likely'd take a bite of
Some visitor in their excitement, which
This human music raised to fever pitch.

But dogs, when they're excited, bark a lot
And do not bite so much; and a human being
Is easier to lead when music's hot
Out of a dog show, where the shock of seeing
A maddened scottie running free has got
Him paralyzed. The attendants run 'round freeing
The visitors, who clap their hands and cry,
"O great sextet, descended from the sky!"

Now Huddel could continue with his plan
Which was to go back to the dog show when
The place was empty and put Ammily Ann
(Ann was its middle name) among the ten
Best spaniels in the kingdom. With a can
There once had been some grapefruit slices in
Of water he washed him off behind Victoria
And Albert Hall, and said, *"Sic venit gloria."*

When he was clean, he had him raise his paw
To make sure he could do it as he'd taught him,
Then took a stone and pared one small left claw
A bit, then in his arms he raised and caught him
And said, "To Huddel you are absolute law.
Go in and win!" "Remember when you bought him?"
His wife remarked, evoking a scene of fleas
Thickening air and divesting of their leaves the trees.

"He's different now," said Huddel, and he placed him
Inside the Hall back door, and said, "Go jump
And play." Then Ammily turned around and faced him
And let its tongue hang; Huddel felt a lump
Form in his throat. "No, no," he sighed. "He'll waste him,"
Predicted Mrs. Huddel from the stump
Where she was sitting behind the Victoria and Albert
Hall, in clothes that smelled of oil of halibut.

But Ammily, when it heard all the barks
And smelled the smells within, turned bravely wagging
Its tail and ran on in. Then through the parks
Of London, Huddel, with his wife (and tagging
Along their daughter Juliet) looked for marks
Of nature's approbation. His conscience, nagging,
Made him afraid that he'd made Ammily suffer:
"His life was bad enough; I've made it rougher:

He will be found out instantly and thrown
Into the pound and killed by filthy henchmen.
They will not even give him a little bone."
And Huddel wept, all sitting on a bench. Men
And women stopped, but, seeing him not alone,
And also because of the halibut oil stench men
Can barely tolerate, passed on their passages,
Delivering money, flowers, cards, and messages. . . .

Is that snow falling, or is it confetti . . . ?
AMMILY ELECTED GREATEST DOG IN ENGLAND,
The banners read; HE HAS NO OWNER, YET HE
MUST HAVE AN OWNER SOMEWHERE. Does a thing land
In Huddel's heart, and is it joy? Upset, he
Runs to the Mall, though it is night, to ring. "Land
Sakes alive!" the maid calls from her shutters.
"I'm Ammily's owner," Huddel proudly mutters.

"Come back tomorrow, Sir," calls the domestic,
Young, in a nightgown with white frilly lace,
"Unless you want to come in till the best tick
Of old Big Ben ticks, dawn on his high face,
And all of London's clocks from east to west tick
The very stroke of six with stubborn grace—
There's fish and beer and my own comely person;
Full many a man has spent the night with worse one!"

How could, I ask you, Huddel hesitate
To take the lady up on such an offer?
He lived his days beneath the iron weight
Of his own nerves and his fat wife, who off her
Big bed but rarely moved, then to berate
Her husband; and, besides, he was a cougher,
A belcher, and extremely ugly looking,
As well as scrawny from his wife's poor cooking.

"I'd love to," Huddel gasped, and was admitted
Through a small door by the white-handed beauty
And led into a chamber. Poor dim-witted
Huddel, to think it anything but duty
To high and criminal dog-world forces pitted
Against him that could make this English cutie
Undress and give her body bright to him
While most of England was quite dark and dim!

While he was dozing in a haze of joy
(His first in fifteen years) the false maid bound him
And dropped him down a chute, which they employ
For dropping laundry. When he woke, around him
Were dogs of every kind, both large and toy.
One dog, who seemed intelligent, unbound him
With teeth and paws, and led him to a corridor;
And Huddel went, because to stay was horrider.

This corridor was lined with pipes of white
Which, when you touched them, burned you. They descended
A flight of steps, then came to a dim light
And followed a passage which quite quickly ended
In a blank wall. The dog guide with a slight
Paw-pressure opened something, and a splendid
Vision of furnaces broke on Huddel's eyes,
While in the distance, much to his surprise,

He saw an opening, small, square, and blue,
For which dog guide immediately made
And reached by leaping. Huddel ran there too
And jumped and pulled his body through. He stayed
Suspended then, which only could be true
Because the surface he was on was laid
On a higher level than the one he left;
Suspended there, he felt of space bereft.

The dog guide meanwhile had crawled on ahead,
And Huddel followed. Both came to a sphere
And tumbled down—out came the dog's tongue (red!)—
Where there were shades of green both dark and clear.
Meanwhile the maid is wakened from her bed
By a most fleshy great big purple sneer—
Dog Boss! "Where is he? Did he come?" "He did.
I dropped him in the basement as you bid."

"Good work, Corinna! here is fifty francs."
(He always paid in francs and thus was famous
For paying everyone in francs. The banks
Were glad to get the business, and his name was
A sacred word in British banking ranks;
'Twas as a financier his chiefest fame was,
But "Dogs" were why he lived, his love, his art,
His cup of tea, his dawn, his apple cart:

He'd rather pound a colleague into smithereens
Than harm a living dog; he'd rather murder
The House of Commons ((wouldn't cause a shiver—beans!))
Than lose a dog show ribbon!) When he'd heard her,
He opened a red trap door, and with a withering
Laugh descended a big wooden girder
Carved out with steps; but, when his eyes became
Accustomed to the dark, screamed a foul name. . . .

III

If the last canto ended suddenly,
It was to give the reader some relief
From such a dark and heavy history
As that of Huddel, who has come to grief,
As he is bound to do unerringly
If of desires ambition is his chief.
But what of Dog Boss? Surely he's ambitious,
And yet to him Fate's often seemed propitious. . . .

Dog Boss, or, more exactly, Hugh Fitz-James,
Was born in Southwerk at East Epping Chickens.
His mother was the famous Martha Flames,
Known for her acting in the works of Dickens
And for her singing voice. His father, Hames
Fitz-James, was a poor boatman from North Grickens
Who met the actress ere she gained celebrity.
Attracted by his strength and his moral integrity,

Martha Flames married Hames at Wop-Wop-Hepping.
They lived in happiness upon a houseboat.
Then one day Martha, through the deck door stepping
Attired comfortably in a housecoat,
Told Hames that she was pregnant; to East Epping
Chickens then they sailed and set up household
Half on the river, half on shore. And Hugh
Was born exactly on the date when due.

He was a baby as most babies are,
Sweetsmelling, touchy, young, and ignorant;
But as he grew he seemed quite under par
In certain ways: he would not talk, he'd grunt.
In certain other ways he seemed a star,
However, since no matter what he'd want
He'd find a way to get it very quickly.
One day a bearded sailor named Old Blickly

Boarded the houseboat part of their new dwelling
When Hames was not at home, and put his arms
Around the mother's waist, with force compelling,
And drew her to him, saying, "Oh those charms!"
Dog Boss was there, a child of five; tears welling
In both his eyes, he ran to shore to farms
And cried for help, but none could understand him.
'Twas summer, blazing. Then a cool breeze fanned him,

And he saw at his side a German shepherd
With wagging tail, who understood! They hurried
To where the lust-crowned living-boat was tethered
And found the pair. The shepherd roared and buried
His teeth in Blickly's thigh, whose muscles severed.
From that day onward, sailing down the Surrey'd
Be nothing to the boy, without a dog;
Sheep could not substitute, nor could a hog.

So for ten years he grew in fog and blizzard
And, when eleven, went to London, where,
Dining on nothing but cold tea and gizzard,
He worked all day, while in the night's despair
He studied to be a financial wizard.
At last he reached a skill beyond compare
In juggling figures and in making millions.
At seventeen he joined the firm of Trillians,

Trillians, Trillians, Trillians, Trillians, Trillians,
Trillians, Tull, and Trillians, Limited;
He had a capacity for gaining zillions:
His mind was quick, and if a thing by whim it did
Its whim brought in the sterling. Though such brilliance
Does not seem easy to the world, to him it did:
It seemed his natural means for gaining what
He wanted—being dog-man on the spot.

He also learned to speak, by listening
Each night to phonograph recordings of
The works of English poets, in the spring,
Read by great actors, and concerned with love,
War, and duty, birds upon the wing,
And here and there a dog. His face above
His muscled body was quite big and purple
And bloated up and puffed out in a circle.

His body's self, by time that he was twenty,
Got all puffed up and bloated too; he dressed
In clothes of pink, with rings and spats a-plenty,
Sometimes dark pink lapels, sometimes red vest,
And always thought of that day on the Trent he
Had chased away the mother-bothering pest
By help of dog. His personality
Was quite disgusting, as we soon shall see,

If we've not seen already. He'd been twisted
By that awful rape attempt upon his Mom
And Shepherd's deed, which made his eyes get misted
With joy at sight of dog and him get dom-
Inated by his rage when men resisted
The slightest thing he said: he was most om-
Inous when he was crossed in canine business—
His head would swell, which caused him a great dizziness,

And all his limbs cried "Kill!" It was as though
He were continually acting out
That early scene and always had to know
His dog was best, so all would come about
Just as he wished it, which would make it so
That he would never have to have a doubt
About what had been done to Mom—thus Ammily,
By winning, was destroying his whole family!

"Blasphemy, blasphemy, blasphemy again!"
He shouted from the girder as he plunged
His eyes into the dog abyss. "Oh, when
Shall my sweet prey be in my hands?" He sponged
His pulpy purple brow. "From out this pen
My foe has 'scaped!" he shrieked, and then he lunged
Amid the dogs, who licked his hands and barked.
"Where has he gone, my friends?" Fitz-James remarked.

From out the breathing canopy of cellar dogs
A cellar dog of cellar dogs appeared,
An old white mastiff, wiser than his fellow dogs,
Whose eyes held Huddel while he disappeared.
"Come, follow me," he barked, and black and yellow dogs
And Dog Boss too into that passage veered
Where Huddel had been led an hour since;
And the white mastiff's name was Buddy's Prince.

Oh, Buddy's Prince he had a violet back
When 'neath the shade of sundown shrubbery
He ran, on earth; but now he sun did lack
And was condemned to cellar-doggery.
Of every doglike skill he had the knack
And had no doubt that he'd know just where Huddel'd be.
Oh, Buddy's Prince he knew a violet shade
Before he to a cellar dog was made!

And there were many spitzes, colored white
And blue, like perfect skies at four p.m.,
And tense police dogs, geared to slash and bite
And Saint Bernards all full of purple phlegm,
And dachshunds swinging sideways with delight,
And Pomeranians alongside of them.
Oh, all these dogs had known sun's orange bliss
Before they'd been condemned to dwell like this!

And Buddy's Prince was gathering consciousness
As he led Dog Boss onward: who'd condemned them
To live without the sun and grass, and press
Their padded paws on cold cement? who'd hemmed them,
The cellar dogs, so in? and why? unless
There were some universal scheme which M'd them
To ups and down. . . . He barked, "That must be it!"
Good thing for Dog Boss, who would have been bit

Had the white mastiff guessed that it was he
Who had established for his private reasons
This cellar of enchanting doggery:
Hugh wanted someplace, where, despite the seasons,
The hours, the days, the wind, the sun, the sea,
He could be happy, far from human treasons. . . .
Not only dogs, of course, but also humans
Were domineered by this neurotic nuisance.

He had to north, to south, to east, to west
Agents who searched continually for
Such dogs in every climate as were best,
Skye dogs in Skye, and sea dogs on the shore,
Which he had sent to him at his behest.
Some agents worked for pay; some, fearing gore
If they should disobey, were slaves of Hugh;
And some were bound to the big purple stew

By family bonds, and sacrificed their happiness
To his impulsive passion! Now let's cross
The ocean and go straight to Minneapolis
Where a quite distant cousin of Dog Boss
Receives a wire from him, which says "Go canvass
For spaniels in North California's moss
And DO NOT MISS THE SAN FRANCISCO DOG SHOW."
He took the train at once. However, a hog show

In Tucson stopped him. It was so beautiful
When, steaming in the station and having nothing
To do for twenty minutes, out into the cooty-full
Arizona air he walked, to the rustling
Of Arizona's shacks and trees, and, dutiful,
Friendly, ribboned, red, white, blue, and bustling,
A field of hogs broke on his sight: they stood
Grunting, each one attached to a post of wood.

A bronco rider lounging in the area
Explained to Pemmistrek (that was his name)
How Western people called the hogs: "Right there ya
Have what's called a *chick*, and in that same
Vicinity is what we call a *terrier*—
Ya see? that twisty one—and there's a *scrame*,
That great big black one covered with white spots
Who's penned close over by them wooden grots.

Here in the foreground is a *pullet*—that's
Another word for northern female hog.
These *Lenas* here are used for bathroom mats
When they're no good no more. Ya see that log
Depending from that grot? They look like cats,
Huh? ha ha ha! They're hogs, though—even dogs
Are fooled sometimes. They're called *reverberators*,
Because they eat so many durned potaters.

Ya say ya come from Minneapolis?
I guess ya never saw a *coper* then . . .
Ya see that hog out there which all a-dapple is?
Well, that's a *coper*. This here's a *bantam hen*,
This one right down in front. What? Indianapolis?
I heard of they disaster . . . must have been
How long ago?—Oh, MINneapolis. . . . Pard'ee,
My Stetson makes me just a little hard, hee

Hee, of hearing"; then he took it off.
He was sparse-haired, the cowboy, sandy-brown
In hue, both hair and skull. He, with a cough,
Resumed: "We got a million hogs in town,
I guess. I guess that that don't happen of-
Ten. Well . . ." and he looked at the nearest mountain;
"They's not too many things a man can do."
Pemmistrek nodded. What for him was true,

At any rate, was that he'd stay in Tucson
To see the hog show through. By all he'd seen
He had been swayed, and by the cowhand's views on
The names of different hogs. "Oh for fifteen
Years I've been Dog Boss' slave—there's what to muse on!
Now suddenly the earth seems fresh and green—
I'll throw away his yoke! By what we love
Spontaneously, we gain awareness of

Our freedom and the realizable world!"
And so he lingers. Oh for Dog Boss now
The times are bad: a relative has hurled
The yoke off, and his puffed-up purple brow
With little tiny beads of sweat is pearled
As Huddel he pursues. Full many a chow
Would set his dish a-tremble, drinking joy,
If Fate this bloat neurotic would destroy.

But still must Europe suffer from his presence
Some little space, until two lovers find
Each other after long debate, and pheasants
Are seen upon a wall, which to a blind
Viale leads, inhabited by peasants.
Then one shall turn as yellow as a rind
And be too heavy for six men to carry;
Another shall be stone before he marry.

Meanwhile in China, where, brought by a boat
After such wholly horrible adventures
As one is liable to when one's afloat
Inside a coffin with a girl (for trenchers
And pistols hide beneath each pirate coat,
And they've still ammunition when you've spent yours)
Is Andrews, who, from Doris rent asunder,
Is wondering if she might not be Down Under.

So next day he sets off from Canton, seeking
Her whom he loves, beneath that Asian sun,
First in Tahiti, where he goes round speaking
Of Doris to them each and every one
Outside and in their huts famed for not leaking
And hearing their reply, *Athpataltun*—
"We have not seen the stranger." Then at dusk
He leaves their isle in his canoe of tusk.

As to Samoa he doth gently steer
He sings this song, which it is joy to hear:—
   Samoa, O Samoa,
    O blazing ocean island
  My sweetheart I shall find on you!
    Dip, my paddle!
   Stroke, my shoulder!
  Let us hurry through the ocean.
  No reason for delay can I conceive
    Not to reach you, O Samoa,

  On which my little sweetheart lies sleeping!
    Samoa, fair Samoa,
  From far off I see your green shoulders
    And your sand-brown arms!
     O beautiful island
  Be to my Love's head a soft cushion!
May she dream of me and of my race through the blue ocean
    To find her on your breast,
    Samoa, O Samoa!

As he was singing, an enormous fish
Tipped his canoe and, seeing Andrews struggling,
Swam under him, and with a great big swish
Came to the surface with the human snuggling
Upon his back, more scaly than you'd wish
For an extended voyage. With a rug, ling-
Ua franca, and a little more security,
There would have been more comfort, though less purity:

For this, an absolute pure trip on scales
Across the blue Pacific, was a passage
Such as one reads about in fairy tales
When sprites must cross the ocean with a message.
There was no cabin, and there were no sails;
For food, Andrews by luck had quite a dosage
Of vitamins along, which he was taking.
He saw the sea, and shores where waves were breaking.

The fish he rode on was approximately,
Oh, fifteen feet in length and three in width,
So Andrews could sit on its back quite neatly;
And when he did his figure partially hid the
Scales where he sat, scales which were colored subtly
With every rainbow tint—but those that did the
Most service were pink, yellow, red, and white
And blue, the bright blue of a summer night.

The fish was human, as you may have guessed
From how it acted, since the other genera
For human beings rarely do their best:
One simply can't rely upon a hen or a
Shark to see one through at one's behest;
But human beings, acting from a yen or a
Moral obligation, can be helpful. . . .
And yet, how could this many-scaled and kelp-full

Big speedy fish be human? When it spoke,
Andrews fell off its back in dumb surprise
And had to be retrieved. It tried to joke
To make him comfortable, but his eyes
Remained enormous through its speech. It broke
Out laughing, "Friend, you ought to realize
That everywhere you go, on land and sea,
You'll find us human animals, for we

Resemble you in everything but looks.
It isn't easy for us, though, neglected
By our own species and ignored in books
Of scientific inquiry, dissected
By no one; and, too smart to bite on hooks,
But rarely seeing those who have rejected
Their brothers of the underwater reef—
But, still, it doesn't cause us too much grief.

We have occasion now and then to aid
You others of our species, and we have,
Besides, the whole broad sea, in which we've played
Since we were children—or, if we're giraffe,
We have the jungle, where our necks have swayed
Against the broad and yellow seismograph
Of afternoon, whose heat can melt the hoof
Of one who is accustomed to a roof.

Or, if we're spiders skating on a pond,
We have the pond; or if we're butterflies
We have the garden and the field beyond;
And if we're birds, we have the singing skies.
I am a human fish, and am more fond
Of ocean than of any paradise
I've heard you humans dream of"—and he dipped
His face down slightly and his tail-fins flipped:

"O Ocean, Ocean, salty, cool, and green!"
And then: "Perhaps you're marveling at the fact
I have so many colors—if you'd seen
Some other human fish, you'd not react
So forcibly to me. The thing I mean
Is that, though human beasts and fish have lacked
The human shape they have a certain voice
In how they look—this splendor was my choice.

A lot of fish were choosing white and yellow
When I was in creation, but I decided
That something standard, since I was a fellow,
Would hold up better and be less derided
In time to come, and chose to be envelo-
Ped in many colors—blue, white, pink—and prided
Myself on being, when I was in motion,
The most delicious vision in the ocean. . . .

But I am much too talkative. Where are you
Going, and can I help you to arrive?
I'm sorry that I tumbled your canoe;
It was my fault—I do have such a drive
To look at human humans; and so few
Come paddling out so far, I always dive
(If I can use the word) up to the surface
To have a look. I'm clumsy as a porpoise,

As you can see, because I tipped your boat—
But only when I'm anxious. But relate
Your story, telling wherefore in this moat
Of Castle Earth you circumnavigate."
But Andrews was as quiet as a stoat:
He still was absolutely stunned. . . . A great
While later he felt sunlight in his eyes,
And the fish cried to him, as one who cries:

"I'm sorry! Can you hear me? Are you sleeping
Still? It's just too much for you; it's stunned you;
But here's a beach where you'll be in good keeping
Among your fellow humans. When you've sunned, you
Perhaps will see the trip you've made, the leaping
Of waves o'er half the world, and rocks that shunned you
Because I steered you perfectly. . . . But how
Can I get you ashore? Aren't you conscious now?"

Andrews said yes, but he was half unconscious
With shock. The fish observed his state, and swam
To a large flat rock jutting, strewn with conches,
Into the bay, and flipped him off. "I am
Sorry," he said, drowned out by sounds of launches,
Steamers, and planes, distracted by a clam
Who floated past, "to leave you; but you'll be
Contented here, as you shall shortly see,

I hope, because it's famous as a place
Of recreation. I, who did not know
Exactly where to take you, from your face
Deciding you were European (though
Fish-eyes are often wrong) to Europe did race;
So here you are, where balmy breezes blow,
On the Riviera (the Italian one). . . ."
And so he left him, lying in the sun.

Some Italian children, swimming off the rock,
Discovered him, and with their slim dark arms
Lifted the stranger in a state of shock
And carried him away from the bay's alarms
(All full of pulpy things that sting and block)
To a café, where espresso coffee's charms
Soon brought him to himself. "Oh, where have I been?"
He sighed, and they gave him a big clear glass of gin. . . .

Let us return, however, to the game
In Cincinnati, which has now resumed.
Ko is awake, and now warms up his lame
(From sleeping on it) arm. . . . Well, I assumed
That play had started; it would be a shame
To miss what's happening in hog-perfumed
And sunny Tucson, where Dog Boss's cousin
Suddenly felt the pulse of life in pulsion.

We have a lot of time, it seems to me—
The players have to get back into shape;
And in the blazing Cincy sun a sea
Of faces from each tier, each fire escape,
Is forming in the stands, inexhaustibly,
The good word having been sent out by tape
That Ko was waking up, the game'd be played;
But till all enter it will be delayed.

To Tucson, then! where leaving his hotel
Was Pemmistrek, who in the lobby stopped
To get some hog show pamphlets, which they sell
In drugstores, but which hotel patrons popped
Into their pockets free; and they had swell
Descriptions of the show and how it topped
All other demonstrations of its kind. . . .
O Tucson, Tucson, only one who's blind

Is unaware, when in your dusty streets,
How strangely beautiful you are! your curbs
Dusty and white, and the restaurant where one eats,
Full of its maple furniture and its herbs
Lining the wall, and the shoeshine boys' leather seats
On the curbs, and the park where no one ever disturbs
The movement of the feet across the paths,
And your hotel gardens, gardens with bird baths,

O Tucson, Tucson! Here a match is struck
In the bright clear sunlight; there a dog goes down
That dusty street; and the newspaper truck
Pulls up, and out jump two strong sunburnt brown
Young men to take the papers down; and the cluck
Of a hen reminds one that you are a town
Not utterly removed from nature. Pemm-
Istrek was walking down Tucson's main stem

Enjoying life more than he ever had
And counting on the hog show to increase
His joy, until perhaps he'd be so glad
That he could merely stare at trousers' crease
And clap his hands for joy! "How am I clad,"
He sighed, "for this great day which brings me peace?
Perhaps I should go buy a brown fluff suit."
And so he did, of Mexico's mills the fruit.

And then he bought some shirts, and then some ties—
One with a cactus pattern, black on pink,
Of which he specially was fond; there flies
Upon another of his ties, I think,
A duck, who's being followed by the eyes
Of the hunter standing at the left-hand brink
Of the fronting fold, who aims a rifle toward it;
From how it looked and from the way it soared, it

Could be imagined what an excellent duck
It was—its colors were purple, brown, and white.
The background of this tie (which cost a buck)
Was dark and shining green; the hunter, bright
Brown and purple. Stepping past a truck
Beyond a garden stretching to his right,
Pemmistrek found the street again which led
To where those hogs to hitching posts were wed.

Numerous cars were hurrying down this street
(Numerous for Tucson, in any event)
With grown-ups in the gray sunlit front seat
And children in the back. The blue sky bent
Above the housefronts, tender, hot, and sweet,
Like a tremendous burning azure tent.
Keeping in the shade, then, Pemmistrek reached the place
Where the hogs were, and he mopped his orange face.

"You'll want a ticket," said the man inside
The ticket booth; "six bucks and thirty cents."
Pemmistrek's blue puff coat comes open wide
And out his wallet comes. His hand, intense,
Takes out the bills, with which is satisfied
The ticket taker, in a certain sense.
Now with a string of tickets which includes
All hog show privileges, with some other dudes

He enters the great gate. Oh what a brave
Display of hogs and colors meets his eye!
Here are a group of scrame, here like a wave
A group of green-glad pullets; here some sky-
Blue copers. Up above them all does wave
The Hog Show Flag, on which white letters cry
Against a background of severest red.
Pemmistrek reads it, tilting back his head:

TUCSON HOG SHOW: EVERYBODY WELCOME.
A kind of wooden boardwalk runs around
The entire area, along which they sell gum,
Hot dogs, popcorn, ginger ale, and pound-
Cake, cotton candy, hamburgers, and talcum
Powder for the stains which you are bound
To get upon your clothing as you eat.
And every once in a while there would be a seat

Along this boardwalk, where, facing the sun
Which was high in the sky, or turning in another direction,
One could sit spellbound till one had begun
To wish to move again; then with one's confection
Clasped in one's left, one's right along the rail would run,
And one could seek the hogs of one's election
(Thus farmers when they walk about their barnyard
Seek some the hen and some the cock, or barn-bard).

When you had come unto the second ramp,
A big red sunset bellowed into view,
And the hogs' backs turned purple, yellow; damp
With water, some were like a prism too,
Reflecting many colors—oh, they vamp
The searching eye with green and lobster-blue,
And Pemmistrek was lost in contemplation,
With many an old and many a new sensation.

Far in the distance were the perfect mountains,
And in the middle distance were the plains—
Most of them desert and devoid of fountains,
Some not, where honest farmers grew their grains;
If Pemmistrek had looked, he would have found tens
Of thousands of green prickly heads sans brains
With big tough leaves and sometimes bright pink flowers.
Instead, he stood there in a trance for hours.

When he awoke, the sky was big and dark,
The stars too far away to be of use
To help him find his way. The only mark
He thought he knew, amid the night's abuse,
Was that shack outline, entrance to the park,
Or so he figured, where he might work loose
A bolt and free himself—or, and why not?
Some old nightwatchman there would let him out.

He made his way toward the outlined shack,
And, doing so, he found it best to leave
The boardwalk, which, it seemed to him, went back
And doubled over, like a wooden weave,
And all in all was not the shortest tack
To take to reach the shack. But to achieve
The shack directly it was necessary
To pass through hogs, a-grunt and temerary.

He felt a pressure first against his thigh
And then against his arm! Some giant hog,
Or so it seemed to him, was passing by. . . .
He sat down, frightened, on what seemed a log
But soon began to move; he gave a cry
And leaped into what seemed to be a bog,
But it was just a puddle . . . then a snout
Against his ear made him stand up and shout.

Proceeding calmly, then, he was aware
Of heavy bodies every place he went;
He patted them and soon felt every care
Vanish! he felt so happy as he bent,
While still proceeding, and patting patting where
The hogs' heads were. . . . "Oh, this is what was meant
By 'Walking in the darkness 'mid the living,' "
He sighed, here kisses, here caresses giving.

And it was Christmas, Christmas in his heart!
The animals were friendly, he was happy,
And in this ecstasy night played its part—
Had it been daylight, he'd have felt quite sappy
To see how much of what he felt was art:
For there were no hogs there with ears so flappy,
Nothing but sandbags and an occasional dog,
With, in the distance, grunting of some hog.

For he, in walking off the boardwalk, had
Immediately left the hog show by
A minor entrance; and, in brown-fluff clad,
Was actually now in a supply
Dump, which if he knew he'd be less glad.
Now, coming to a fence, he gives a cry
Of joy and sorrow both, of understanding
That pleasure, which is ever so demanding,

Demanded that he follow through his plan
And leave the hog show, though he had enjoyed
His midnight walk there like a crazy man;
Or else with aftermath would be alloyed
His perfect moments. "Ah, farewell, I can
Already see you in the dazzling void
Of day—so beautiful, but lacking in intimacy!"
The morning star then showed him that day's imminency.

"Goodbye, dear hogs!" and through the door he passed,
As one who, if he could, would turn and say
"Forget not me," out into the sparse-grassed
Hog-filled terrain where he had spent the day
And was immediately almost gassed
By the foul smell of rotten mud and hay.
Then something rushed against him, and he fell;
And the hog's teeth were sharper than its smell.

What happened was that he had left the dump
By another entrance to the hog exhibition;
Thinking he'd left the exhibition, the bump
Of the hog against him he took for an auto collision,
But when he felt sharp teeth he gave a jump
And circled his enemy warily in wrestler position.
"Hog, what the hell are you doing outside the show?"
He shouted, while the hog walked to and fro

With blood upon its teeth. "Aren't you my friend
Like all the rest of the hogs?" The animal, frightened
By Pemmistrek's shouts, moves off. And then from an end
Of cloud the moon appears, and the whole field's brightened.
Pemmistrek sees the great expanse where wend
The hogs about their posts, and is enlightened. . . .
He rushes back to the door he left, and sees—
The dump! then, weeping, falls upon his knees

And curses life, and on the bitter boardwalk
Strikes his poor knuckles till they split and crack:
"Oh you who were my very most adored walk
I'll rend to splinters!" Smack smack smack smack smack!
But, bleeding, stopped; and, as those who are floored walk,
Walked out into the night, but walked, not back
To where the entrance was, but toward the peaks
And plains, where you could hear the coyote's shrieks.

"Somewhere out there is something. That, I feel,"
He said, and kept on moving. When he'd reached
The boardwalk's end, he climbed a fence of real
Wood, green as of rowboats which are beached,
And fell to earth. Just then a piece of steel
Zinged past his head, and facing him, with bleached
Blonde hair, at thirty paces, was a girl
Whose body was as pleasant as a pearl

(The face included) and who held a knife
In her right hand, and with her left hand tried
To keep her wrapper closed, which, for the life
Of her, she could not do, so there was spied
A rose-pink hue encalloused by no strife
Into sweet soft strict curves all modified.
"Get out!" she said; but Pemmistrek, distracted
By her pink body, sighed, "How have I acted

That you should treat me in this awful fashion?
Why, you don't even know me! If I came
Over your fence—" But then a fit of passion
Quite conquered him, and, like an angry scrame,
He rushed toward her, totally irration-
Al—the knife-point stopped him. "What's your game?"
The girl demanded. "None," said Pemmistrek,
"You're just so beautiful." "Well, what the heck,"

The girl said, picking up her wrapper now
So that it would not drag upon the walk,
"Come on inside and have a little chow,
And when you've eaten some we'll sit and talk."
There was a robin on the willow bough
Who 'gan to sing. "It's almost dawn; it's awk-
Ward, being alone, and at this hour: you frigh-
Tened me." Already in the distant sky

Above the desert Pemmistrek could see
The city of Paris forming in the clouds:
Cloud-shapes of Tour Eiffel and Rivoli,
The Tour St. Jacques, its gargoyles tiny shrouds,
Old Notre Jame, Ivry, Île St. Louis,
The Boulevard St. Germain with sad young crowds
Pushing toward the river; Odéon,
Concorde, Champs Élysées, Palais Bourbon,

And, in that wrack of whitest whisperies,
The Cité Universitaire; and here
The Gare du Nord; there, blackened St. Sulpice,
Suggesting storm. But now it blows quite clear
And straight: St. Étienne, or the Tuileries!
Now Luxembourg and Buttes Chaumont appear,
And Trocadéro, white as whitest snow,
And the Musée Grévin, the Parc Monceau;

Here is the statue of George Washington,
And here the little replica Statue of Liberty
And the Allée des Cygnes. . . . "There was a bun
From a Paris pastry shop," thought Pemmistrek, fidgety,
And went inside the house, his looking done.
But while we leave him to the receptivity
Of his new friend, let's look some more at those
White shapes in blue which ever clearer grows.

By concentrating on the Rue François
Premier, which is discernible to the left,
One sees a figure portly as a shah,
And—yes, you've recognized him by his heft!
It's Hugh Fitz-James—and here, see in the Bois
De Boulogne that skinny shape bereft
Of every grace, which moves from tree to tree . . .
Oooh, what a wind! and now we cannot see

Paris at all in the clouds, for they've dispersed—
But that that figure in the Bois de Boulogne
Was Huddel (by nature and society cursed)
I would suppose. But what strange fate has thrown
Him there? and Dog Boss? Can it be the worst
Has happened? Meanwhile, driving through Bourgogne
Is Andrews. What his voyage has to do
With theirs, I'll rest, and then explain to you.

IV

To Cincinnati, though, I feel compelled,
To start my canto, since a sort of promise
Was made that, when confusion'd been dispelled
And in their seats had settled kids and mommas
To see the game again, to see who felled
Who and who felled who felled who—quick as commas
The fielders on the field—that we'd return
To Redleg Field to see the ball game burn.

Besides, Ko's reputation is at stake,
A source of great concern to those who know him.
What starting pitcher ever had worse break
Than Ko's, in hitting Higby, which did show him
The responsibility he had to take
For his fast pitching talent! Would it slow him?
This was the question dominating Slater
And all the fans, to whom the vendors cater.

Meanwhile to the University of Japan
A cable had been sent, explaining things,
And asking for encouragement; and Dan,
The clubhouse boy, into the clubhouse brings
A message reading *Ton wai yakki san*
Three hours later. Slater on the wings
Of hope flies quickly out to sleeping Ko,
Reads him the note, and sees him rise to throw!

"What does it mean?" asked Higby, when Slater told
The story in the dugout. "Can you understand
The Japanese language?" Slater merely rolled
His eyes, and gestured with his gloveless hand
Out toward the mound. "I read it to him cold;
It worked. That's all I need to know—it's grand!"
But what was in the message Ko well knew
And why he pitched beneath the sky's clear blue.

The entire student body of the University
Had cabled to him their encouragement;
Inyaga, whose intemperate perversity
Had made Ko groan, now joined the Dodger management
In hoping he'd wake up and with a diversity
Of pitches expose the Redlegs to the disparagement
Of all true fans, humiliated with strikeouts.
"I'll pitch," Ko sighed, "and I'll have no more blackouts."

And then, for one or another reason, he thought
Of that first day in Tampa, when he'd come,
An untried stranger, in a ball hat bought
Ten thousand miles away, and how the hum
Of the Dodgers' playing had crept in, unsought,
The dreams he had in the bullpen; and the strum
Of his heart when Slater had said, "Let's give the kid
A chance." "I'll do whatever I am bid,"

He thought; "I'm grateful to them. Just as long
As Higby shows that he's to health returning,
I'll pitch my fastball. Stinting would be wrong
When all these men for victory are burning—
Slater, De Bruins, Cooper, and De Jong,
And countless others—and my friends are yearning
In far Japan for a personal victory
For all of them, as symbolized in me."

And so he threw. And if he looked at Higby
Occasionally, it was but as one
Who looks up from his hoeing at the fig tree
And smiles, and wipes his brow, and in the sun
Continues hoeing. Soon a Dodger victory
Seemed almost certain, for each Redleg gun
At Ko's swift mastery lapsed into silence;
And in the field, unnerved by the pitches' violence,

They all made errors, so that by the end
Of inning number four the score was tie—
Sixteen–sixteen. Then Dodger friend on friend
Came to the plate and either lofted high
The ball until to Vine Street it did wend,
Or else hit low, when fielders with a cry
Would leap away. How many times the plate
Was crossed is too fatiguing to relate.

The Dodgers won, of course. The game was called
At one a.m., although the Reds protested,
Justly, perhaps, that the Dodger team had stalled
For over three hours and thus had manifested
An anti-sporting spirit; that they had mauled
A poor old catcher, poisoned an umpire, and divested
Another of his senses by serum, and thus deserved
To lose the game. But the Dodger win was conserved

Temporarily, at least, and oh, next morning
The Dodgers had a beautiful One–Nothing
Against their name, although it was a warning
Against too much unwarranted chest-puffing
That four teams had the same; but it was charming
To see the *one*, the *zero*, and with loving
Attention to be looking at them still
When noontide sunlight did your chamber fill,

And walk out in the street, if you were Ko,
And feel the buildings beating with a heart
That knew you, knew you! and to watch the slow
Movement of the streetcars, where, apart,
They climbed upon the hill, and then to go
With burning face out to some park where art
Has ordered nature—Eden Park, for example—
And see Kentucky, where the gamblers trample;

Then climb to Clifton, where the dazzling sun
Beats down upon you 'mid the drugstores, and
Past campus grasses till you come to one
Of the streets which leads to Vine Street, which, with grand
Bravura and agility, seems to run,
Irrespective of the way the town was planned,
From in the center to bright Clifton hill—
Plain German houses and a dark slum chill.

Or you could take another street descending
The hill into "downtown"—most of them lead
To someplace near the ballpark, where you're tending
In time for pitching practice, which, indeed,
You scarcely need, and later to be lending
Your cheers, to make the Dodger crew succeed,
From on the bench, where you shall pass the night game
Unless you're called on for that falsely bright game.

But now it still is afternoon, and there's
No need to worry yet about your tasks.
You stand on a stone landing, free of cares,
And board a streetcar. "Where?" conductor asks.
"To College Hill," you say, but he prepares
You for a shock by saying, "You see those casks?
That's where you get the orange twelve which goes
To College Hill." Then out of the car there flows

A mass of people—who would have believed
That there could be so many! almost six—
But none of them joins you as you walk, relieved
To know the car to take, toward the sticks
In front of the store of casks. Now there is heaved
Into your sight a blue eleven—nix!
You need the orange twelve; and in five minutes
It comes: its track noise is a noise of spinets.

You enter it and pay your dues—a dime—
And as a paying member you are moved
From Clifton out to where you hear the chime
Of the College Hill Memorial High Behooved
And Welfare General Church, where there is time
To pray and think. The streetcar's wheels are grooved
And cannot leave the track unless they hit
An object, or some brute with little wit

Pushes the whole car sideways. . . . What's that jostling?
Ko rubs the streetcar window and looks out:
An elephant from a circus parade is bothering
The streetcar; many people are walking about
Confusedly, and arguing and posturing.
Then, over goes the car! and Ko no doubt
Is hurt, for he has landed on his arm—
Worse luck! for pitchers that's a major harm.

He staggers to a little luncheonette,
Trying his fingers out: they seem to work,
But of his elbow he's not certain yet,
Because it pains him as though cut by dirk.
"I'm going to call the management, you bet,"
Ko sighed, "and get their doctor." With a smirk
The waitress looked at him, a pimply thirty,
With stringy hair, and apron rather dirty.

"Have you a telephone?" asked Ko. "Oh, ouch!"
"No, Buster," said the waitress; "what's the matter?
Your elbow hurt or something? There's a couch
Back in the kitchen you can lay on." At her
Right the kitchen was; her apron pouch
Was filled with change. "Just, please, a glass of water,"
Ko said. Then in came Benjamin De Clover:
"Were you in that car the elephant just knocked over?"

But who De Clover was and what he wanted,
And of the termites living in the car
Ko had just left, and plants that grew in front, it
Would idle be to tell when now there are
Big doings in Bourgogne, where in a stunted
Simca, speeding toward his lucky star,
Is Andrews. After several hours of rest
In Italy, a letter he'd expressed

To his old chief in London, who had wired
There was a Simca for him in San Remo
And that although officially he was fired
For laying off the job too long, the same old
Wages he could have if he aspired
To trap a criminal fat as a hay-mow,
Who now, the Force believed, was on the Continent
In Paris, France. Five minutes Andrews pondered it

And then decided Yes, for he was all
Disturbed by seeking Doris, and the strange
Experiences he had had. The call
To duty might be just the needed change
To give him strength again and make his pall
A rosy hue. "It also means I range
Across two countries in a fast new auto,
And may find Doris, as I've simply got to!" . . .

Sitting at his seaside desk, he wired "Yes."
And now that he was driving through Bourgogne
He visited the townships to express
His hope that Doris had been seen. No one,
In all the gray French streets where to excess
They drink the juice of circles filled with sun,
However, had seen her. And to Montrachet
He came exhausted at the end of day.

From Montrachet to Paris in two days
He sped his course, through deadly drab Lyon
And dark cold cities which deserve no praise,
Though one can eat a passable piece of *thon*
For lunch, and then their wine deserves the bays,
But all in all this section is quite *con*
And one arrives in Paris with relief
At its blonde smiles like sunlight on a reef.

Here, Andrews, disappointed, to be sure,
That he had not found Doris, settled down
To study his new task, perhaps the cure
Of his despair. How long could Fortune frown
Upon his efforts, Fortune which with pure
Inventiveness had brought him to this town
That Pemmistrek had seen in Tucson's skies
At dawn, more blue than his dear Doris' eyes?

But Paris now was Rue de Rivoli,
And Avenue de l'Opéra, la Place
De la Concorde, and not those tear-filled swee-
T and lovely eyes of Doris, which philos-
Ophers would lay their quadrants down to see;
Nor were her eyes the sky above the bus—
Paris was Paris, and through its stone ways roamed
A dangerous crook to capture, purple-domed.

For it was Hugh Fitz-James, as you have guessed,
Who was the man that Andrews had to find.
But why was Hugh a criminal? the best
Financial head in London, what a mind!
And usually they forgot the rest,
That he was ruthless Dog Boss, power-blind,
Who wreaked his will on men and helpless pups
Throughout the town of London's downs and ups. . . .

But Juliet Huddel, seeing her mother's lethargy
At Huddel's five-day absence, had reported
The case to Scotland Yard's Inspector Smethergy,
Who left his chair the moment that he heard it:
"At last we've got Fitz-James—perhaps!" Such energy
He put into the orders that he ordered!
"You, Daws, to Fitz-James' office; you to the Victoria
And Albert Hall; and you, secret girl-agent Gloria

Galelba (Juliet was not in the room),
Trail little Huddel, to make sure that this
Is not a trick." Himself in Morris zoom
To the concierge cottage at Albert Hall. "What is
It?" cried Corinna, lovely, with perfume
Shrouding her body. "Not for physical bliss
I come, Corinna," shrieked the brave inspector;
And neither door nor beauty could protect her

From Smethergy, who got a full confession:
How she was hired by Dog Boss, and how Huddel
Had been abused. "It's vice and it's aggression,"
Said Smethergy. "I've always said that blood will
Tell! I knew we'd get him." But the question
Was *how* to get him. "Splashing through the mud will
Not help," thought Smethergy. . . . "My dear Corinna,
Put on some clothes, and we'll go out to dinner"—

And so they did, and she confessed some more—
I.e., about the secret passage which
The dog had opened through the wall-hid door
That Huddel entered wearing not a stitch
Since he was dumped directly *dopo amor*,
And where he had been followed by the rich
And influential Hugh. "Once past that panel,"
She said, "it runs beneath the English Channel;

And, though there is one opening at Cherbourg,
Most passengers go straight on through to Paris—
The former really is a sort of bare, poor—"
"Enough!" said Smethergy. "Could you prepare us,
My sweet, a little map, and with some care, poor
Corinna, indicate exactly where is
The Cherbourg exit and the Paris exit?
Here is some paper." And Corinna makes it,

The map, and puts her oval head upon
Her flattened hands, and weeps. . . . When Andrews' letter
Arrived, three agents had already gone
In vain to search for Dog Boss. "He'll do better,"
Said Smethergy at the airport, searching for dawn;
"When there aren't any girls, he's a go-getter!"
So that's why Andrews has the horrid job he
Has got, more dangerous than that of bobby.

In Rue du Vac, inside a vast hotel,
Dog Boss sat thinking. He was dressed in orange
And yellow, thinking this would help to fell
The preconceptions of his seekers, discourage
Identification, for he knew quite well
That he was being followed: with incorrig-
Ible vital spirits, he had already snuffed
The life of two with knives, and another puffed

With deadly poison. "Ha ha ha, ho ho,"
He laughed, remembering it; and was regarded
By the other people sitting in his row
Of lobby chairs as one who is retarded.
His face, which always had a purple glow
In England, now with blue cosmetics larded,
Was hard to know for certain, but the bloating
Was unmistakable still beneath this coating.

He was wearing a morning suit, with vest and pants,
Spats, coat, and tie, and a top hat which shone
A brilliant yellow in the clear light of France;
His knees they had the texture of a stone—
His pants material so rough—and danc-
Ing slippers clad his feet, with soles of bone;
Picked in the soles with dots of white and pink
Were pictures of gin bottles, Dog Boss' favorite drink.

"Here, boy," he called, and Buddy's Prince came trotting
Across the lobby, gayer than a bird
Since he left the cellar where he had been rotting,
And most attentive to Dog Boss' every word.
"Let's go," said Hugh, and, quickly, past the blotting
Pads and chairs, they move like a big herd
Of something into the street. Huddel, whom they
Were searching, was in Luxembourg Gardens that very day.

His dog was with him too, Pyrethrum's Sandro,
Who loyally had led him beneath the waves;
They'd tried the Cherbourg exit, found a sand row,
An abandoned green puff suit, and a few staves;
And Huddel, after asking, "Can I stand ro-
Ving through that tunnel, which is dank as graves,
Again?" decided it would be less ominous
To be in a large city—more anonymous.

And so to Paris, where the tunnel concluded
Just off the restroom of a large café
On Boulevard Montparnasse; thence green-puff-suited
Huddel and panting Sandro found their way
To restroom, bar, and street, and then intruded
In a nearby hotel, with front of gray,
Which was quite cheap: they had a little room
With wallpaper, dog-box, bed, and stale perfume.

Their custom was to go each afternoon
To the Luxembourg Gardens and enjoy the green
Of all the trees, the statues, and the un-
Iversal loveliness of some unseen
Presence, which make these Gardens such a boon
To mankind, whether in a limousine,
Like Dog Boss, riding hard to them, or whether
Out with one's pet, poor loyal friends together.

Sometimes they'd watch the fountain, a huge spurt
Exuding water over an amorous pair
Above a black stone puddle; and the squirt
Would sometimes reach them in that gentle air,
Blown by a Paris breeze—it didn't hurt!
And oft Pyrethrum's Sandro drank his share
Of water from its brim, and saw reflected
His collie face, to collie form connected.

If you should ask me just exactly what
The nicest place in Paris is, I think
I'd say here in these Gardens, at a spot
Not far from where old Sandro takes a drink,
When sun is shining and bright gardens blot
The grass. . . . But meanwhile Dog Boss, 'mid the clink
Of taxi ashtrays, yells, "J'descends ici!"
The driver stops. Hugh pays. "M'sieu, merci!"

"Come, boy," says Hugh, and Buddy's Prince, a-tremble,
Races his master to the garden gate
And beats him easily: Hugh isn't nimble,
But solid, heavy, ruthless, packed with hate,
And just about impossible to tumble.
Then Buddy's Prince, with mastiff-step elate,
Leads him into the park. There in the April
Sunshiny mist, they circle many a table.

"Where's Huddel, Buddy's Prince?" Hugh often murmured
To his companion with mosaic vision. . . .
Meanwhile our Andrews, drinking a cup of wormwood,
Sat on the verge of a complete decision
In a café not far away. A germ would
Occasionally come into collision
With his wet cup, but none remained to infect
The agent, whom the Heavens should protect.

"I've got to find him," Andrews said, "or else
I'm done for. But I've searched the city over
For purple jowls that hover over pink lapels,
And I've not found them, no, not in a grove or
Field of Bois, nor in the streets where bells
Of old blue churches clang, nor by the stove or
Inside the bar of any restaurant—
No, nowhere is the Dog Boss that I want!

Oh, were I but a cloudlet and could hover
Above this city of Paris and remain
The sky-long day attentive as a lover
To the streets and the parks, and the Seine that is tall as a cane,
Oh then could I find him, this big pink-purple shover
Whose image is imprinted in my brain!"
Then, seeing in the distance grass and flowers
And iron grillwork—"There's a shape which towers

In all directions, and it may be he!
He's dressed in yellow, yes, that is the truth,
And orange too, but never did I see
A man so big he would not fit in booth
Of any size that you could possibly
Construct, till I saw this one. Oh, my tooth!"
Then, leaping up, and leaving forty francs
Upon the table, toward the park he banks.

Dog Boss, aware, by something in the air,
That he was being chased, retired into
A flowery enclosure over there
Beside the gate you go into when you
Leave Boulevard St. Michel; and the despair
Of Andrews, who arrived on double shoe,
Was great: he stood there wailing in the traffic
Of the Boulevard, near yellow flowers seraphic.

"I've lost him! Was it all hallucination?"
And Dog Boss, Dog Boss bending down beneath
The mass of yellow flowers, with some elation
Was smearing poison on Buddy's Prince's teeth.
"Go bite him, boy," said Hugh, and his sensation
Was of contentment on that city heath.
Out trotted Buddy's Prince, but he was hit
By an automobile, which shook him up a bit.

He seemed unhurt, though: he got up at once
And ran into the park. "Hist, hist!" Hugh whispered,
"Go get him!" but the dog not even grunts,
But runs straight on. "I'll bet he really *is* hurt,"
Says Hugh; then rising, Andrews he affronts
And hits him on the head and in the gizzard.
While Andrews falls, Hugh chases Buddy's Prince
Through alleys' green and dew-wet leaves that rinse.

But Buddy's Prince, whose mind is disarrayed
A little bit, will not let Hugh catch up;
But, dreaming of the days when children played
With him and he was a cute little pup,
Dashes insanely. . . . Meanwhile, in the shade
Of afternoon, which holds them like a cup,
Sit Huddel and his dog, Pyrethrum's Sandro,
Upon a bench, amidst a rather planned row

Of plane trees. Dog Boss passes—Huddel, though,
Is not aware how close he is to death,
But sees the sky above, a big blue O
Framed by the planes, and draws a happy breath,
The while Pyrethrum's Sandro from below
Seems to be breathing less and less and less;
And now its breathing stops, and Huddel sees
A message in the dust between his knees:

HURRY TO ITALY, written by the ants;
Now Sandro starts to breathe again, and it
Is evening! darkness falls on Paris, France,
And everyone cheers up a little bit
At the thought of a drink, and a bit at the thought of the chance
To talk to girls who through the by-ways flit
In blackest smocks, and some in bluest mink
In huge cafés where waiters bow and blink.

So, on to the river! There is no need to stay
In the Luxembourg Gardens all night, nor on the Boul-
Evard St. Germain, where the newsprint faces are gray,
So come to the Seine, that river, follow the *foule*,
And stand on its banks, for it still is warm with the day—
Now put up your collar, for you are growing cool. . . .
Here Huddel, Dog Boss, and Andrews, each at a distance
Stand leaning, drawn by the sweet air's insistence.

Prince has recovered and stands at Dog Boss' side;
Andrews is better, though he feels quite low;
And Huddel perplexedly looks at the tide
Wondering whether to Italy he should go.
Across the Seine can be identified
The various buildings that Paris has to show;
But soon it's dark, and they're invisible. . . .
And with that change, our scene is changed as well.

It is high summer in the desert where
Dog Boss is roaming. How has he become
So hapless, fugitive? We left him there,
A few days back, beside the Seine, which some
Believe the finest river anywhere,
With Andrews not far off and feeling glum;
Then toward Les Halles big Dog Boss took his way . . .
But Buddy's Prince behind him some did stay

Because of a lame foot he'd gotten in
His frolic; Andrews recognized him and
Followed him past the stores whose fronts of tin
Were fastened for the night, until the bland
And milky streetlights showed him some blue skin
Above lapels of yellow. His command,
"Stop, or I'll fire!" was answered by a shot
Which missed him, but, as chance would have it, got

The hapless Prince, who fell into the gutter.
Andrews took cover in a doorway. Dog
Boss, seeing what he'd done, began to splutter
And leap about insanely like a frog
On the Rue St. Merri; then, like a cutter,
Completely senseless, steered in the slight fog
To Place de l'Opéra, and stormed the building
Till in the Place lay many a quaint old gilding.

Andrews arrived too late: the harm was done,
And blackened statues lay on the warm walks
Which round the note-enclosing building spun.
Then toward Gare St. Lazare Hugh madly caulks
And shoots at the great clock with his strict gun,
Then plunges on a train. Andrews, who talks
To passers, "Have you seen him?" is too late
Again, and stands behind an iron gate

While Dog Boss' train goes spiralling away.
Andrews prepares to follow. . . . So they both
Are in the desert: Hugh in Arabia does stray,
While Andrews in the area of Gla-Tòth
Vainly goes searching down each sandy way.
Hugh meanwhile's going wild, has made an oath
To destroy everything in the whole world
Since he'd destroyed his friend, white hair uncurled.

A psychological malady, you remember,
Made it imperative for Hugh to be
Both friend and master of each taily member
Of the family Dog, because that shepherd three
And thirty years ago, in warm September,
Had saved his mother from bad infamy:
In having killed white Prince, it was as though
He'd killed his father—so the theories go.

One also might interpret it, more simply,
By saying that he'd left his mother now
Defenseless—Martha Flames, so soft and dimply,
But dead for fifteen years—without a chow
(To use a metaphor), however limply,
To keep attackers off. He saw the prow
Of his dear family boat, he saw the fiend
Attack his Mom, and in the desert screamed!

It is a fact, however, that there's not
An awful lot in deserts to destroy.
It's probable Dog Boss had picked the spot
Because its utter blankness gave him joy;
When there's not much to do, it seems a lot
When you have done that little—and so, ahoy,
Camel! bang! and nomad, bang! and tent!
With wild and puffy fury you'll be rent . . . !

Meanwhile in Cincinnati, after Ko
Had gotten back into the clubhouse, it
Was ascertained amid great sobs of woe
By Old Doc Champ that Ko would have to sit
The season out, for elbows they heal slow,
And he on his right elbow had been hit. . . .
However, Ko'd seen Benjamin De Clover,
Who in the diner'd said, when he came over,

There was an exercise that Ko could do
If everything else was unsuccessful, which
Might cure his elbow. . . . B. De C., as you
Perhaps have guessed, was serving out a hitch
With Car and Circus Life Insurance Coo.
Which had to pay the damage if the pitch-
Er sued them, as he would, at Slater's urging,
If from his arm that pain would not be purging;

Aware, then, of the psychological value
Of magical cures suggested by a stranger
Who comes from nowhere, does not try to sell you,
Just speaks, then fades away like the Lone Ranger,
The Car and Circus Life employed it. Shall you
Declare them wrong? What matters is that pain should
Go away—and Ko, who exercises
From 12 to 2 and 4 to 6, arises

At 7:10 without a trace of pain.
"I'm well!" he phoned to the astonished manager,
Who, moving to the clubhouse windowpane,
Sent up some words of thanks (these, though, a tanager,
Who then was flying over, took for grain,
And pecked at, so they fell). Umpire Ben Bannister
Walked through the orange light with the smiling news
That Ko could pitch again, healed were his thews;

And in pants factories lights were going on
To herald breaking day, and pantsmen moved
(Smoking already, though it was but dawn)
Among the swatches of plain and herringbone-grooved
Materials, and spoke of what had gone
On in the clubhouse—for, as it behooved,
The news had come to them while it was green,
Via the radio newscast at 7:15;

And in the terminals where the huge bus
Reposes on its suffocating tires
The word went out, like a great stream of pus,
That Cincinnati's fondest sport desires
Were likely to be thwarted, and the cuss
Of many a lounger greeted the radioed wires;
The streets, where serious traffic had begun,
Glittered and sparkled in the morning sun,

And the Ohio River, which was wise
From days of steamboat transportation, rose,
It seemed, an inch, and in its measured rise
Was like a man who slightly older grows—
They say that you can see it in his eyes—
Still, though, to the great River dashed its flows;
And from blue Newport, passing over it,
Kentuckians joked with pessimistic wit

About the chances of the Cincinnatis
Against the Dodger wonder: "They don't make 'em
Kin hit thet kid!" they offered, light and gratis,
To the river's morning air; and "Shore he'll take 'em!
Cain't nobody else, though, punctuate them batters . . . !"
And soon it was noon. Meanwhile at El-Bar-Hakem
Andrews had come on an important clue,
A fragment of human skin pomaded blue.

Its color, of course, originally was purple;
"So Dog Boss surely can't be far ahead,"
Andrews murmured, drawing a big circle
In the dust-thick street, then touching his hot head,
"I wonder, by the time I get to Europe will
I permanently look all feverish-red?
And Doris, if I ever find her, can
She love such a flaming emaciated man?

But now I'll stop in this complete café,
Complete with bugs and darkness, where there may be a
Clue to Dog Boss' whereabouts, who, today,
May be in El-Bar-Hakem, and this day be a
Shining one amid the hosts of gray!"
But Dog Boss was ahead, destroying Arabia;
And nothing to his fury could say No—
The sand swirled up wherever he did go.

Meanwhile in Kalamazoo we must begin
The following canto: driving into town
After traversing part of Michigan
Was Pemmistrek's car (he'd paid two hundred down
And still owed seven hundred for the can),
And with him, dressed in stripes of blue and brown,
Was she whom on the outskirts of the hog show
He'd met—they now together on a jog go!

V

If you have ever driven in Kalamazoo
You'll know the way the road that leads you in
To the center of town has curbs sometimes of blue,
Sometimes of green or white, and as you spin
On four good wheels some houses look quite new
And others old, but all of them make you grin
Because they are so calm—then, there's the name
Of the city, which is its chiefest claim to fame.

I know you'll speak to me of overalls
And furniture, as folks in Willimantic
Tell one of thread, and in Niagara Falls
Of coal deposits, and in gray Atlantic
City of hydrostatic telephone calls;
But all of what they say is rather pedantic,
For what is nice in Kalamazoo's its monicker,
As in Atlantic City Miss America.

Some towns, of course, are famous for two things:
Nome, for example, for its ice and snow;
And Petrol City for its chicken wings
And for, of course, its oil (or if you go
To Bakersfield, there's oil and hornet stings);
Pea Gulch Springs for the restaurant of Joe
The Indian, and the place where you can buy
Ice from your car, as you go riding by;

Detroit, for hideous ugliness and cars;
Chicago, for its lake breeze and its El—
Chicago actually also boasts its bars,
But we cannot consider very well
The cities now that merit three gold stars
(We lack the time), but there in a hotel,
Or off the street, you drink and spend an hour
In an airplane, forest, soap-mine, gulch, or tower. . . .

But back to Kalamazoo, where Pemmistrek
And Alouette (that's his companion's name)
Are wending according to their road map's beck
(Does she remember when like an angry scrame
He rushed at her in Tucson? or the wreck
Who dragged his feet into her house, the same?
They have been very happy, though, since then,
Though neither'd like to do it all again

Because it was, at first, a tortured time)
And Pemmistrek, aloud, "We ought to turn
Left on Azalea Street, Alouette, them climb
Petunia Street, upon which we sojourn
For seven blocks, then dodging from the grime
Of Kalamazoo's industrial part, where burn
The overall works, drive six soft blocks on Rose,
Which into the dear, sweet center of Kalamazoo goes;

Then for an evening at the Trask Hotel,
Five hundred rooms, and each of them with bath,
Rugs, ink, iced water, and a bellboy-bell. . . ."
"You're right," said she; "just as you say's the path,"
And, driving through a nice suburban dell,
Their car pulls up before the homely Trask.
A porter takes their luggage from the back
Of the red Chevrolet, and in they tack

To the main lobby, where they settle down
At the registration desk, to spend a while
Giving their names and giving the names of their town
And watching the manager quite quickly smile
And beckon to the bellboy, who to the brown
Bags most immediately comes, and he lifts them with style,
And leads the pair to a moving box which sheds
Them after sixteen flights, with tipsy heads.

Next day the love-fatigued and pleasant couple
Who wished to visit Michigan's urban all
Decide Grand Rapids is a good example
Of a furniture city where they can have a ball.
So off they drive! Their radio's on: "A double!
It's almost certain Slater's going to call
His 'miracle hurler' in. Yes, now he's beckoning
Out to the bullpen, as we've been expecting.

Fans, just as soon as there was any threat
To the Dodger lead, we thought we'd see this boy
Who not so long ago was a bad bet
To ever pitch again. Oh, there was joy
In Brooklyn, which the dirty rivers wet,
When he was cured, a joy without alloy . . . !"
"Let's turn it off," said Pemmistrek; "it's time
For lunch," and out the light red door they climb

Into the lovely air of springtime Michigan.
Robins are singing, and a luncheonette,
AUNT SUSIE'S TRUCK STOP, promises many a thing to them;
Their gullets already in the soft dry air are wet
With thoughts of what Aunt Susie's liable to bring to them:
Baked beans with ketchup, cooked as a croquette,
Or roast stuffed breast of veal, with mashed potatoes,
And mayonnaise salad with yellow, hard tomatoes. . . .

Near Florence, in a meadow filled with violets,
Dog Boss reclines upon a bed of stone;
Around him, as far as you can see, are toilets,
Discarded ones, of porcelain and chrome,
Some of them shattered as if hit by mallets,
But most of them the way one has at home:
A vaselike cup descending in a neck
Which fastens to the bathroom floor a speck.

And there are also birds—large healthy robins
And teentsy sparrows, bobwhites, cranes, and storks,
Pelicans who could keep the works of Hobbes ins-
Ide their beaks, and birds with heads like forks,
Kingfishers, hummingbirds who dance like bobbins,
Upon the loom, or in the splash like corks;
And all of these are flying about and landing
On various toilet parts large views commanding.

As you remember, we saw Dog Boss last
In a less pleasant scene and a worse climate,
When through Arabia he raging passed
Like a blue mountain no one'd wish to climb at—
So, how has he in Tuscany been massed,
Where violets and toilets take their time at
Creating a completely pleasing picture?
What was the ecstasy, and what the stricture?

Let us go somewhat backwards, speak of sickness
And hot pursuit—then we'll to Florence later.
Now Huddel's face, and Sandro's, its small thickness
And its long bigness, as if seen through water,
Appear through shimmering air, as in the Preakness
The final horses' noses. . . . To the crater,
Then, or near it, to Pompeii, let's force
And spy them. Here an old man shoes a horse

And Huddel watches him with fascination,
And here a truck goes rocketing through the dust
And Huddel sees it with a strange sensation
Of recognition; here a young girl's bust
Appears to him and causes him elation.
"I must find out what's going on, I must!"
Cries Huddel, with Pyrethrum's Sandro at
His side. And here a man puts on his hat

And Huddel's filled with dreams. Then there's the Bay
Sparkling as if it weren't just a dress
For sand and rocky bottom green and gray
That stretches all the way to Inverness
And then to Boston, down to Uruguay,
And round the Cape to China and the rest,
Then back to Naples. "Here it is quite strange,"
Said Huddel, "for the water seems to change

What's under it, and all's transformed into
One shimmering self!" The sun shone down upon
This statement, which, extending in the blue
Of noon, above a public park's sparse lawn,
Ever and ever much more floral grew
Until it seemed the day itself, from dawn
To melancholy evening, when Dog Boss
Would lie on stone amid that Tuscan moss.

"O Naples, Naples," Huddel cries, "Pompeii!
What a blue sea and Bay, and what a Sky!"
And while he cried upon that street of clay
Pyrethrum's Sandro joined him in his cry.
A donkey, passing close, begins to bray,
And over them Italian sea-birds fly.
The bus pulls up, and Huddel mounts aboard:
He's off to Rome, where Pompey had his hoard.

And, as he goes there with Pyrethrum's Sandro,
He can't believe that he is really Huddel:
His heart is beating like a happy banjo
And all the past seems but a painted muddle
And all the future but a painted sandal
Lying atop a big white laundry bundle.
The bus goes squealing over asphalt tops,
And into the Tiber Valley now it pops.

Huddel descends, and he and Sandro seek
A pensione near some large piazza
Where they can live for *pochi lire* a week.
Said Huddel, "Sandro, this way! There are lotsa
Houses over there," and off they squeak.
They end up near the Forum, with some mozza-
Rella on the table near the bed. . . .
And toward the Appian Way was Sandro's head.

Beyond it there is nothing but the country;
And Sandro, while his head was pointed there,
Pointed his tail toward, in Rome, the one street
That can compare with it for dazzling air
And pure long brightness, clarity, and some sweet
Mysterious event the gods prepare—
For Sandro's tail, which wouldn't want to fool ya,
Was lying pointed at the Via Giulia. . . .

The Via Giulia! now it's just a street!
What was it ever, though? And down it go
Huddel's and Pyrethrum's Sandro's feet
To seek the Tiber's big cemented flow;
But just as they are leaving it they meet. . . .
Dog Boss! whose visage is as white as snow.
Some horrible disease has ravaged him
And made him get what is, for him, quite slim:

A hundred kilos, or about sixteen stone.
His flabbing face, it had an orange mustache,
And he was wearing a blouse of green chiffon
And trousers of a rather dark pistache.
From time to time he gave a terrible groan.
Huddel, on seeing him, quick as a flash,
Ducked into a doorway until the horrible specter
Had passed. Toward the Palatine was its vector.

Felled in Arabia, felled by a germ,
Dog Boss had struggled to El-Bak-Bar-'Ab
To get the plane for Rome and put a term
To all his miseries with some great jab
Of antibiotics beneath his epiderm,
Which now had turned to quite disgraceful flab.
But though he had the best of care procured,
The doctors didn't leave him reassured:

"You'll have to wait and see. No one has ever
Been cured of 'it' before, but this new product
May do the trick." Dog Boss, who was quite clever,
When he was not just hopelessly neurotic,
Saw he was going to leave this life forever
And what remained to him was episodic
At best. His rage was gone: he was most calm.
When he'd passed Huddel, he paused beneath a palm

And said: "He thought I didn't recognize him.
I did. He is forgiven. I was afraid
To frighten him, indeed, to terrorize him,
And so I to this tree-hid spot have made
To give him time to breathe. Now I'll apprise him
How my vendetta has aside been laid
For more important things: the confrontation
Of death, which has so high a reputation. . . .

So I was wild for dogs . . . ha ha, ha ha. . . .
It seems so strange to me now; and yet I know
They've been my whole existence—like a shah
I strode among the mastiffs. . . . Well, Sir, go
And ask forgiveness . . . there's an *au delà*. . . .
But what's this breath that rocks me to and fro . . . ?
Stop—little boots it. . . . But, where is Sir Huddel . . . ?"
And now he chases over many a puddle

Of sparkling street to offer his forgiveness.
But Huddel, hearing heavy pounding steps
On that delirious asphalt, seized by lividness,
Amid the Roman crowd's *oh*'s, *what*'s, and *yep*'s,
Rushes toward a tomb, that, for its bigness,
Its rednesses, its roundnesses, and depths,
Was known to all. And there, reposing with
Pyrethrum's Sandro, seemed a thing from myth.

And then came Dog Boss, coming along the Tiber,
Limping, I fear, and puffing very hard,
With orange mustache and yellow albino eyebrow
And groaning every time he landed hard
Upon the pavement! But let's let that slide now
And turn to Andrews. He sees vultures starred
Above some scattered scraps of Dog-Boss flesh,
Which makes his world look new, as through a mesh

The brilliance of the sun. "I can go back
To Europe!" Andrews said, and clutched the fluff
Of his gray coat, but did not see the track
(Now covered up by sand) down which did puff
Six hours earlier Dog Boss. That clack clack
Of vultures seemed to Andrews proof enough
That Hugh Fitz-James had met with a catastrophe.
And so he went away from the horrible masterpiece

Of Arabia. To Athens then he came.
From here he wires his chief Dog Boss is through.
Then out into the sunlight like a scrame
He wanders, seeing etched against the blue
The Parthenon! Though feverish and quite lame,
He walked to it immediately, new
With hope, he knew not why, that he'd see Doris
Before the day was over, and the chorus

Of Athens' buildings seemed to him to sing,
"Your love is far from you but you will find her
And place upon her hand a silver ring,
And then with weak and sunburnt arms you'll bind her
Unto your breast, and into bed you'll fling;
Then when you wake you'll kiss her and remind her
Of all that happened while you were without her
And how each moment made you think about her,

And—" But just then a gentleman dressed in red
Accosted Andrews. "Can it be . . . ? It's you!"
Astonished Andrews to the poet said. . . .
And close behind was Doris, dressed in blue
And wearing a peacock hat upon her head—
Green, red, and orange and yellow feathers strew
The fanned-out tail, while both the head and beak
Are blue, dark blue, and orange colors streak

The breast and sides; apparently it's hollow,
For it would be too heavy to support
If it were solid like a stone Apollo. . . .
But it's alive! it's starting to cavort!
And then as Doris walks it does not follow—
It's always on the rampart of that fort
Where it cavorts. But it was just above her
When Andrews saw her, and that's why the lover

Supposed that she had on a peacock hat.
The rest of her was pure and simple Doris,
However; Andrews had no doubt of that—
Just as when entering the Plaza de Toros
One knows which side is *sol*, or as a cat
Knows which gray spot is *mouse*, or when, in *Boris*,
The tenor sings "Marina!" you know who
Marina is: the one he's singing to.

And he was overcome, as in an ocean
Of hopes and doubts, and when he heard her voice
So insupportable was his commotion
That he sat on the sidewalk, not by choice,
But literally clipped by his emotion,
And Doris' legs and Dah's from there a clois-
Ter seemed, where he would like to spend his days;
And he stared, stunned, at the street's differing grays.

But soon beside him on the sidewalk there
Was Doris, dressed in blue, and with a light
Green coat on, with her beauty past compare
And with her understanding deep as night,
And took his hand with one of hers, yanked bare
From a green glove, and said, "Are you all right?
You look a little feverish. . . ." Andrews said,
"I'm happy," and in two minutes he was dead.

Though Andrews had not had the same disease
That Dog Boss did, he had a similar one
For its effect: to bring you to your knees
Within a week and make you cold as stone
When it lies always in the shade of trees.
"What can," wept Doris, "Dad, what can be done?"
Meanwhile, in Rome, Huddel was catching cold
In the shady tomb, which also had some mould.

Pyrethrum's Sandro, when he heard Huddel sneeze,
Ran up to take a peek outside the tomb
Where was bright sunlight; poking out, he sees
The white-faced flabby green-clothed dean of doom
Being picked up among the Roman trees
That front the Tiber, which cement doth groom.
"Ruff, ruff," he said, and Huddel, sniffling still,
Came to the door with hesitating will

And saw his enemy being carried off
In the direction of the Piazza di Spagna.
"Come, boy," he said to Sandro, with a cough,
"Let's see what's happened." Exiting the monu-
Ment, they follow, while the Romans scoff,
As in a Crucifixion by Orcagna,
At such a strange procession. Boss is taken
To American Express, to see if he'll waken.

And after that they carry him to Cook's,
And finally to the British Embassy,
Where the proconsul with a few quick looks
Sized up the prey. "Good Romans, this is he
The British nation's sought through staves and stooks,
A very star of criminality,
Dog Boss by name, or, rather, Hugh Fitz-James,
Son of the famous actress, Martha Flames. . . .

I never will forget her *David Copperfield*—
She was not quite so portly as her son—
'Twas late in life she came into her proper field,
The theatre, and yet she got so much done!
As Little Nell 'twas clear that she could top her field
Whenever she wished; or, changing sex for fun,
As Mr. Pickwick she received the praise
Of critics wherever the English language sprays

Its marvelous influence." The Romans stood
In hairy wonder at this rhetoric.
And then Fitz-Williams trounced his desk of wood
Beneath his fist, and cried, "Our thanks! Now, quick,
Take him inside there to that bed so good
Where he can lie: perhaps he's only sick
Instead of dead, in which case proper rest
Would be what would recover him the best—

Then . . . Justice!" Huddel, hearing from the corridor,
Swelled up with patriotism and, now secure
That he was safe, walked through the streets much torrider
Than hallways, with a new enjoyment pure,
Greater than that he'd had before—thus horrider
The fate that lay in store for him: for cure
For that which seemed his sniffles there was none—
He had "Mould Fever" and his days were done. . . .

Huddel dropped dead upon the whitewashed stairs
That end the Corso, called "The Monument";
Pyrethrum's Sandro, trying to bite his hairs
In maddened grief, to Dog-Elim was sent.
And the British consuls, pulling up their chairs
To the consul table, spoke of the event:
"Regrettable. They have no sympathy
For animals in balmy Italy."

Balmy it was, and Dog Boss he was dead,
And Huddel dead, Pyrethrum's Sandro hanged,
And it was balmy, as the consuls said:
The white of blossomed plum and pear harangued
With peaches' pink; and poppies blindly red
Fell through the fields round Rome, where streetcars clanged;
And every slopy place bore gray-green olives,
And girls were white and curved beneath their collars.

And Doris, who was fairer than them all,
Sat holding Andrews on an Athens street,
Remembering the barge, the coffin small,
And how she had been saved by Uncle Pete,
Skipper of the *Merry Christmas*, after a brawl
With Pirate Jules, who'd pulled them from the fleet
And dashing waves, then tried to force her charms,
While Andrews in the hold had come to harms

At pirate hands, and at the time of rescue
Had been thrown out a porthole and not found
(He had been saved by Captain Papapescu,
Whose lighter for the China coast was bound—
But Doris had thought him dead); it was grotesque, you
Can see, to be with him, and hear the sound
Of his dear voice again, then watch him die
A second time, beneath that Athens sky.

And she had loved him so. Well, how explain . . . ?
They took him to the hospital, of course,
And he was dead. And, looking at the grain
Of the sidewalk, Doris felt the total force
Of grief, which like hot sun deadened her brain.
Her father, Dah, was purple with remorse
For having thrown the children in the sea,
Which had brought on the whole calamity.

They had become quite friends with Uncle Pete
And, at his invitation, had been going
About with the *Merry Christmas* (and the Fleet
Boasted no better craft, all white and glowing
With cleanliness). Now Pete suggested Crete
As someplace that was capable of sowing
New seeds of interest and a cure for care.
So off they go upon the ocean bare,

But Doris' life is over (so she thinks),
And Joseph, having seen the Parthenon,
Decides next morning as he sits and drinks
Some hot ship-coffee, that from that day on
He'll make his work "extended," with the links
Of verbs and prepositions—thus begone
The danger of ever harming Doris, too.
So Action Poetry sinks into the blue. . . .

Dog Boss, when it was noticed that his skin
Was purple underneath and that his corpse
Showed no sign of decompositiòn,
And that there was still sparkle in his orbs
(Though he was dead), was taken to the Min-
Istero della Pubblica Istrorps-
Ione Direzione Generale
Antichità e Belle Arti. "Golly!

He'd make a great Etruscan," Direttore
Ottaviano Della Pergola
Exclaimed, on seeing Boss and hearing story
Of how been dead some time. "Oh la la la,
He'll make a fine Etruscan, yes, *Signori*,
So it's off to Florence this *domenica*:
There's a new project that I have in mind:
A field of toilet bowls—you know, that kind. . . ."

Everyone nodded quickly in agreement,
For Pergola was known for his bizarre
And yet entirely practical ideas.
His eyes were twinkling like a silver star,
And his whole face grew whiter than a Feenamint
In his excitement. "That's the way things are
In Etruria!" he gurgled, and he shrieked,
"Remember that big fountain here that leaked,

And how we fixed it with the horns of oxen?"
And everybody smiled. Meanwhile, the air
Was growing sweeter than the smell of box in
The month of May, and was beyond compare
Before they'd even finished up the coffee
Which had been brought to them to stem despair,
Which often follows great enthusiasm,
As death comes riding often on a spasm.

And in this air so sweet the men decided
On this and that, and how, and such and such,
And each of them grew terribly excited
When he was in the street outside the Hutch
(A nickname for the Ministry), delighted
At having been at last enabled to touch
Some truth about Etruscans through the genius
Of one of them. So now explained the scene is

Of Boss in Florence on a stony couch.
Huddel's corpse, meanwhile, turned a brilliant yellow,
But really bright, a cadmium you'd vouch,
And the undertaker said, "I teenk dis fellow
Is happenink sahmtink strenge"—then, screaming, "Ouch!"
It was dropping Huddel's corpse that made him bellow:
It landed on his feet as if a gun
Had shot him there—it seemed to weigh a ton.

Its texture was like clay that has been baked
And double-baked to give it a high gloss:
A yellow statue, there was nothing faked!
And whether to set it up where two paths cross
Not far from Villa Giulia, or to make it
A model for ceramics, at a loss
The Ministers ponder. The undertaker's feet
Were mended free, which really was quite sweet.

Andrews, however, was not found for years
To be a work of art, because his body
To everyone perfectly natural appears
And to be decomposing rather quickly.
Actually, though, his body rather clears
Than decomposes, and becomes, aesthetically,
A perfect thing, whose every line you follow
With thumping heart—a white granite Apollo

Which, when it is discovered, takes its place
With what at Delphi and Olympia
Is most excruciatingly in space,
Whose lineaments remove you from where you are
And make no face a stranger to your face:
Someday you'll see it near the Parthenon,
Its eyes toward Crete, its large and perfect eyes. . . .
But to Ohio now our story plies

Where fans are roaring wildly in the eaves
At Ko's great exhibition. Never has
A pitcher turned the batters down in sheaves
The way Ko's turned them down. And the base paths
Are empty, empty. Now and then there weaves
A Dodger in for water, to the razz
Of teammates—otherwise, nothing . . . but the smack
Of balls in the mitt of one who throws them back:

The catcher! Gabby Hartnett at his best,
Or even Basil Higby never had
A more excruciating catching test,
Nor Big Bill Dickey with his home-plate pad,
Than this: to catch those balls that are expressed
With speed that makes the Redleg sluggers sad.
For Ko has struck out twenty-four straight batters,
And all would see how he will wind up matters.

Now at the plate is Vladimir Mischensky.
Strike one! strike two! strike three! And in the pants
Factory, office-boy Insommelschensky
Cries, "It's more beautiful than a romance!"
And cleaning woman Olga Maravensky
Looks up a moment from the stream of ants
She's sweeping from the Art Museum lobby
And sighs, "Oh baseball is my favorite hobby!"

And hunched in London, listening by short wave,
Are Chief Inspector Smethergy and Juliet
Huddel, who in her attempts to save
Her Dad had found a husband. Smiling coolly, yet
Caring deeply, Smethergy from the cave
Of his great chest said, "They may get unruly yet,
Those Slavs—I've always said that you can't trust them."
And, stamping on the mahogany floor: "Boy, bust them!"

Valcowsky batted then, whom Smethergy
Derided, feeling the increasing comfort
Of his tremendous chair, then made an effigy
In paper of all the Reds he one by one burnt
With green-tipped wooden matches, savagely,
Hoping to make the players feel so sunburnt
They couldn't hold their clubs. Strike one came in.
"Juliet, dear," said Smethergy, "give me a pin."

But nothing happens from his nervousness,
Which on the baseball game has no effect.
It was completed just as you might guess
With two more strikeouts. And the Dodgers wrecked
Their clubhouse out of simple happiness,
Which Baseball Boss declared was not correct:
So each and every Dodger had to pay
A hundred bucks for what they did that day.

This had a negative effect upon
Their wives, who questioned Slater: "What's the idea
Of that?" and "Why is Ko the only one
Who isn't married? that don't seem fair neither!
A bachelor, it's easier to pay that sum."
Then Slater smiled and leaped upon a streetcar;
"The reason Ko's not married," Slater said,
"Is that—" but then the orange streetcar fled

High up a hill and passed a brighter green one,
And carried Slater into Cumminsville,
Where in the street a scrame was loose, a mean one,
Who knocked the streetcar over and down the hill—
A way of traveling very like to bean one.
When Slater, dazed, emerged, there waiting still
Were all the wives, to whom he said, "You see,
I always felt it wasn't up to me."

But Ko came up just then, and on his arm
Is someone we have seen before—but where?
It is a Kansas girl, fresh from her farm,
And, naturally, she's completely bare.
"I wish to marry, Sir, and what's the harm?"
Said Ko. And Slater, after many a stare,
Conducts them to the Cincinnati Municipal
Building, where they all become invisible. . . .

Meanwhile the entire continent of Asia
Was moving sideways unpredictably—
Mountains and other places where you graze your
Sheep, if you have sheep, fell in the sea,
And Burma had the very strange sensation
Of being where Hawaii used to be;
Hawaii, meanwhile, feeling simply great,
Was speeding toward acceptance as a state.

This movement opens up a whole new ocean
Between where Asia now resides and Europe,
And sailors sail it with a wild emotion
Of new delight, and waiters pouring syrup
On Trans-New-Ocean steamers get the notion
Of buying boats themselves to start a tour up.
And sailboats, tramps, and tugboats rush into
This brand-new sea, or sky, of fairest blue. . . .

Within a week, a great wild trip is planned
For all the Dodgers, to appear in this
Newly contiguous Asia. What a grand
Exalted feeling Slater finds it is
To after a two-hour ride look up in the stand
And see Tibetan faces, hear the fizz
Of mountain-goatca-cola, with a periscope
Look at the sea, like much uncoiled blue rope,

And feel the mountain air, which is refreshing
The local players not so much as you
Because they have it whether they are threshing
Or herding, it's what they're accustomed to,
And therefore does not set their glands a-meshing
The way it does the raving Dodger crew,
Who, used to lowland air and lowland smells,
Run onto the field as if their limbs were bells!

And Ko, of course, is Asia's new sensation—
A local player who is better than
The all-stars of American civilization;
And Joyce his bride, dressed, for the trip, in tan,
Is happy, sharing Asia's admiration
For Ko. "He's more," she cries, "than just a man:
He is a champion too!" Tibetan faces
Gallantly glimmer on her girlish graces.

De Bruins has retired, and is replaced
By Pemmistrek, who, after touring Michigan
Exhaustively and tracing what could be traced,
Decided he would seek a sports position.
"I think one travels better if one's placed,"
He told Alouette; "one gets the travel wish again."
But this intensive joy of Asian living
So close to home has all his senses swimming;

And Alouette's, as well, who has some capital
She got from selling all her goods in Tucson,
And walks New Ocean coast, with plans to map it all
And choose a site where voyagers profuse on
The beach will be, then take her dough and slap it all
Into a huge hotel, the Munster Mooson,
Which she will build—for stylish folk in scores
Already are speeding to New Ocean's shores.

"It's absolutely the only place to bathe,"
They say; and "It's entirely unspoiled!"
"You can walk around as naked as a lathe
And no one sees you." "When the water's boiled
It is quite good to drink," and "If you pay the
Beach boy, he will keep you freshly oiled
For fifteen cents a month." "Oh, do let's go—
Just think: blue waters and those mountains' snow!"

The earliest tourists had to sleep in shacks
That Alouette and Pemmistrek set up
Hastily on the beach. Oh how like wax
That beach is, and that water, with its slup
Slap slop, how cool, whose sparkle stings like tacks,
But after's green and gentle! And with rup-
Turing intensity Alouette completes
The Munster Mooson, which completely meets

The most exaggerated views of what
Deluxe hotels should be. And Slater said,
"Pemmistrek, you're a millionare! Why not
Retire?" But Pemmistrek just shook his head
And kept on coaching first. It was a spot
He liked; he liked, before he went to bed,
To walk New Ocean Beach and watch the waves,
Like Reds struck out by Ko—or Cards, or Braves.

But the sinking of American capital in
Tibet's new beach was criticized by many
Tibetans home or going for a spin;
So Alouette retracted every penny
She'd put into the Mooson, and where Chin
Chou Lai, a local guide, had told her Pemmy
Of brand-new inlets formed by strange monsoons
Set out with him across the spacious dunes.

Meanwhile the *Merry Christmas*, which was hired
By Amaranth, who'd heard it was in Crete
And knew it for the one craft he desired,
Sailed up the broad Missouri. Uncle Pete
Stood at the mainmast, pulling the poopsail, tired
But happy, chosen out of all the Fleet
To serve the King and cross the ocean's curls
And rivers' rapids, so that Kansas girls

Might be revealed to Amaranth, make him Ah!
And oh! then cause a change across the Ocean.
Belowdecks, writing poetry, was Dah—
Not Doris, though, for she had got the notion
Of being dropped in Athens, which her fa-
Ther willingly acceded to. His devotion
To her and all she wished to do was absolute
Since the unbearable coffin-Andrews episode.

She's had a premonition. And meanwhile
She stands amid some Roman columns musing—
Oh Doris! swatch out for that peristyle!
She ducks—she made it! It, some fragments losing
Through weather and slow time, could have made vile
What's beautiful and living; smashed and oozing,
What now walks toward the Parthenon with a smile.
In London, Shrump, and Bixter Beets meanwhile

All England's girls, once word's been cabled through,
Are tossing panties, blouses, and brassieres
Into the Thames, the Trent, the Avon blue,
The Suggye, and the Afton, to the cheers
Of Englishmen, who crowd to get the view.
"England has altered once again," say peers.
Then Scandinavia, not to be outdone,
Unclothes its men and women every one.

So that one sees a nude man eating smorgasbord
In Stockholm, and three naked girls of Bergen
With bodies worth more gold than all the Borgias' hoard
Standing beside a telescope with an air-gun
And looking at the sky; and where an orchard's board
Pathway leads to trees a young American
Stares dumbstruck at two naked maids of Denmark.
In Florence, meanwhile, someone's made a pen mark

On Dog Boss Statue, and there's great confusion
Because Etruria mayn't be tampered with
Lest there should be destroyed art and illusion.
Therefore the malefactor's put to death,
And Dog Boss scholars drink some sweet infusion
To toast the government's health, then take a breath
Of that sweet Tuscan air and perfect breeze
From the young white-haired blossoms of old trees.

O Tuscany! without you there would not
Be any Dante, Petrarch, or Boccaccio!
There'd be no Dog Boss Statue and no grot-
Toes in the Boboli, no red Masaccio
In Santa—I forget the name—and what
About the Arno shining like a watch—oh
That would also, nay, could not exist!
Meanwhile Ko pitched. Ya Wakki swung and missed.

And Amaranth sails for Asia. Meanwhile Ko
Is pitching, pitching, pitching, and he's caught
By Sanford Yu, a rookie. In Athens Do-
Ris climbs the Acropolis steps and, having bought
A ticket, enters it. And meanwhile Jo-
Seph Dah comes up on deck and bows. "It's hot,"
Says Amaranth; "don't bother bowing, please."
Huddel, meanwhile, is flaking at the knees. . . .

The Duplications

I

One night in Venice, near the Grand Canal,
A lovely girl was sitting by her stoop,
Sixteen years old, Elizabeth Gedall,
When, suddenly, a giant ice-cream scoop
Descended from the clouded blue corral
Of heaven and scooped her skyward with a loop-
The-loopy motion, which the gods of Venice
Saw, and, enraged, they left off cosmic tennis

And plotted their revenge. They thought some outer
Space denizen or monster had decided
To take this child, perhaps who cared about her
And wished to spare her heart a world divided,
Or else who wanted to hug, kiss, and clout her,
And, lust upwelling, the right time had bided,
Or something such—so thought, at least, the gods of
Her native city, famed for bees and matzoh.

Venice, Peru, of course, is where it happened,
A city modeled on the Italian one
Which was all paid for by Commander Papend,
A wealthy Yugoslav who liked his fun.
The Com had sexual urges large as Lapland
And was as set for action as a gun
In madman's hands who hates the world around him—
But Com was filled with love, his heart all pounding!

And so he'd made this North Italian jewel,
Canals and palaces on every side,
An urban re-creation, not renewal,
A daring lust's restatement of life's pride;
Huge bumboats carrying marble, masks, and fuel
Clogged South American streams, till Nature cried
"Some madman's building Venice in Peru!
Abomination beneath the sky's blue!"

In protest of his act, waves shook the earth:
Shock and resentment over this new Venice!
And Central South America gave birth
To hideous monstrous bees, so huge disfenes-
Tration would result when their great girth
Against some building window hurled its menace!
So, windowless new Venice had to be.
But there was one thing that could stop a bee

Of overwhelming size: a matzoh placard
Placed on the shoreside gilding of the house.
It must of course be large, huge as the Packard
Driven for Canada Dry by Mickey Mouse
Attempting to establish the world's record;
Minnie at his side, and Gabby Grouse,
A brand-new character who's been invented
Since Disney's death—they think he'd have consented.

Walt Disney dead! And Salvador Dalí lives!
Paul Éluard gone, and Aragon still alive!
How strange the breathing tickets that fate gives—
Bees dance to show, when entering the hive,
Which way best flowers are, but are like sieves
To death's mysterious force. Oh you who drive
The car, stop speeding; breathe a little longer.
Create, and make us gladder now and stronger!

As Papend did by carrying out his plan
"Venice in South America," an almost
Perfectly accurate copy. Yet one can
Discern things here and there I think would gall most
Other Venetians: bees and the whitish tan
Enormous matzoh placards which some tall ghost
Might use for palace walls. O strange piazzas
Of South America, deranged by matzohs!

How was it known, you ask me, that the busy
Bees would stop marauding if confronted
With matzoh placards? Well, it makes bees dizzy
To look at matzoh. If more details are wanted,
See *Matzoh-Loving Bees* by E. McTizzy
Where all's explained: the stinger's slightly stunted
Or blunted, I forget, by the bakery pleating
Of the matzoh, made in this case not for eating

But civil defense. So with this problem over
Com could proceed to build his city and bring
Into it thousands of young girls fresh as clover
And beautiful as an ancient Mexican ring
With jewels red as the hat of Smoky Stover,
And to these girls he offered everything
Our sad world can provide: drink, clothes, and money,
And, when he could, his love. Like some wild bunny

He made love over fifty times a day,
Never becoming sated, bored, or sleepy.
"It's just life's great experience," he'd say,
"That's all! Preferring other things seems creepy
When I can sweep into the disarray
Of limbs and golden hair, then plunge in deep. We
Live but once: let us not live in vain.
Sailors, come home! Here is life's bounding main!"

And, saying so, he'd lunge into some beauty
And, panting, pass a half an hour or so
Coming and crying "Ah, this is my duty!
Someone must make the human radar glow
Continually, or else the Cosmic Cutie
Will kill us! This I absolutely know!"
And so he'd theorize and love inceasingly
With pleasure growing in his soul increasingly.

Why did he want all this in Venice? Actually
I do not know. I'm not sure he did either.
I'd guess the city just aroused him sexually
As Mommy's breast arouses the pre-teether.
One's lust is bound by fancy, not contractually:
To rouse it even while one takes a breather
One needs an optimum spot, and so for Papend
The place was Venice—that's just how it happened.

He'd thought of Samos first, because he'd seen there
A beautiful city—he could not remember
Its name, but everything had been so green there
And the sea'd seemed a huge light emerald ember;
Also there was that temple to the Queen there
Of all Greek gods, even Hera; in September
He'd cabled to his manager in Split
To start creating Samos, that was it.

And then by chance, purely by chance one evening
He'd found himself in Venice, where the sheer
Beauty of everything set him to grieving
For having chosen Samos. It was queer
To change his mind so suddenly! but leaving
The café where he sat he phoned Vladmir
Komslavul with these words: "Abandon Samos!
Put Venice in its place. *Allons-y! Vamos!*"

And Venice had been born in old Peru,
A most unusual South American city
Where all Commander Papend did was screw
And give sweet things to girls, all of them pretty
As everything in nature is when new
And not decided on by a committee
But fresh and gravely formed by nature's process
Which shuns the minuscule and the colossus

In making human creatures—So, the gods
Decided to take vengeance on that scooper
Who'd taken the young beauty. "I'll give odds
It was some interplanetary snooper!"
Opined one other girl. "Our lightning rods
Do not keep off, as stun-ray keeps a grouper,
Strange alien eyes from gazing at our bodies
While we disrobe in Venice hall and cottage!"

It was discovered to have been, in fact,
No interplanetary plot but rather
What André Gide called "a gratuitous act"
Of cumulus clouds, which, when they are together
For a long time, sometimes overreact
And form some kind of scoop, which is a bother
If it behaves as this one did. The girl, though,
Was found unharmed though puzzled by her furlough

Among the clouds. Meanwhile in Greece, near lines
Which run from Theseus' temple to Poseidon's
Let's turn our gaze, like Heaven's, which divines
A motor vehicle with an inside ins-
Ide its outside larger than the spines
Of dinosaurs, which men with subtle guidance
From bits of bone and dust have put together
Inside museums to resist the weather

So we can walk around them saying, "Jesus!
What if them fuckers walked around today?"
And now and then a guard comes up and teases
Some little chap with "Did you see that, hey?
It moved! The thing's alive!" which so increases
The pleasure of the people there that they
Laugh to themselves at both the boy and guard—
So huge this automobile was. "Take a card,"

Said Minnie, as they drove, to Gabby Grouse;
"Mickey, how many do you have by now?"
"Dear, I can't play while driving. Here's the house!"
Gabbed Mick. "Look, dear," mouthed Minnie, "Clarabelle Cow
Is cropping grass as evenly as a louse
Creeps through the hair of evening. And a bough
Heavy with honeysuckle hangs above
Our nest of nozzling and our lair of love!"

"Truer were never spoken mousy words!"
Sang Mickey as he drove the gleaming Packard
Into the barn. Above him busy birds
Conduct their songfest, and not one is laggard.
"Clarabelle's milk has been too full of curds!"
Cries Pluto, running to them. Thought a faggot
By some, this dog was said to favor fellas
Of every species when he lived in Hellas.

But Mickey didn't give a damn! He smacked
Pluto between the ears and gave a whistle!
Clarabelle Cow came munching up. Mick whacked
Her on the ass and said, "I picked this thistle
In far-off Zululand, my love. Half-cracked,
I've brought it from that bush like an epistle,
Clarabelle Cow, for you! Now, food and rest!
Tomorrow we must be at our rodent best!

Come on! We've got to get this car unpacked
No time for fooling now; we have one night
And one night only, one, to be exact,
One twelve-hour span to seek our souls' delight
And then before Greece's hellish dawn has cracked
We must be on the road again in flight,
In glorious flight, world's record speed to try
On all the roads of Greece, for Canada Dry!"

"Oh, Mickey, can't you stay here more?" cried Clara,
Hot for some consummation with the mouse;
"They say upon the shores of the blue Cari-
Bbean Sea is a pagoda house
Where mice love more than Deirdre did in Tara!
Oh, that I there could shed my milky blouse
And be with you a weekend or a year!"
So saying, she rough-tongued his rounded ear.

"Clara, beware!" cried Minnie. "I'll not let you
So carry on with Mick while I'm alive!
Even if you make him now, he'll soon forget you
When we go speeding off upon our drive
Over the million roads of Greece. Upset you?
Too bad! He's mine! You, just when we arrive,
Start making cow eyes at him. Your tough luck!
Alone with him tonight I'll squeak and fuck!"

Meanwhile the brilliant red sun in the sky
Of Western Greece now turned a fiercer pale.
A cook in Athens throws an eggplant pie
Against a restaurant wall; he missed—a nail
Appears now in his forehead where the guy
Named Alfred Funz the pie hit could not fail
To take revenge by shooting it from a pistol
Which shot but nails: its barrel was of crystal,

So that a person near enough could witness
The passage of the nail from end to end
Of the Greek gun, which ended physical fitness
For whomsoever—husband, wife or friend—
Its missile struck. From manliness to itness
It turned the waiter, caused his knees to bend,
And flung him straight into the *au delà*—
Hard punishment for throwing moussaka!

A meaningless violence seems to plague the world
Which world cannot get rid of. Men debate
In great assemblies, with all flags unfurled,
The cause of peace, go home, and fill with hate
And get their rifles; brows with sweat empearled,
Feeling some insult to their purse or state
Or that some person is too much unlike them!
It's hard to see why that should make them strike them!

Hard punishment for any on this earth
To have to leave it in his early years
Before he's had his soul's and body's worth
Of ecstasy and action! hard for ears
To have their function stunted from one's birth;
Hard for the eyes not to see what appears.
Hard are the changes brought about by violence
And even, sometimes, by some fact of science—

The change, for instance, of a man to glassware
By trocadminium phosphate steriodinus,
A horrible substance scattered on the grass where
Two characters from *Ko*, one fair as Venus,
The other once a coach, in Provence ask where
A picnic place might be, safe from the keenness
Of the wild, whistling Mistral. They are shown
A field, by an old man with head of bone.

These two are Alouette, a Tucson belle,
And Pemmistrek, her lover. They much voyaged
Through Michigan, then o'er the ocean's swell
To vast New Asia, where Alouette encouraged
The tourist trade with an immense hotel,
The Munster Mooson, which was then disparaged
By certain persons as imperialistic,
Which didn't please Alouette, who was a mystic

Of sorts, who thought of love and only that.
The Mooson she had built because a panther
Came to her in a dream and ate her hat,
Then stood up on its hind legs like a dancer,
Then changed to a hotel, all cool and flat.
Next day she brooded; then, "I've got the answer!"
She cried, and started building. When, however,
She heard that version of her deed, she never

Had one day's doubt that she should leave her holdings
To a New Asian outfit, if, of course,
It was all right with Pemmistrek. What foldings
Into his arms, and kissing her with force,
And saying "What, to us, my love, are mouldings,
Are bellboys, elevators, Kleenex, coarse
Americans in short Bermuda pants?
How better far fresh air and high romance!"

They left—she her hotel, he being coach,
And toured New Asia, then to Europe via
The Trans-Siberian Express, steel roach
That runs so far, runs, almost, from Korea
To Aix, where they are now, and now approach
Their deadly destiny. What an idea!
A chemical that makes a person vitreous!
Horrible change, from flesh and blood—and piteous.

On lying down in it, Pemmistrek immediately
Feels an absurd sensation in his thorax,
Stares at his hand and finds it, inconceivably,
Transparent, through which he sees fields of borax,
Light green. Then his whole body glazes evenly,
And he, though conscious, can perform no more acts.
The sun shines down on him, as you'd expect, from
The sky, and shows all colors of the spectrum.

And Alouette, who loved him so, and had
For such a while, seeing him turned to substance
That could not feel nor see, know good from bad,
Nor walk around, nor eat, nor answer questions,
Began to shake, like one who has gone mad
And changed, herself, all tremblings and convulsions,
Into a giant bird—metempsychosis
Due to ornithological neurosis.

One goes along, and one is feeling pleasant
And normal, certainly, and full of life,
When suddenly one feels an effervescent
Sub-epidermic tingle, like a knife,
Then feels stark feathers pushing, one is Desmond
Or Betty Lou no more, no more the wife
Of Doctor Fosgrove of Three Fifty-Two
Hyannis Lane, no more Gentile or Jew

But absolute pure bird—asocial malady,
That frees one from one's culture! Curious case!
It almost always started as an allergy
With a slight hint of feathers round the face—
One ended up like something from mythology
Which guards a hill or other sacred place.
It lasted days, or months, though meditation
Could speed its cure, as could the imitation

Of a bouquet of roses (this is an ancient
Orthodox Jewish ritual which survives
Chiefly in jokes and in one smallish painting
By Pisanello, with beflowered sides:
A young, rose-costumed rabbi with a fainting
Woman in a green wood). Now she decides
To act, at once. "For maybe he can shake
This illness off, or its enchantment break—

I'll fly him to a hospital at once!"
To pick him up is hard, and to transport
Is harder still. Now through the field she runs
To gather weeds, of which she makes the sort
Of basket which balloonists who do stunts
Are fond of leaping out of, or, at court,
Ladies pile plums in for the delectation
Of him or her who rules their sovereign nation.

So Pemmistrek is tied inside the lock
Of twining Provence weeds, and Alouette takes
Him, windowy, to Rome. And there, with shock
And microsurgical laser beam that shakes
His flesh free from the vitreous parent block,
He's cured! He moves—and breathes. Dr. McSnakes,
Who did the work (amazing!), does the best
He can to help Alouette: "Poor child, with breast

Of down, and downcast wing, who overspread
My chair, would that I knew a certain cure
To turn that bird's head to a human head
And give you back your feminine allure—
I would, but I cannot. I can, instead,
Assure you, though, that you will change. The pure
Dry air of Rome this time of year should help
You to come back to womanhood. Eat kelp

And drink a lot of water. Try to find
A synagogue. Your friend will have amnesia.
There is no way a man can keep his mind
Intact when packed in vitreous anaesthesia
As he has just now been. If you are kind,
However, and let him live in love and leisure,
His memory will come back. This morning, though,
It's as if he'd been born an hour ago."

He opened the great window, and they flew
Together over Rome. Then down together
They walked about, and he found nothing new
Or strange about the fact that she was feather
Where he was flesh, or that her legs were blue.
He felt so strange amid that ancient heather
Of Palatine and Capitoline, knowing
The whole of human life within him growing—

Surprised by joy, impatient as the wind,
Full of the amorous passions of a man
And all the careless ease of youth. He grinned.
"Can we be happy here? I think we can.
Dear feathery friend! Oh, were you trunked or finned,
Or both, I'd love you equally!" "My plan,"
Alouette said, "though's to change to girl as soon as
I ever can. It's nicer." Then when noon was

Upon the Palatine, where these two wandered
In happy delectation of a future
That could not be far distant, as they squandered
Sweet words upon each other's tint and feature,
Pemmistrek bumped into a white unlaundered
Rough marble portal faint with architecture,
Which opened, when he touched it, dark and wide,
And he fell in, then closed, he trapped inside.

He fought to open it but fought in vain.
Once in each hundred years that door would budge.
It was designed by Archibald of Spain—
A famous architect who held a grudge
Against Pope Leo Seventh ("The Insane")—
To capture Leo's mistress, Ellen Gudge
Of England, whom he'd meet upon this hill
Each Monday night, in weather warm or chill.

The Spanish builder had slipped a phony note
In Ellen's door, which told her on that night
To wear a big warm fuzzy winter coat
And at their rendezvous turn to the right,
Descend, and at the marble mountain goat
Turn left and press the buzzer with delight
Which she would see in front of her, and enter
The door which opened. When he this had sent her

The guileful Archibald had gone inside
The Roman cave to wait for her. She was
The most, since what time Cleopatra died,
Beautiful creature ever dressed in fuzz,
Which even women never have denied.
And so when Archibaldo heard the buzz
He felt not only vengeance coming to him
But also fire-tipped tremors running through him!

Alas! the one who entered was not Ellen,
But a clove-covered steaming Chinese fish
Who picked his bones in whispers. Trojan Helen,
Whether on mountain's top or ancient dish
Adorned with fruit trees you abide, or, dwelling
In some obscure hut, wrinkled, hear my wish:
That no man, filled with passion, feel again
What Archibald of Spain experienced then.

Grant this, and grant no more. The Pope, of course,
Had long ago found out the Spaniard's plan.
He had a thousand spies whom threats of force
Obliged to work incessantly. "The man
Is crazier than I!" With no remorse
The Pope commissioned Papal Chef Wang Fan
To bake a poisoned Chinese walking delicacy
To kill the fool who threatened his fake celibacy.

And so he had. The manner of his killing
Is too repulsive to report. Instead
Let's follow Pemmistrek, who will, God willing,
End up in Finland, where the passage led
The Door had let him into. But that milling
Throng he sees immediately ahead?
Those ocean's waves, that sunlight on his pinky—
Yes, in two minutes he had reached Helsinki!

That cave was built in a mysterious way
And Archibald of Spain had been a genius
Far greater than the greatest of his day.
What puzzles me is that our high school seniors
In science know the work of Ludge, Dubray,
Pistaki, Meyers, Einstein, Fox, Veisenius,
But do not know this master of illusion!
And now a boat sails up with a profusion

Of female beauty on it. "Who are you?"
One lovely cries, attired in open shirt,
With long blonde hair and features almost new.
She was an Early Girl, made from the dirt
Of Western Finland by MacShane Depew,
A wild American chemist who to flirt
Was all he cared about, and he had found
A way to make young women from the ground.

In Western Finland there's a soil called *simma*
Pronounced like Jim plus *a* though with an *s*
Instead of *j* (that is, it isn't *jimma*)
Which, with an ounce of water, more or less,
And a dash of white pepper from the Hima-
Layan Mountain States, sends up a Bess,
A Sally, or a Benedetta Croce—
Young beauty to impassion the unstodgy,

The valiant men of earth. More than he needed
He could create, since he had lots of pepper
And plenty of soil, and so Depew proceeded
To send such girls all over, like the skipper
Of this cave-entering boat. The one she greeted
So gaily was unconscious as a kipper:
The speed and force of what had happened to him
Struck all at once and violently threw him.

Were these girls like those girls who grew up from
A babyhood to childhood, adolescence,
And then more perfect state? Were they more dumb?
Shyer? More awkward? Or more full of presence?
And from what culture did they seem to come?
What traits, if any did, betrayed their essence?
Were they more innocent than ordinary
Girls? More giving? More relaxed? More merry?

O strange, sweet girls of whom the chemist thought
Who more than other scientists took pity
On those who live for beauty! But I ought
To hurry now to Rome, that brilliant city,
Where Huddel, who so valiantly has fought
Against the tight embrace of Zacowitti,
The Beljab God of Death who smiles at nothing,
Awoke, and broke out in a high, loud buzzing.

If clarity is what we seek in life,
Then life's a disappointment and a fraud,
For nothing's ever really clear, not wife,
Or home, or work, or people who applaud
The finest work you do. But if a knife-
Like deep sensation worthy of a god
Is what you're after, life can furnish plenty—
Some earlier than, some at, some after twenty.

There is the proud sensation, for example,
Of sinking in the ocean in a car;
Or being thrown against a Gothic temple
By an outrageous omophagic czar—
No one should ever feel that he has ample
Experiences which light him like a star:
Stark naked hens and roosters playing cricket,
And Juno, Mars, and Saturn in a thicket.

Of such events the coming back of Huddel
To life was surely one for many people
Who found the trip to Rome well worth the trouble
Although at times the climate made them feeble.
He gave, to all who watched, the thought that rubble
Itself might take a jog around the steeple
If but its atoms came to that decision;
The pleasure this thought gave banned all derision.

In fact this statue, dear to the enlightened
And ignorant alike, was now betraying
Sure signs of coming back to life, which frightened
Old ladies, so that one could find them praying
In the S.S. *Annunziata* night and
Day: what once had died should be decaying,
Not coming back to breathe the air of Rome
And pinch and kiss its girls and take them home.

Most Romans loved it, though; to them it seemed
That life was good again! And Huddel felt
(He had felt nothing for a while), he dreamed,
Or did whatever, that a rope or belt
Had loosened from around him. He esteemed
The sun was hot but not enough to melt
His form completely; he was still half dead
And rather liked this state. The doubters said,

"You must also suppose that Notre Dame
Will start to dance a jig in La Cité,
That Eiffel Tower will make a grand salaam
To all of Paris' tourists one fine day,
And that the Winged Victory will come
Flying along above our sidewalks gray—
If you believe in all of these events,
Then Huddel redivivus makes good sense!"

Buses, however, emptied every several
Minutes, green and yellow buses filled
With famous tourists—Dr. James McDeverel,
Expert in shoulder transplants; Harmon Schild,
The "buggy doctor," known as Richard Feverel
In Zurich Klinik's Literary Guild;
And hordes of others, leaping from their taxis
In sweaters, jackets, cutaways, and maxis,

In minidresses, cashmeres, rubber suits,
Some laughing, others crying, some with amulets,
Consumptive women and presumptuous brutes,
Miss Ellen Foster Tay of East Los Angeles,
And the Italian army's young recruits,
Looking at Huddel, which so far was thankless:
No arm he raised nor shoulder braced nor torso
Bent in a semicircle toward the Corso.

But now . . . he did! He turned all April blue
(The color of the dry air after rain).
A child cried, "Mother! Look! He's coming to!"
And, sure enough, from vales of No-More-Pain,
No-More-Remorseless-Plans-for-Things-to-Do
And No-More-Love, No-Justice, No-More-Brain,
Someone was rising there! His fingers flexed,
His eyes shone wide, which earlier had been x'd

By deadly Zacowitti. Huddel leaped
Down from his platform base. He felt so strange
In heart and head and leg and arm, so steeped
In puzzling new vibrations at the change
Of state that had come over him! There beeped
Horns everywhere; as at a rifle range
Shots rang all around; from pure excess of feeling
Men wept and cheered; and temple bells were pealing.

This mad crescendo made a car nearby
And its Italian occupants who'd been
Chasing a rare mysterious butterfly
Which had the power of speech drive over in
Excitement, thinking that the reason why
So many minds had gone into a spin
In Central Rome, with many a helicopter a-
Bove their heads, could but be Lepidoptera

Five Hundred Sixty-Five, the one they sought.
"A butterfly!" their chief, Gorso, imagined
He heard somebody say, and cried, "We ought
To head that way! that crowd there—like a pageant—
They must have found our creature!" Overwrought,
He sped the Fiat in a crazy fashion
And hit poor Huddel, shattering him. To be
Killed twice is to be dead eternally,

They say. We'll see. He fell. Then Rome grew blurry
With deadly thunderclouds. To quit that sky
For shelter now was everybody's worry
Save for the crazy scientists who try
To find their bug amidst the storm, and scurry
All round the place where Huddel's ruins lie.
Then suddenly these ruins, by some force
Triumphant welded, swifter than a horse

And stronger than a lion, leap together
And strike the crazy hunters where they run.
Hit by that hand and nearly dead from weather
They raise their hands for mercy, every one,
Then see before them like a speaking feather
The butterfly they sought with axe and gun:
Five Hundred Sixty-Five, both red and white
Its moving wings, how sure and quick its flight!

"I'm sorry that I can't be staying with you,"
The butterfly observed, "but I'm obliged
To go wherever mercy is at issue.
You know you didn't find me: I arrived
When your survival was so frail a tissue
That if I hadn't come you'd have capsized
Beneath the deadly blow that Huddel gave
And found in Rome an awful, watery grave.

Give up your quest for me. I can't be gotten.
Go be the consolation of the poor;
Convince the man of shame that he's not rotten;
Perfume the harried worker in the sewer;
Bind up the wounds of youth with gauzy cotton;
And make the days of hell on earth be fewer!"
While saying this, Five Hundred Sixty-Five
Stood poised above their heads, as if to dive,

Which then it did. Strange that a creature which
Has neither man's intelligence nor feelings
Can hold a view of life that is so rich!
So moths that leap at lightbulbs on our ceilings
So maddeningly that we turn off the switch
To sit in darkness with the apple peelings
And half-filled brandy glasses in the evening
Of summer days might cure us of all grieving

If we could but hear their philosophy.
However, none of them can talk, which is
Why Enzo Gorso and his cohorts free-
Ly gave up love and laughter, bed and bus-
Iness to chase this stunning wingèd flea,
The talking butterfly and moral whiz
Five Hundred Sixty—but you know already
And must be wondering what Huddel, heady

With new-found powerful life, was up to while
These hunters heard a bug philosophizing.
He felt as full of mysteries as the Nile
And felt the strangest force within him rising.
Vowing to live this time in a new style
(More wildly free and much more enterprising)
He turned from those he'd struck, and, turning there,
Finding new strength he rose into the air.

Pursuing what he takes to be a parrot
That calls him by name, Huddel descends
The Valley of the Tiber, while a carrot
Grows up in Houston, and while Pemmistrek's friends,
His new friends, that is, Early Girls, inherit
The job of curing him. "He has the bends!"
Cries one. "But no!" "He's darling!" cries a third.
And Alouette flies, far off, a helpless bird.

If she will find the passage to the snowy
City where her lover is and if
He still will be the Daphnis to her Chloe
If she does not, somehow, de-hippogriff
It's hard to say. Bedazzled by the showy
Beauty of these girls who make him sniff
For losses dim and foggy in his brain,
He goes off with them on a Finnish train.

It takes him to the north of Finland, touted
To be quite fair. He felt he was in love
With Early Ann, and they made love about it.
She was afraid, though—gave an anxious cough,
Looked at him, closed her eyes, wept, smiled, and pouted.
"What's wrong?" he asked. "Was I too rude or rough?
I'm sorry if I was. You made me happy!"
She stood up in her blue and white serapi.

"I-I like you too," she said. "But I'm afraid
Of what may come to be." And as she said it
A strange fine mist exuded from the bed
On which the two had lain like persons wedded.
"I fear it is some city we have made,"
The artificial beauty wept. "I dread it.
The old gnome in the peach tree prophesied it."
Into his arms for comfort then she glided.

"What? City? I don't understand a word,"
Said Pemmistrek. "The prophecy was this,"
Said, brightly, Ann, "that each time it occurred
An Early Girl responded to a kiss
And lay down with the fellow she preferred
And held him to her hard for emphasis,
The double of a city would appear—
A ringer for the chilly real one, beer

Exuding from its barroom taps, and trolleys
Ringing down its urban streets, bananas
Sold by vendors from high carts, and college
Students dreaming up some pure Havanas
Where love would govern all, not francs or dollars,
And alligators in the fake savannas
Of its aquarium or giant zoo—
And many another subtle detail too—

But something would be wrong, some little change
Which made a person wandering there feel crazy
Who thought he was in his true city; strange
Events would make his sense of things grow hazy—
Beds, for example, at the stock exchange.
Sometimes it was just air, which made one lazy,
So that all action had a different rhythm,
As if one had a hippopotamus with him

Who would not move too fast. Sometimes the light
Was what was different. Viewed in solid pink
With polkadots of yellow, Paris might
Be beautiful, but not quite what you'd think;
In such a city one would welcome night,
If night could change those colors, or strong drink."
"How strange it is!" "One love gasp can achieve it!"
Said healthy Pemmistrek, "I don't believe it!"

But, actually, forming at his side
Was Philadelphia, white as the receiver
Of a new "sandal" telephone, the pride
Of Bell's insane inventors, and the savior
Of those with feet which talk. This town was wide
And high and windowed, and no true believer
Could tell it, save for color, from the town
In Pennsylvania, where it settles down;

So that there are two cities right together,
One the old Philadelphia, one the new one.
The new has all bright white or snowy weather,
And it is hard to say which is the true one;
Each smells of rope and roofing, leaf and leather,
And each sends mixed sensations coursing through one.
Each time, good God! that Pemmistrek makes love
Will some new city hit us from above?

The earth in that case will be like an album
Filled up with stamps and no blank spaces showing—
A huge refectory of urban paldom—
And then on top of one another growing
These duplicates would hold the earth in thraldom.
Only the top ones would have sun or snowing,
So most would not be light at all, or airy,
The truth—good news!—is that they're temporary.

Into existence suddenly released,
They'd stay until the sun had done its job
By rising once and setting, then decreased
Until they vanished, causing those to sob
Who like new places. To the west and east
And north almost as far as penguins mob
The crumbs Kaploona empties in the drifts
And south as far, men saw these city shifts,

And, startled by them, often I would guess
Leaped into bed themselves with female citizens
They'd felt too shy with earlier to express
Their passion with such wholesome lack of reticence.
"What? Harold! Why?" "I really love you, Tess!"
So Cracows, Nices, Zurichs, Bombays, Patersons
Inspire what without the control of birth
Will soon exhaust the resources of earth.

O Birth Control! How radiantly superior
You are to Love Control! O arms and legs!
O pelvic threshold! Exquisite interior!
O breasts for which the thirteen-year-old begs
And marvels over when they soon appear to her!
Thigh, calf, and foot! O delicate as eggs,
You, wrists! and face, how can I praise you properly?
Besides, it's all been done by Akopopoli,

Who, though, unfortunately, wrote in Greek,
Which I can't read, so doubtless plagiaristic
Is somewhat of the praise which here I speak.
Still, repetition is characteristic
Of greatest wisdom: what said Christ the meek
Not said before by Prophet or Greek mystic?
He simply put it in a different order.
So Pemmistrek will every day embroider

The planet with new cities. He knew not
What life was like, therefore it seems to him,
Amnesiac, that this strange life he's got
In Finland's snows among the cherubim
Made by MacShane Depew, a heavenly lot
Of love works none would choose to merely skim,
Is Everyman's. Now pausing in his flight
On Samos Huddel lands to spend the night.

I don't believe I made entirely clear
What sort of matter Huddel was composed of
After his second recrudescence here
On earth where men are usually disposed of
Once and once only, even when quite dear
To gods who have the power to change them. Most of
The Greeks the Greek gods saved were made divine,
Not given human life a second time.

In fact, it seems a questionable gift;
One might, I think, like something slightly altered
When one came back from death, the slightest shift,
Something, at any rate, so that what faltered
The first time round would get a little lift
And have more chance to feel itself exalted.
Huddel, indeed, was not the same he once was:
Half flesh, half concrete, flying into sunsets,

He had the strength of seven men; he could
Lift two-ton weights above the people's heads;
His slightest touch would splinter stoutest wood
And he could take the Dodgers and the Reds
And hurl them into center field for good.
But here he was on Samos, and the Feds
Were fearful that if Soviet Russia found him
They'd build a whole new war machine around him.

"Think of him mating with those Soviet maidens!"
Said Arragaw DePew, a slithy G-Man;
"Those Rooskies know just what to do. In cadence
Every hour some new threat to a free man
Would be begun inside the girl he laid ins-
Ide the Birth-Rate Building. Unless we man
A nuclear sub to cut him off at Samos
We may lose everything!" *"Te gaudeamus,"*

The choirboys sang in Rome, and "Try to find me!"
Stout Huddel sighed, intuiting the project
The American government had. "No one assigned me
To fight for any side. Of life the object
Is to be strong and glad. Three births remind me
That I was meant to live. No sub or prop-jet
Shall force me from this Asiatic sea—
Above all else I prize my liberty!

O Liberty, you are the only word at
Which the heart of man leaps automatically!"
As Huddel spoke, the folk on Samos, stirred at
The way he spoke and what he said, ecstatically
Began to shriek with pleasure. "I prefer dat,"
Said Mugg McDrew, the sub commander. "Practically
Makes dis ting a cinch! We'll just pretend
Dat we're Greeks too, den take our little friend!"

The sub, already there beneath the harbor,
Now opened up, and ten Americans swam
Ashore and started searching for the garb or
Part of garb that, aided by the ham
Inside each one, could help them play the barber,
The farmer, and the chief. They gave a damn,
These gallant boys, enough to risk their all for
A blow against the Reds, more vile than sulphur.

When they are all attired in stolen clothes
And walking through the Samian crowd, which, cheering
Huddel, to the left, then right side flows
Like a Ferrari with a melted steering
Wheel, they see a maiden like a rose
All pink and white toward the temple veering
Where Huddel is declaiming—"Watch out! You
Are being trailed by agents from the blue

Aegean, or whatever sea it is!
They want to trap you, so beware!" Then Huddel,
Glancing around, saw one who fitted his
Idea of a phony Greek—unsubtle
His idiot disguise! He blew a kiss
To his sublime informant, who was trouble
To those who thought to make a capture here,
And struck the fake Achaian with a spear

Which was a part of Hera's holy temple,
Something he obviously should not have done,
For it made all the earth of Samos tremble!
A giant earth- or sea-quake had begun,
Which made the Samians, screaming, disassemble.
An act of sacrilege, the only one
That Huddel ever did, caused this upheaval
Which smashed the classic with the medieval

And smote the Samian robber in his cave
And threw the Samian shepherd from his mount
And shot a thousand dead up from the grave
And broke more water jars than I can count;
And, while the island cracked, a tidal wave
Like a huge copy of *The Sacred Fount*
Smashed everything in sight and then retreated,
Leaving old Samos totally depleted.

Yes, there was nothing on this island now:
No eagles, no bazoukis, no percussion,
No moussaka, no blossoms on the bough
Of the delightful pear tree where the buzzing
Of bees made glad the lad who led the cow;
And all the persons who had been discussing
The ways to solve their personal problems are
Gasping at sea and cling to any spar.

Life's simple in such crisis situations,
Provided they don't last for very long:
Such fortitude, such sympathy, such patience,
Such pleasure in a patriotic song!
Too bad that just by decimating nations
One usually has such things. It's wrong.
One ought to live as nobly every minute
As these folks did at sea while struggling in it

To stay afloat and find their island home
Just one more time, and then, they vowed, forever
They'd be obedient to the speechless dome
And parchless eye of heaven; they would never
Do any bad or selfish thing, nor roam
From Samos off to any place whatever.
These vows were heard by no one but the fishes
Whom usually they fried and served on dishes

With lemon on the side, and sometimes rice.
These edibles, though, found incomprehensible
Their human language, which did not suffice
To make the fish do anything more sensible
Than swimming out of earshot. Fish are nice
In being, though we eat them, not revengeful.
I think that we would probably be meaner
To those who washed us down with their retsina!

However, back to Huddel, who was flying
Above the wavetops, seeking the beauty who
Had warned him of the U.S. agents. Spying
Her floating near, he scoops her from the blue
And flies with her to Africa. Now sighing,
Now cursing violently, Mugg McDrew
Cruises the choppy sea in loop-the-loops
To save his Greek-costumed aquatic troops.

He finds them, all but one, a boy named Amos
Frothingham, who, wishing to escape
America's Secret Service (though it's famous,
To guns he much prefers the girl, the grape,
The pear tree and the plough, and so on Samos
Decides to live, and was in such good shape
That he could swim against the tide) had swum
Alone to shore again, but was struck dumb:

For Samos, Samos was not what it was!
A million people jammed its dusty streets!
Construction pierced the ear with hideous buzz!
Enormous libraries, with busts of Keats,
Shelley, and Colonel Pepperidge, sheltered fuzz
Who searched for foreign spies among the treats
That literature offered! Traffic lights
Changed hue, to promise multicolored nights!

What was this transformation of an island
City to a metropolitude?
The taxi and the steam drill pushed the silent
Sea aside and smashed the island's mood!
How could that be? I think a Danish pilot,
With engine trouble, with his parachute
Came down to earth in Finland and so flattered
An Early Girl, so many kisses scattered,

So many a light caress placed here and there,
That she succumbed to him, upshot of which
Was this new form of Samos. What a scare
It put in Amos' bosom! "No such switch
Is possible!" he cried. "It isn't fair!
Just at the moment I decide to ditch
Urban America, it comes back to haunt me!
I'll kill myself! Oh God! Life doesn't want me!"

And, saying this, he ran into the sea
To drown himself—at least, he thought he did,
Thought he was running blindly, terribly
Into the salt sea where nobody lived;
He ran from two till quarter after three,
Stopped, opened up his eyes, and saw what gift
His life had given him: the old, true, empty
But beautiful Samos, at whose harbor entry

The Samian citizenry now climbed ashore.
The tide had changed for which they thanked the goddess
And vowed that none would violate ever more
Her sanctuary. Meanwhile in Nevada's
Gambling halls, the odds are five to four
That Mickey Mouse will conquer the White Protes-
Tant Anglo-Saxon rats who are his rivals.
The mice, both he and she, are better drivers,

The gamblers say; and many a bet is made
By those who can't afford it, kids in sneakers
With wistful looks, who all night long have prayed
For Disney's two to win this crazy Preakness
Through all the roads of Hellas. Undismayed,
Terence and Alma Rat have shown no weakness,
But, driving just as fast, with less support,
Intend to win. In Athens, in Earls Court,

And in the drowsy empires of the East
Interest is high, and television offers
Daily two-hour reports, a visual feast
To all who love the contest. Mickey proffers
A candy bar to Minnie. "Brewer's yeast
Is all I'll eat today," squeaks she, but softens
And takes the bar and takes a bite. "My diet
Is less to me than keeping Mickey quiet

In mind and heart so he can be victorious,"
She thinks—while Donald in the back seat's dozing
As they pass Delphi, famous for its oracles,
Descend to Thrakis, famed for early closing,
Then speed with trembling wheels to Crete the glorious
Across the "Bridge of Spray," made by the hosing
Of people on the islands on the way;
This would not work in San Francisco Bay

Because there are no islands there to hold
The people spurting water; but there are
So many isles (twelve thousand five, all told)
Of Greece, there was no problem; so the car,
Supported by this water brave and cold,
Could brightly beam along, a daytime star,
Bearing two noted mice of black and one
Of yellow duck, whose name, you know, was Don.

O Donald Duck, if ever you could know
The destiny that waits for you in Crete
You'd urge your best friend Mickey to go slow
And exercise the webbing on your feet
To leap into the blue sea air, for though
Your life with him and Minnie seems complete
Soon a most horrible wedge will drive between
You and your friends. Meanwhile the beckoning green

Of fair Heraklion with its Labyrinth
Spoke to them from afar. "Land, land at last!"
Said Mickey. Minnie said, "And it's a cinch
We'll all be glad this watery ride is past,
Although it was exciting!" "May the tenth:
Two thousand miles—eight hours." Don smiled and laughed
Then passed the book to Minnie: "Let Terence Rat
Just try to beat or even compete with that!"

And Donald's doom was on him in two days. . . .
A Chinese gentleman named Hu Ching Po
Was interested in living different ways:
Spending the month on Crete, he wished to know
The black, the white, the intervening grays
Of all that happened there. Well, he was so
Surprised to see a duck walk up and speak
To him that he stared madly at its beak—

Or "bill"—men have a lot of names for noses:
"Schnozzola," "target," "ray-gun," and "proboscis";
And "implement for getting kicks from roses,"
Or "helpful, with the eyes, in winning Oscars,"
And "fresh air opens up what clothespin closes."
Whether by cows or beautiful young Toscas
Borne in the midst of face, it has the beauty
Of being both delicate and heavy-duty:

We breathe all day and then we breathe all night—
Sometimes, it's true, the mouth takes over for it,
But mainly it's the nose, when sun shines bright
Or when stars gleam, that does, like Little Dorrit,
More than it seems it ought to do. Our sight
Is veiled by lids, our hands in sleep lie forward
And do not touch, our ears the brain takes care of
By making dreams of sounds we're not aware of—

But nose, you go on breathing all night long!
What was I speaking of? Oh, Donald's bill.
Yes, well, an animal, chicken or King Kong,
Will have a different nose than humans will.
A nose which on a girl might look all wrong
Would on a hen be beautiful; yet still
We think our own of a superior grade.
Don's was two dots upon a bony blade.

When Hu Ching Po, astonished, saw the beak
Of Donald Duck, and heard him talk, he couldn't
Believe he'd not gone crazy. In a week
They had him out of surgery, a wooden
Brain inside his head, and in his cheek
A "thinking cathode," which would help him goodn-
Ess knows get through life's ordinary duties.
But now to Mickey and his "You, too, Brutus"

Attitude toward Donald, for he found him
In Minnie's arms, with Minnie gently sighing!
"Minnie, goddamn, you've your two arms around him!
I see," cried Mick, "a duck will soon be dying!"
And, seizing a huge rock, began to pound him
(Poor Donald Duck) to death. "I'm not denying
I hugged him hard, but good Lord, Mickey, listen!"
He stopped; he saw her eyes with teardrops glisten.

"Donald—I hope he's not dead yet—poor Donald—
Oh, Mickey, see, he's breathing! yes!" "Come, tell me!"
The barely pacified Mickey cried, "I've coddled
This duck enough! Don't try to overwhelm me
With sighs and tears. Goddamn, I feel dishonored!
What consolation are you trying to sell me?"
"Oh!" Minnie said; then, with a voice like bells,
"He was upset at hurting someone else.

It was the kind of thing we've gone through too—
Don't you remember, Mickey? Oh, you must!
Before the world got used to me and you.
Staring at my small shapely mousy bust
Full many a mariner would go cuckoo;
And you, you were not unaware, I trust,
How many of those who heard you speak your name
Went totally and hopelessly insane.

You know there is a hospital in Switzerland
With two pavilions, Mickey and Minnie Mouse,
For crazy people who go round insisting that
Rats and mice can speak. This crazyhouse
Has services and doctors both most excellent,
Yet no one's ever left it cured." A louse
Leaped through the air toward Mickey's ear but missed it.
Minnie took Mick's left hand in hers and kissed it—

Or, rather, kissed his white four-fingered glove
(These mice have clothing on their hands all year).
"Well, Donald drove one mad today. Oh, love,
Forgive him. And me, too. He felt such fear . . .
I was but pitying him." She kneeled. Above
Her head her lover gave her the all-clear
By making spring-like signs of benediction.
Then both went over to Donald. "His condition

Is grave," said Mickey. "He may really die.
We've got to find a top-flight veterinarian,
And soon!" As through Heraklion's streets they hie,
Let's turn to Huddel and the lovely airy in-
Spiring girl he's found and holds, who fly
Above that substance held by the Aquarian
To Africa, where roams the wild rhinoceros,
That angry brute, and the mild hippopotamus.

Landing in Kenya, girt about by huts,
This pair have scarcely time to greet each other
Or even see each other when there juts
Into the side of each of them a rather
Tremendous deadly spear. "No ifs or buts,"
Thinks Huddel, "life means not to give me breather!"
"What are you doing here?" the natives cry.
"What are you? Are you man? How can you fly?"

Huddel at once sensed he had an advantage
In being strange to them and seeming magic
But tried to tell the truth. "In the Atlantic
An island lies, hight England, known for tragic
Theatre, hot tea, and great Romantic
Poetry. It's hard to find an adjec-
Tive to describe it all!" "Speed up," they said,
"Or ere your story's finished you'll be dead!"

"Well, I am from that island," Huddel moaned,
Pretending suddenly he felt the anguish
Of being far from it. He fell, and groaned.
"What's wrong?" the natives cried, no longer angry
So much as curious. "Perhaps he's stoned,"
One young spear-bearer said, in secret language—
For drug use in the village was quite frequent
And had its own patois. Just then an egret

Flew over Huddel, and he suddenly rose
Grasping sweet Aqua Puncture in his arms
(That was her name) to join that bird. Her clothes
Flew all about, and all beheld her charms
Spellbound, while Huddel in the airstream goes
One hundred miles an hour. Black alarms
Sent up in smoke through Kenya are too tardy
To catch that thrice-born aeronaut so hardy.

Hardy as a Venetian gondolier
When moving slim black boat against the tide;
Hardy as Greek or Trojan charioteer
When war's concussions cast his steeds aside;
Hardy as these and more, and full of cheer,
Huddel once more descends from his sky ride,
This time in Tropical China, a peculiar
African region very like to fool you.

For everyone who lived there was Chinese!
And all the buildings there were Chinese too!
The women wore their skirts slit at the knees!
Some older men resembled Fu Man Chu!
And there were paper lanterns in the trees.
Perhaps it all was caused by you know who,
An Early Girl, caught in the coils of passion;
Or maybe it was made in Papend fashion—

That is, perhaps created by the fancy
Of one ambitious man, to soothe his soul.
Perhaps an old monk skilled in necromancy
Had seen the whole thing on an ancient scroll
And worked, to please his young assistant Nancy
Chang, to make it real and make it whole.
Whatever cause there was for this phenomenon
It amazed Huddel and his belle companion.

They landed, this time, luckily, out of sight
Of the inhabitants, so they had a moment
To look around a bit and gauge their plight.
The people's manners seemed like a good omen:
Everyone was exceedingly polite.
"In such a place as this," said Huddel, "no man
Should do us wrong. Let's see if we can dodge
The carts and crowds and find someplace to lodge."

Aqua, it happened, spoke Italian, which
The people understood, for Tropical China
Belonged to Italy from nineteen six
Till the end of World War Two; and some old-timers
Recalled that epoch with nostalgic twitch
As Bellay France, and Foster Carolina,
Or baby thinking of its mother's breast:
"No doubt about it, that time was the best!"

For Italy had brought a certain order
To Tropical China which it had not had,
And unlike all the countries on its border
Each night its jungly Chinese streets were glad
With sounds of mandolin, flute, and recorder:
Vivaldi then competed with the sad
And Neapolitan songs; here flirted Tosca;
There Norma died; here Pu Tang Fong ate pasta,

While toucans called and monkeys leaped around
And crocodiles went sliding down the river;
The feetchekee bird made a looping sound,
And jungle night at last, that Indian giver,
Took itself off or changed to day: one found
That chilly morn had come and with a shiver
Returned to one's pagoda in the brush,
And then the sun rose with a velvet hush!

They found a lodging, as they'd hoped they would,
A straw pagoda, and they had a chance
To get to know each other. It was good
To hear the gongs and tarantella dance
And merely sit there at their table's wood
And gaze—for the beginnings of romance
Are often very quiet, like a sailor
Drowned in the sea, or like a power failure—

Or rather, its results: no songs, no speeches,
Nothing but stilly silence in the air.
One could have heard the fuzz grow on the peaches
If there had been no one but those two there.
Then finally they spoke. "Experience teaches,"
Said Huddel, "that to find someone you care
A lot about is life's supreme event.
Tell me about you—are you heaven-sent?

Did you descend to Samos from the clouds,
A messenger from Zeus or from Athena?
Or did you make your way through Samian crowds
From powerful Poseidon's wet arena?
Or are you of those mortals doomed to shrouds
Brought back to lovely life by a novena?
Are you love's pattern? or love's syllable?
Whether you are of this or that race, tell—

For I don't know exactly what *I* am:
I have been born three times." Aqua responded,
"I know about your life. An anagram
On an old jar told much, and then, beyond that,
I read about you in the Amsterdam
Gazeeter on the same day I absconded
From the Antiquities Museet. John Ruskin
Was my great-grandfather. I am Etruscan.

Unknown to other folk our leaders had
Worked out a way of keeping men alive—
And women, obviously," she smiled. "Too bad
There wasn't time to save at least, say, five—
Just one. What would, I thought, make me most glad
Would be to see more like myself survive,
But that was then. Now here in this pagoda
Is all I want!" She kissed him for a coda.

And outside they were celebrating Easter
In African Chinese Italian style.
Inside those two embraced. When he released her,
Huddel said, "Let's go out there for a while
To join our joy with theirs in this great feast for
A man come back to life, as I did. Smile.
What's wrong? You're looking worried." She said, "Well,
I am, a little. But—I'll come." The bell

Was sounding Paternosters à la Chang
With Verdian riffs and Congo syncopations,
When from the straw pagoda's door there sprang
These two caught in the enmity of nations.
They joined the streaming multitude and sang
A song of love and youth and their elations—
Unfortunately, staring at them through
A nearby window's straw was Mugg McDrew!

If you are wondering about Aqua's age,
Since she is young and gorgeous, though Etruscan,
And how she got her name, don't skip this page.
Her grandmother had terrified John Ruskin
By talking to him, while the English sage
Was studying her. What is a man to trust in?
He trusted in his feelings—pounding heart!
She was alive, and not a work of art.

Frightened at first, Ruskin became enchanted
With this Etruscan beauty and her story:
Here was, at last, Etruria, not invented
By dry historians, but real. Before, he
Thought history hardly real at all. He wanted
To spend his life with her! She made his glory
But died in childbirth near the Coliseum.
Their daughter was confined in a museum

By envious archaeologists who stole
Her from John Ruskin's carriage at the border—
This loss almost deprived him of his soul!
He'd see his child in dreams, start walking toward her
Then suddenly find himself upon the Mole
In Venice. So she would obey each order;
The archaeologists stuck in her veins
A needle that exempted her from pains

And bodily movement yet which let her grow.
She bloomed apace. Nor did John Ruskin ever
Discover it was she. Why should he go
To Amsterdam or any place whatever
Save Italy? He thought her dead, and so
He stayed, to pour his heart out like a river,
Spending the hours left him, not on tennis
Or careless love, but on *The Stones* of *Venice*.

(That book! the most important ever penned
For Papend and his helpers! All the while
They built their Andean Venice they would spend
Each night stirred and inspired by its style.)
But now to bring our story to an end
Of Aqua's mother—she stayed in the vile
Etruscan Room of Amsterdamsk Museet
Till one day something happened, which is sweet

To tell of and was sweet for her. The venom,
Which had been fed into her veins by those
Who valued stone girls more than girls in denim
And taffeta, wore off, and, like a rose
In the first dawny breeze, near the anemon-
E, her sweet sister flower, in pleasant pose,
She gave a slight, slight shiver and a shake,
Which caused a man to cry, "Am I awake?"

It was the great physician Nyog Papendes,
Commander Papend's father—I am aware
That such coincidences do not lend ease
To readers having perfect faith, but where
The truth is, we must follow. And the Andes'
Doubled Italian city past compare
For love and beauty's founder's father was
The man who saw this scene and felt this buzz

Of love and disbelief. For he had fallen
Quite hopelessly in love with this antiquity,
Or so he thought her, till against the wall in
A state of shock and joy, he felt his rickety
Conventions all collapse around him. Call in
The greatest living experts in propinquity
And they will not find any two made gladder
By being close than these two—or, soon, sadder

At being close no more. He, in the ecstasy
Of that first moment, took her in his arms
And cried, "I have so longed to have you next to me
That I cannot believe this: from what Farms
Of Fantasy or Causeways of Complexity
Have you been now transformed into what warms
Me more than high volcano or deep furnace?"
She sighed, "It is a warmth that cannot burn us!

Oh, take me, love, with you. For I have been
A prisoner in this place so long. And I
Have watched you watching me, which was no sin,
I dearly hope, and hoped before the sky
Would turn to changeful April once again
That we could be together." So they fly,
These two, the dark museum, and two years
Live in a blaze of bliss, and there appears

As product and summation of their love
A beautiful baby girl, who when a tidal
Wave killed both of her parents, being of
Etruscan heritage, was doped with Mydol
And then some stronger syrop, with a shove
Of needle against her arm. And the recital
Of her life, then, is like her mother's: she
Came back to lively motion suddenly.

Her name she'd simply taken from the first
Sounds she heard spoken when she had awakened
And felt her senses tingle. Someone burst
Into her part of the museum shaken
By bitter news and, happily, had not cursed
But cried out, "Acupuncture! they have taken
Her to the Chinese clinic!" She thought, "Oh!
That's me!" and felt her face with pleasure glow.

Then she had run away, hid on a boat,
And gone to Samos, where brave Huddel found her.
Meanwhile in Pucci-styled white llama coat
Half-brother Papend leans upon a counter
And thinks it is a sadly jarring note
In his sweet life, to have not been around her,
His sister, who, a girl saw in her crystal,
Was once again in life. "If but my sister will

Come here, how good for me! I'll seek her out
And speak to her and try to help her manage
The difficulties, which, I have no doubt,
Beset her in a world she must find savage
And most bewildering." He strolled about
Downing full many a glass of Andean vintage
And smiled. "No one can try to find her better—
I'll send out bird and person, wire and letter!"

McDrew knew where she was! For he had followed
Where Huddel flew. He'd left his submarine,
For it was useless baggage, and had collared
A Tracking Helicopter Five Sixteen
Four Hundred and had flown to China hollowed
Out in the midst of Africa. "I mean
To end this matter here!" he cried. "A shame
That I must kill them both, but that's the game

Free life depends on!" Slipping from the doorway
Of his pagoda as the happy pair
Joined in the mingling throng, he saw the shore, way
Down upon his left, and signaled there
With a "Dark Daylight" Lamp, which had a four-way
Beam control—Torch, Sunlight, Sweep, and Flare—
Each type of beam in different cases relevant.
Mugg used the Sweep, and when he did an elephant

Of green transparent plastic raised its trunk
Above the shore and aimed a deadly dart
At Aqua, gauged to turn her into junk
If it attained her flesh in any part.
Signaled by "Sweep of Daylight" Lamps, such sunk-
En weaponry arises. Oh, the art
We waste upon ingenious ways of killing!
When we were babies, just to be was thrilling—

To hold a rattle up, to eat our mommies,
To learn to walk. Then came our childhood pleasures—
Our baseballs, footballs, rag dolls, origamis.
Next, adolescence, with its sexual treasures—
Who then was thinking about killing Commies?
I just wanted to peek under your feathers
At Aaron's costume party, Ellen White,
And think of you and phone you every night

And swim with you sometimes in Karen's cool
Light-blue *piscine*, and kiss you cold and dripping
And hold you in my arms. Oh, why not pool
The intellect of all to make one gripping,
Inevitable, bright, ecstatic school
Whose aim will be to keep such times from slipping
Away from us, so that we'd keep so much
Of happiness from weather, mood, and touch

That we'd be generous of our condition
And give it freely, not be always fighting
Those who we fear may threaten our position—
Like Mugg McDrew, who stands here just delighting
In Aqua's almost certain demolition.
Till such school starts, I know a Mouth, which, biting
The heads off such as he, at least could clear
Some space and time for us to found it here.

This Mouth is part of Akitu mythology,
A creed unknown to most men of the West
But treasured by some experts in psychology
As showing the fear of being eaten best
Of all the earth's religions. No apology
Or prayer will work when comes the Mouth, obsessed
With biting. I must find a way to speak
To this tremendous mouth, or bill, or beak.

It's dangerous, though. I wonder. Mugg, meanwhile,
Stands hatefully amidst the world of men
And women, with a slow, unpleasant smile,
Unmindful of a nearby lions' den,
From which three quick young lions—full of guile,
Nobility, and power—out of ten
Come leaping out, feline, immense, and naked,
Rush to the plastic elephant and break it!

Aqua is saved, the deadly dart it had
Intended for the lovely young Etruscan
Held in its trunk, unsent! McDrew, gone mad
In his frustrated wait for the concussion
Of poison dart and girl, picks up a shad
Seen lying on a fish-store plank and throws it
In fury at the slowly moving pair.
Huddel swerves round and grabs him by the hair.

"Damn you! Who are you? Why'd you throw that fish?
'American commander'? What the hell!
You followed me from Samos! Boy, you'll wish
You never joined the service! Ring out, bell,
And hide his screams!" But, with a savage *swish*,
The lions rushed and took him, like a shell
The ocean takes, from Huddel's hands, and left
Him staring, as if of all sense bereft.

These lions were the agents of a man
Who lived inside the jungle and intended
To rescue people, if he could, and plan
To save the world, afraid all would be ended
If humans had their way. This fellow, Dan
McGillicuddy, one day had befriended
A lion in the Hyde Park Zoo. These two
Had planned and plotted then what they must do.

228

Dan thought it wrong that lions should be kept
In iron cages, and he also thought
He'd like a lion's life himself. He slept
In beds but dreamed of caverns; he was caught
In London's civilization, and he wept
To think of freedom in the wilds. He bought
A ticket for himself to Tropical China
And smuggled Beano on the ocean liner

(That was the lion's name) locked in a trunk.
Installed now in the jungle for three years,
Dan had ten lions in his charge, a monk
Of sorts, who gave his life to calming fears,
To rescuing all who might be pierced or shrunk
Or poisoned. People, wiping off their tears,
Would seek to thank him with large sums of money,
But he said no, which many thought was funny.

In any case, these lions then had brought
A body to the cave where they all dwelled.
"What sort of poor sad man is this?" Dan thought,
Then looked at Mugg's insignia—it spelled
"American Secret Service." "What's God wrought?"
He said; "I'm not too fond of this!" but held
Mugg's wrist to take his pulse, then let his lions
Revive him with their animal medical science

Which operated like the tide-flung leaves
Which, covering, in the fall at Vallambrosa,
The swollen stream, give to the heart that grieves
Small room to grieve in fact; and on Formosa
The wheat was being "set to bed" in sheaves,
A drying process thought by Saragossa
To be the most effective that there was.
McDrew revives, and hears a high, loud buzz.

It was the buzz that people said they heard
The first time Huddel took his second breath,
i.e. revived, in Rome. McDrew was stirred
With thoughts of going after him, but death
Now brightly intervened. Not life deferred,
But actual real and everlasting death,
Unrecognizable and terrible death,
Decay of body, dissolution, death.

McDrew had scarcely been prepared for death:
He'd heard that there was such a thing but felt
It was for others. Now the face of death
Appeared to him and he began to melt;
Within five days he was a cask of death—
All bone, no flesh to cling to it like felt,
And tell the brain the lovely things it felt;
He lay upon the cave grass green as felt—

For this was death; and Dan McGillicuddy
Bewildered by the failure in this case
Of animal medicine to cure the body
Of Mugg McDrew about the cave did pace
And didn't want to talk to anybody.
The Canton *Star*'s reporter in that place
Pursued him day and night, but Dan said merely
It was a case he'd not as yet seen clearly.

He had not seen a tiny light-green insect
Escaping from the heart of Mugg McDrew
Just as he died. Its power was extrinsic
To anything the jungle savior knew.
The Boboli Gardens held the secret: rinsing
Her hair there a young girl with eyes of blue
Reveals it all to a Tiensin reporter:
"When Mugg was young he was a good deal shorter

(How do I know all this? Our families were
Quite close back home in Akron); he would beg
For anything to make him taller"—her
Eyes lowered here—"he loved me"—swung her leg,
Resumed: "One day a man named Doctor Burr
Said he could offer him a certain egg
For fifteen thousand dollars, but that never
Should he go in the jungle, for whatever

Imaginable reason, for the damp
Of jungle days would cause the egg to hatch
And then, instead of lighting like a lamp
His own impulse to growth, it would unlatch
The life inside itself, first cause a cramp
And then cause death. Say, have you got a match?"
The lovely girl requested. When the Tiensin
Reporter bent to see, she ran off dancing

And screaming horrible threats into the air,
"We'll kill you all, we bugs! Ha ha! Forget it!
You'll never stand a chance!" No underwear!
She rose into the sky. "What have I said? It
Was only so I'd understand!" "Beware!"
She rising cried. She saw a bird and met it
With sloppy kiss. "We cure at first but then
We do our fated work: death to all men!"

While this reporter stood in great amazement
(Until he ran to phone his story in,
For which the poor man was put out to graze with
These words, "You have been drinking too much gin
Or vodka on the job. It's out of phase with
A real reporter's duties: it's a sin
To lie about a true, important story:
Life as it is is the reporter's glory!"

And so the world did not find out the truth
Of what Meralda said until much later,
When "insect eyes" were decimating youth;
Then Pong became a noted commentator
Until he felt the praying mantis' tooth
Which made his life reverse, till incubator
Held all of him there was; then he began
Again to grow and so become a man).

In any case as he was standing facing
The sky amid that dry place full of fountains
And with an eye incredulous was tracing
The young girl's disappearing in the mountains,
While he stood there, poor beaked Alouette was pacing
Outside the Palatine cave, with dreamy countenance.
Touched by some unknown impulse then, she rushed
Into a cab, aside the driver brushed,

And with her wings and claws sped the blue vehicle
To Rome's first synagogue, La Mamma Aleph.
Arriving, she flew out, and knocked the pickle
From someone's hand just entering that palace.
Apologizing, she bumped into a beagle
Who started barking frenziedly. "No malice!"
She sang, then flew inside down to the altar.
"Help me!" she said. "Oh, heaven, if the fault were

My own that I'm a bird I would accept
This cruel fate, but since I know of nothing
That I have done of ill in life except,
Perhaps, construct the Mooson—yet that one thing
I soon abandoned—" here she paused and wept,
While rabbis creeping toward her with black bunting
Prepared to make a fast attempt to net her;
"If I," she sobbed, "were evil, I'd know better

What sense this made. . . ." Just then, one rabbi gave
The signals clear: "Five hundred, seven, forty!"
Then flew the crepe, that symbol of the grave!
And one young playful rabbi, Ben Ayorti,
Began to do his "imitations." "Save
The best for last!" cries one who's known as "Shorty,"
"Your imitation of a rose bouquet!"
Hearing this Alouette shivered where she lay

Upon the synagogue's marble floor, although
She did not know the cause. They tied her down
And sent one of their number out to go
And find a truck to drive her through the town
And set her down beside the Tiber's flow
Sufficient miles away. But first the clown
Ayorti does his crazy imitation
And Alouette feels an absurd sensation!

"Help! Let me out!" She has become a woman
Of beautiful form once more. "What was that noise?"
Asks Rabbi Joe; "it sounded really human!"
They lift the crepe and wish that they were boys
Again, and had not chosen to be Roman
Rabbis, but to live for sensual joys—
For Alouette, more dazzling than before,
Lies warm and naked on their temple floor.

Oh for the brush of Rembrandt to depict
The measure of surprise on all these faces!
But Alouette leaped up suddenly and tricked
The crepe around her: she was going places!
She ran outside to where the taxi ticked,
Its driver still unconscious with amazement,
And drove it to the Palatine, but still
Found no trace of her lover on that hill.

How she will ever track him down I can't
Imagine. Feeling awful, she decides
To do what people often do when scant
The hope of help from action, and imbibes
A red Campari soda, which an ant
Imbued with magic information finds
Just as she drinks it down. At once she knows
Where Pemmistrek is, and to the airport goes.

What, although she does know of his amnesia,
She'll feel about his amorousness with
The Early Girls, imagining I'll leave you
For now, and go to Mickey Mouse—and death.
For Donald died. His grave bedecked with freesia
His mouse companions walk away from. "Fifth
To die of those we know: first, Harry Horse,
By measles swept away, and then, by force,

In the Chicago riots, Ethan Mouse;
Then Penny Pig in childbirth; John the Emmett
Burned by a magic lantern." Gabby Grouse
Has flown to be with them in this dilemma t-
O do what all he can, but sorrow plows
Deep grooves in all their faces. At the limit
Of guilt and anguish, Mickey El Ratón
(His Spanish name) says, "I cannot go on!

Minnie, if you and Gabby have the heart
To finish up the race, go on and do it.
Me, I feel burned in every mortal part;
I can't do anything, I can't go through it.
But you are free. Here, take the keys and start
The Packard up. I'd hate to think we blew it
Because of what I did and felt!" Her tears
Assured him she would share these lonely years,

These mournful years with him. Gabby said, "Well,
Well, yes, all right, I'll do it, but alone!"
And did heroically. But he fell
From Caesar's cliff. The Packard hit a stone
And leaped to ruin. He hit a church bell
Two miles below, which made a curious tone.
He lost his human powers but was well-met;
The kindly vicar kept him as a pet;

And until London floats in Chios' bay
And Big Ben tolls to passing lobster seekers
And brilliant light is lapped in London gray
He will remain a common grouse, whose features
Are lighted not by reason but by day
Alone. As for the celebrated creatures
He'd left on Crete, they sought a mountain village
To work as common laborers until age

Would whiten them all over. But their dreams
Could not be realized. The daisied slopes
Of Minos' realm grew rowdy with the screams
Of journalists and tourists, and their hopes
Were doomed, they knew it, once the gaudy beams
Of world publicity, like telescopes,
Had found them. "Minnie," Mickey said, "we must
Be gone from here!" She brushed away the dust

That running down the Cretan road to shun
Some crazed photographers had sprinkled over
Her mousy garments all, and cried, "There's one,
Perhaps one way!" "What is it?" Mickey drove her
To where they took the plane to Washington,
Where, in a building dear to Smoky Stover,
They were transformed from living things to comics
By a new drug, which flattened legs and stomachs

And flattened arms and faces, though the eyes
Are left with bright expressions, and the lips
Still curve in two-dimensional surprise
At what this new life offers. Minnie's hips
Are sensuous still, though of a smaller size
Than those with which mouse gloves once came to grips.
King Features' famous doctor, Georges La Berle,
Did this in part to please a certain girl

Who loved new funnies. So, they've looked at us
When we've picked up a newspaper that carries
Their new adventures. On a train or bus,
Going to school, at home, or picking berries,
Quarreling, loving, making such a fuss,
Their lives go on in print from Nome to Paris,
Where nobody can get to them, just read them,
Not touch them, get an interview, or feed them.

Meanwhile, on Samos racing, at the wheel
Is Amos Frothingham. He's found a plot
For taking over Greece, which he, a real
Greek patriot by now, resents a lot.
Added to what most native Greeks would feel
Is his conversion's fire, which they have not.
At the Archbishop Bastilokiokos'
S Palace he gets out and picks a crocus

Inside which is a bug that stings him hard
(One of Meralda's killers? What a horror!)
Which he ignores and slaps it off, and, barred
At first from going in, goes by the barrer
By showing him his Secret Service Card—
Then to Bastilokiokos, mighty warrior
For Hellenism, his head and shoulders bulging
With energy, to him the plot divulging.

On hearing which, the Prelate smacked his blotter
Hard with one hand, picked up the phone, and said
"Bring Postiopos to me!" "Glass of water,
I beg of you!" sighed Amos, then was dead.
The crocus insect was Meralda's daughter
Whose bite was lethal if she bit your head.
So Amos's work was done. They give a feast.
"Here was one good American, at least,"

Wet-eyed Bastilokiokos sadly says
Above the body—"all we most have treasured
In our imagining of the U.S.!
Delightful generosity unmeasured
And free to all, a spirit which said Yes
To what was Greek, found its own land a desert
Because of lack of liberty!" And there
They built a statue in sweet Samos air

Of Amos, who had lost his life while serving
Democracy and Hellas! From the prow
Of ships the world shall see him in the curving
Of Samian marble—none shall make him bow
Or compromise, or aught be but unswerving.
And whosoever wakes on Samos now
May be by him inspired. Let us, however,
Seek out soft African Tropical Chinese weather

Of brand-new spring. Aqua says, "Let us hurry—"
(And caroling natives round about them sung)
"And we can see the Easter Service. Murray
Fitzgibbon writes that when the Cross is hung
From the high bamboo altar, tons of curry
Flow out of Mount Kabogo mixed with dung."
She handed him the guidebook. "Here it is."
He smiled. "How great!" They hugged and had a kiss,

Then ran to the cathedral quickly as
They could. The crowd was vast and oriental—
Ying Pu has more brocade than Yeng Pu has,
But both have quite a lot; and banjo rental
Was doing quite a business on the grass.
"Like England," Huddel thought, once sentimental,
Twice burned, for as he entered the cathedral
A giant pygmy stuck him with a needle.

"For Hengland!" cried the pygmy then, and vanished,
While Huddel slumps on the cathedral floor.
These pygmies from that country had been banished—
One was not used to see them anymore.
But sometimes they disguised themselves as Spanish
Marines and sought the "freedom of the shore."
They made themselves look taller with the help
Of special "sea shoes" stuffed with sand and kelp.

Huddel ran out into the crowd but lost
The pygmy in it. "When will we be free,
Sweet Aqua, of such persecution, tossed
Upon a sea of terror such as we
Have no way merited? Perhaps the frost
Of Arctic zones would give to you and me
The kind of private joy we both deserve!"
"Yes. Take me!" To Helsinki then they curve

And with no middle flight. So high they soar
That clouds are far beneath them, and the vapors
Invisible from earth. They spy a shore
Of softest white where little winds play capers
And have the thought to settle there. Why more
Reside on earth, where just to read the papers
Each morning makes one almost give up hope?
This shore was white as sparkling Ivory soap

But Huddel found no solid part, and she
Who flew with him said, "Dearest, what of nourishment?"
"Skylark is good," said Huddel, "and it's free!
And over there, look! in that cloud, that blurrish one,
Je crois qu'il y a légumes des cieux!" Why he
Began to speak in French, to the discouragement
Of all who do not know that language, I
Have no idea, but vegetables of sky

Indeed there were: cloud parsley, heaven's beet
Celestial rutabaga, wind tomatoes,
Gale cucumbers that grow at heaven's feet,
Au delà carrots, spirit world potatoes,
And other produce nurtured by the heat
Of cloudless sun. Sometimes in the Barbados
One has days such as here were all the time;
And sportsmen after a long mountain climb

May glimpse a moment of the sweet, pure grandeur
That Huddel and Aqua both now felt pervade them.
You may walk into cafés and command your
Cognac and coffee, but the man who made them,
That billionaire who might not understand your
Problems in the slightest, he would trade them
His cognac industry and his plantations
Could he be guaranteed but these sensations

Which Huddel and his Etruscan girl were feeling.
Sometimes a person, billionaire or hobo,
Will see a young girl caught twixt floor and ceiling
Or on Lake Leman in a sparkling rowboat
And think, "Ah, she's the one, who, by unsealing
The strongest feelings in me, strong as cobalt
Bombs in chain reactions, will enable
Me to rise up above the highest table

In trigonometry or logarithms
And find the free joy that I seek, at last!"
Then, by loud vows or jewels bright with prisms,
Each wins the girl and binds her to him fast;
At happy best, afloat with paroxysms
After the act, the world seems cool and vast—
These instants, though, are hedged by daily living,
Which gets us at the same time it is giving.

So that one often feels hemmed in in spite
Of having one's desire; and then one sees
Another girl upon another night.
One's head is stirred by the cool café breeze;
It is not serious, one is not bright,
But yet it seems if one could take *her* knees
Between one's hands and kiss them, one would find
The true and vast space of one's secret mind!

And so one carries on, as Kierkegaard
Describes in *Either/Or* (that's the right title
As I remember, though I find it hard
To get things right when rushed by the recital
Of new events continually! Pard-
On me, then, if I'm wrong), with what is vital
Being a thing continually sought for—
At death it's this that we have come to naught for!

This airy place where Huddel was with Aqua
Gave these sensations every single minute—
So mourners walking down the Via Sacra
See their love's grave and feel they're buried in it
Themselves, they feel their loss with such alacri-
Ty. Goodbye to lobster and to linnet—
Their very being's caught! So this fresh air
Caught their two souls, as if it caught their hair.

II

After a two-year interval, in fact
It's almost three, once more I come, dear Muse,
To write this work, and hope it's still intact,
And you will generously not refuse
Your sweet assistance—which I haven't lacked
At all till now, but had—that I may fuse
What's in my mind and what is in the spectrum
Of earth outside with my typewriter plectrum.

Not that I want to limit it to earth,
Since it had outer space in also previously,
As well as grief, solemnity, and mirth,
And persons acting virtuously and deviously.
This follow-up of mine to *Ko* had birth
Fourteen years after, when I suffered feverishly
And feverishly wrote, to make an equal
Turmoil which came from me and caused a sequel—

Which intermittently I went on writing
With pleasure for two years. And, after that,
I stopped. I found some other things exciting
And left this epic I'd been working at.
And now the world has changed again, inviting
Me back to love, and Aqua Puncture's hat,
To Huddel's heart, to Papend's heat, and to
The mystery of Minnie Mouse's shoe;

To Alouette and him she would return to,
To Amos's statue, larger than a room—
This stanza is a help, a splendid churn to
Make oppositions one, to bring Khartoum,
Venice, and Oz into the self-same urn; to
Put silverfoil and rags on the same loom
Along with silks and wool and mud, to weave
A fabric to deceive and undeceive.

The problem is, Can I pick up my story
And carry it convincingly from where
I left it trailing an uncertain glory
Through the humming, bee-filled Venice air
And plunk it down again as in a dory
In my now elder words, perhaps more bare
Of connotation and my mind less leaping
Than when I saw you last when I was sleeping

And saw you blossom for me every night
Just like a girl and also like a field which
Was filled with flowers, daisies yellow white
And roses pink and white, a florist's yield which
Would make him think a horrid world all right—
So were you to me. Well, that loss is healed, which
Is not to say that I no longer love you,
Because I do. But I've stopped dreaming of you

In that particular way, which made me wild.
To wit, and to resume, I wonder if,
As I've grown further from the actual child
I used to be, I still can leap in skiff
And hope for the same wavy, undefiled
Trip through the aether like a hippogriff
I have had once, or several times, or always.
I think about these things sometimes in hallways

But when I reach the room and there's the door
And there's the typewriter with paper waiting,
I leap into my place, and, lo! before
I've had a second more for meditating,
I've filled up pages flitting to the floor
On which what seem like countless truths I'm stating;
Then darkness comes, or supper, and I stop it.
Next day the fear once more is, Can I top it?

So, I suppose, on thinking the thing over,
Yes, I can take up where I left it lying
My poem which from the white cliffs of Dover
To Tuscany, where someone's hair is drying,
Goes quickly as a beam of light, that rover
Without compare, and with some honest trying
Continue my narration of the fallacy
We find by being born into this galaxy.

This galaxy in which—a fine word, *galaxy*,
Giving a sense of clean wide-open spaces
In which there's nothing much to cause an allergy,
Which, bringing itch to throats and pink to faces,
Can get a person dropped from the anthology
Of health and beauty and ongoing graces;
And, as a word, it's a good test of diction;
Though it has overtones of science fiction,

Which, like all other special kinds of writing,
Is often dull save to aficionados,
As ravens, bats, and graveyards are exciting
To those who like to have their sex in grottos
But not to most, who fear the vampire's biting,
The sluggish worm, and the gravedigger Otto's
Hard shovel hitting them, or his bad jokes;
So psychedelic art's for one who smokes

Or eats the cactus bud or drops the acid,
And motorcycle jokes for one with bike
The trouble with these genres is they're placid—
One knows right at the start what they'll be like.
Dog tales may please the owner of the basset
And barroom tales enthrall your Uncle Mike,
But those whose taste in things is more demanding
Prefer a story built on understanding

And not, like science fiction, seeing only
How new discoveries have changed conditions
So that you squeeze a module when you're lonely,
Or have your interests altered by physicians
Who are themselves machines, not flesh-and-bone-ly.
Such stuff is dull and can't compare to Titian's
High-flying saints or works of Proust or Byron,
Which are more complicated in their wiring

Just as I hope this work I'm writing may be,
In which it's true I found that *galaxy* suited
My meaning as a nursery fits a baby
Because its atmosphere's unconvoluted
And full of time and space and dark and day, be-
Cause it's grand and at the same time muted—
My characters, God bless them, have real lives in it
Like bees someplace with galaxies of hives in it,

Which there were not in Papend's Venice. Well,
I must confess that I don't quite feel ready
To leap back into things just yet and tell
How this and that were—I still feel unsteady:
Sometimes I ring with insights like a bell—
At others I feel close to Zacowitti!
I think I want to stall to tell you more
Of what I've felt, since on Hibernia's shore

I walked each day with Homer Brown and wrote
So many pages leading up to this one.
We'd see green fields so worthy of our note
That I at least was tempted to go kiss one.
But didn't, since I'm neither sheep nor goat,
But tried instead distilling all the bliss one
Feels in such happy times into my eight-line
Poetic sets with a late-sixties dateline—

And which will be resumed, but not this second.
I said I want to say things, and I do,
To catch myself and you up on the fecund,
Or fecund-seeming, life this long-lapsed Jew,
To whom the Talmud Torah had not beckoned
Imperiously since nineteen-forty-two,
Lived since that time, but most to tell you of
That Irish time I wrote this, which I love

To think about, but I have never done so
At length at all because of life's fast pace
Which, starting off with waking, makes me run so
That I am short of breath and red of face
By evening, as if Tempus held a gun so
That Fugit could escape. Oh lovely lace
Of memory, that we can hold and contemplate—
How much of you mind's attic does accommodate!

There must be miles of you that are still folded
And stacked away in trunks I'll never get to!
Some people claim that some of theirs have molded—
I must confess mine I have not known yet to:
What I have Lear'd or Tristran-and-Isolde'd
Is with me still, each sit-down and each set-to,
For me to find the temporal space to climb to
And speculate about and find the rhyme to.

I want to do this now with those six weeks
I spent in Kinsale working on this epic
Which of things unattempted boldly speaks
In verse Orlandic, Don-Juanesque, and Beppic:
Of how Alaskan toucans got their beaks,
And why the waters of the vast Pacific
Are blue at dawn and pink by half past seven;
Of how things are on earth, and how in heaven—

A work perhaps I never can conclude.
It's my own fault—I like works to be endless,
So no detail seems ever to intrude
But to be part of something so tremendous,
Bright, clear, complete, and constantly renewed,
It totally obliterates addenda's
Intended use, to later compensate
For what was not known at the earlier date.

So, Memory, back! to those sweet times in Cork, which
Have not yet gotten my complete attention,
And, Muse! help me to find that tuning fork which
Makes anything it touches good to mention.
I'm starting up this work now in New York, which
Is as unlike Kinsale as hypertension
Is unlike pleasant calm and sunny weather—
By verse I hope to get them all together

And most specifically by verse concerning
The days I spent in Kinsale. Well, I've said that
At least two times already and am burning
To carry on this discourse with my head that
The world calls poetry and I call yearning—
If you don't mind, do please forget you read that:
It's far beneath my standards and I worry
You'll think it's me—it's not—I'm in a hurry

To catch my feelings while they pass me fleetingly
And so don't want to stop at every boner
Like scholars who er-umly and indeedingly
Lard everything so much you wish a stone or
A rowboat's oar would batter them obediently
Then magically fly back to its owner
Who thus would not be punished. I like catching
Pure chickens of discourse while they're still hatching

And so, unhushed, rush on. I had a bedroom
In that three-story house which the Browns lived in;
Each day I wrote my poem in the said room
While Betty Brown diced, sliced, and carved, and sieved in
The kitchen which was under it. The red room
Across the hall from mine, designed by Rifkin,
Homer and Betty dwelt in, and the other
Room on that floor was Katherine's, whom her mother

Would sing to sleep two times a day or once,
Depending if she was in a napping period;
When she was, there was one nap after lunch
Or sometimes none, at which time cries were myriad
And I would set my elbow with a crunch
Upon the desk and, like a man much wearièd
By journey long across a perilous waste,
Put head in hand and groan as one disgraced

By having lost all natural zest for living,
All inspiration, talent, luck, and skill.
I've always thought I should be more forgiving
And not be seized by the desire to kill
When someone interrupts me at my knitting
Of words together, but I'm that way still.
I've not, however, murdered anyone,
I swear, as I am Stuart and Lillian's son.

How moved I am to write their names, how curious
They sound to me, as Kenneth does, my own one,
Which, though I'm no more Scots than Madame Curie is,
I like for the plain clear Highlandsy tone one
(Or I) can hear in it. Some names sound spurious,
Like "Impsie," or Sir Lalla Rookh Ben Lomond.
Some are invented; some we choose by fantasy;
Some hoping to inherit; some, romantically—

If, for example, Dad once loved a lassie
Named Billy Jo, he might call baby Billy,
If baby is a boy, or if the chassis
Of that small creature shows that it is silly
To think she's the same sex as Raymond Massey
And may one day play Lincoln, perhaps Tillie
Might satisfy his crazed nostalgic need
To see his old flame at his wife's breast feed.

In any case, names are a sort of token
Which parents give a child when it sets out
Into life's subway system, which is broken
And filled with people eating sauerkraut;
We pass the turnstile when our name is spoken
But it's the train that hurries us about,
I.e. our brain, brawn, energy, and genius,
Whether we're named Kaluka or Frobenius.

So names begin us, but—On with my story!
If I have interrupted interruptions
Of interrupted interruptions, glory
Will never be my lot, but foul corruptions;
For that which feeds upon itself grows gory—
But there, again, enough! All my productions
Are subject to this peril; let's go on.
Already in the east I see the dawn

Growing more quickly than the flush of red
Upon the back of Lisa who has lain
Four hours naked in the sand instead
Of going to the store at Fifth and Main
To buy some pinking scissors as she said
That she was going to, wherefore her pain;
And out of the vague silence of the night
Come slippery sounds of birds, not yet in flight.

So did the mornings greet me in Kinsale,
Often, when I would read all night, or, oftener,
When I would have some nightmare by the tail
Which crushed the woof of sleep like fabric softener
And brought me naked to the shade, where pale
Aurora seemed, as Joyce said, to be "doffin' 'er
Glarious gowrments to receive the Sun"—
Those garbs were pink and red. O Day begun,

How energizing so to contemplate you
Before the full awareness of the twenty-
Four hours we have to know you makes us hate you,
Sometimes; sometimes one minute of you's plenty
And makes one wish to ante- or post-date you
Just so you go away—but in the denty
Sweet early scuds of dawning, how delicious
You, Day, can be! so that, sometimes, ambitious

Poets have hailed you at your birth with names
Like Monday, Tuesday, Thursday, Friday, Sunday,
Saturday, Wednesday, Pottsday, Day of Flames,
Day of Decision, Pet and Family Fun Day,
All Fools' Day, Hallowe'en, Christmas, Henry James
Commemorative Reading Day, Clean Gun Day,
Happy Hog Day, and so on, as if, by calling
You names, one might prevision your befalling

Or something of that kind. Well, at the window
Sometimes I'd stay awhile and sometimes hurry
Back into bed whose sheets like very thin dough
Were slightly rough for sleeping (made by Murray)
And doze again, then later would begin to
Get dressed for breakfast, which, in a great flurry
Of soda bread, we three would eat together
With Katherine Brown, in the cold Irish weather.

Then after that quite often I would run
Along a kind of sidewalk that ran upwards
From where the house was, up to where the sun
Would have been closer if in the cloudy cupboards
It did not hang away till day was done.
Then homeward, past proud dames in Mother Hubbards
And former Irish exiles who'd found out
That Budweiser was nothing to the stout

Served at "The Spaniard" on Saint Bernard's Hill.
Sometimes "Good marnin" would emerge from these
I passed, and sometimes not, for they were still
And I was running, it was not with ease
We could converse. My lungs with breath would fill,
My heart with beats, and then my mind would seize
Sometimes a phrase or line that made me race to
Get back in time so I could find a place to

Put it into my poem in time to carry
With it all its inspired associations.
One's words, though, once excited, mate and marry
Incessantly, incestuously, like patients
Gone mad with love, so even sometimes the very
Words I would lose enroute spawned duplications
Stretching as far as sight. Back at my desk
I'd sit then, breathless and Chirurgeresque

With lacy inspirations and complexities
Made up of breath and heartbeats and confusions,
As one may have of fish as to what sex it is,
As to which of my *trouvailles* were delusions
And which could guide my poem as sheep executives
Ideally guide their flocks, toward such effusions
Of epic lyric life that I would find
The sole true story of man's secret mind.

A large ambition! Strange that words suggest to us
That we can do such things. And strange the feeling
That we have done it sometimes; strange that Aeschylus
Probably felt the same beneath the ceiling
Of the Greek room he wrote in for the festivals
Of le Théâtre Grec. And it is healing
The thought that one is capable in some way
Of being in control on this huge Stunway

Of our existence. Anyway, I'd sit
Un-Aeschylean, certainly, at that
Table I used for desk, and stretch my wit
In such way as I could. There was a flat
Quality to my living there that fit
The kind of thing that I was working at;
Friendly but not involved with anyone
Not lonely, but, whenever I wished, alone.

And there were, doubtless, certain real connections
Of other kinds between my life and work
About the Early Girls with belle complexions
And Papend more licentious than a Turk,
And Huddel who can fly in all directions
And Mugg McDrew who now in Death did lurk—
Some ways in which cool Kinsale did concur
With Aqua, but I don't know what they were.

Well, maybe, this: a kind of a suspension
Of everything except my poem, which filled
The spaces action left with pure invention
Of characters beaked, snouted, nosed, and billed.
Then, too, there was that sweet unnerving tension
Travel creates, the worst parts of it stilled
By being with my friends. And then there was
The foghorn, so like Inspiration's buzz.

Enough! My story's sun should now come out, when
I'm feeling I am fit to make it good—
How happy, though, I've been to write about then,
That time I walked on Kinsale's sea-soaked wood
With Betty and Homer Brown and had no doubt then
That all would be completed, as it should
Have been. How glad to think again of walks
I took with Homer and, at night, the talks

With Homer and with Betty, while we heard
Sitting in the garden chairs above the house
Halfway to where "The Spaniard's" barmaids spurred
The local gentry nightly to carouse
With dark black Guinness—in the garden burred
With tiny burrs no bigger than a louse,
The seabirds calling—really did they call?
Or was there nothing in that sound at all

But bird phonetics, sea phonetics, what?
And if someone had come to me to say,
Wishing, perhaps, to put me on the spot,
"Just what's the content of your work today?"
I could say, "Not abstractions, though it's not,
Either, the sounds of birds on Kinsale Bay,
But human sounds, make of them what you want to;
Saying unto others as I've been said unto—

Trying to put into a usable range
A vast amount of matter, form, and tone
(Which is what human noises are) to change
What seems disparate into what alone
Can make us happy: re-possession. Strange!
That we should be so different from a stone!
But since we are, I'll go on writing this way.
For other modes, see Dryden, Pope, and Disney;

See Wordsworth in his rustical abode;
(Not Shelley though for he resembles me
In twitching off his story like a toad
So he can dream of what it is to be
A crag of icy flame or a lone road
Amid the Apennines, or a blue sea
Of expectation and despair) see Cowper
A very quiet but consistent trouper

Of Things That Really Happen, in the Order
In which they do. For all of these and most
Of those who wrote before the Abstract Border
Of this odd twentieth century was crossed
A Structure had to be of stone and mortar
Or it could not exist. Let's drink a toast
To Rimbaud and Apollinaire and laughter,
And all who, learning from them, have come after

To practice this new art. The purpose of it?
I think I have already said, but one
Keeps asking. It is to help people love it,
Their world, I mean, which has such means to stun,
Confuse, and kick. But one can be above it
And in it all at once, it can be done
If poets do what I believe they're meant to,
I.e. the whole of what they feel give vent to."

"Farewell!" With this digression from digressing
I'll go back to my story. Though not all
Of what went on in Kinsale—it's depressing
To think what's gone from summer by the fall—
Is talked about, I've gotten back the pressing
Desire I had, as lofty as a wall
And twice as strong, to write. So let this vanish
Into the mountain air above the Spanish

Part of the Pyrenees and, even higher,
Where we left Aqua Puncture and her lover
In flight from death and strengthened by desire
Among the curious clouds, where they discover
Sky nutriment of all kinds they require,
At which they have looked wildly at each other
Hoping a hopeless hope, that they might stay
There in that soft perpetual blue-white day.

"*Légumes des cieux!*" breathed Aqua. "Well, but still
We've found no place that we can sit or stand."
Huddel said, "Over there, this little hill
Of cloud. Try! Yes! It's solid, love, as sand
Firmed by the grand Atlantic's azure spill!"
So they two sat down on it. With her hand
Aqua touched his. "If we could find more solid
Cloud, might we . . . ?" Her with his hands he collared

And kissed her hard: her mouth, her lips, her eyes.
"We can! We will!" He walked and looked around.
He found one mile-long stretch, a grand surprise,
Which seemed to be as solid as the ground.
"That's it! Wait here! I'll go get some supplies
From earth—" but, thinking, then: "They can be found,
Perhaps, right here." He smiled. "We may not need
So very much," he said. Aqua agreed.

This was a good decision, since beneath them
(Just fifteen feet beneath) there was a pack
Of sky piranhas in a mood to eat them,
If they had seen them, on a watery track
That went from Rome to somewhere east of Eden—
Some colored green and blue, some white and black.
The leading one, Piranha Ninety-Six,
Had taught her fellow-fish some aero-tricks

Which made them capable of "swimmo-flying,"
A mode of locomotion known in Dallas
On the Aereal Lakes, built by a dying
Billionaire to fête his girlfriend Alice
On one of her young birthdays. She, untying
The laces of her stays, cried, "Oh, a palace
Of airy pools!" Then in each other's arms
These two were happy, till he left her charms,

That very year, for death. His girl went on
To be the world's great star in this aquatic,
Celestial sport. How many a summer dawn
Saw her fair form amidst it, she the product
Of human kind, yet equal to the swan
In water, dove in air. An old despotic
Aquarium man had taught his prize piranha
The trick, as well. Now, pale as a Madonna

Of Piero's, Aqua saw them and was shaken—
"H-Huddel, l-l-look—" With her right hand
She pointed to the fish, which now had taken
A downward turn, and soon their deadly band
Had swimmo-flown away and left forsaken
Them, glad to be. And now they walked and planned
A new existence in the clouds till when
Something might draw them to the earth again.

It's difficult to stay away forever
From something we have lived with all our lives,
Or most of them. All find it hard to sever
Relations with their husbands or their wives.
So with our native planet. And what bever-
Age ever shall, with sharpness as of knives,
Give us that high, like Legions back in Rome again,
When we return to earth, of being home again?

Now, though, they feel contented to remain
In their sky nest forever. For, aside from
Their love, what had life offered them but pain?
Oh pleasant place. Far off from there now glide from
Blue to blue-white the sky-piranha chain
Of Ninety-Six, which anyone would hide from
Who knew the eating habits of these predators,
Sea-homnivores of sky. Meanwhile the editors

Of papers everywhere observed the progress
Of the Great Hellas Race, now much diminished
By Mickey's absence, which encouraged codgers
Who'd bet on him before to say, He's finished!
The Rats will win, as surely as Buck Rogers
Will conquer Killer Kane. As if a tin dish'd
Move sideways from a dog, while they were speaking
Tobacco moved across their jaws. And, squeaking,

Terence and Alma Rat enjoy the full
Fanfare of earthly stardom. They are left,
They only, left! as in the ring the bull
When matador is missing, it bereft
Of everything but Toro in the cool
Of Spanish afternoon! He felt so deft,
Terence, at his red steering wheel, and stormed
Up and down roads which Grecian hillsides formed.

"Oh, Alma dear, this is the only life
That's fit for such a couple, whose ambition
Is to be more than merely rat and wife
But to exceed in glorious condition
The sun itself, which glistens like a knife
Upon us rats in summer! The ignition
Seems to be out of order—help! What's happened?"
The car stopped. He looked ghastly, as if rat-penned.

"Terence, what's wrong?" cried Alma. She looked over
And saw a deadly serpent on the seat
Just beside Terence. "I am Herman Clover,"
The serpent said, "come, listen to me, Sweet."
Then made a gesture to draw near which drove her
To the Toyota door on quick rat feet.
"What—why—who—ah!" she cried. He coolly said
"Don't worry about your rat. He isn't dead.

I gave him just a little bit of venom,
Enough to stop his driving. He'll be fine.
He will awake with a slight taste of cinnam-
On in his mouth, and you, dear, will be mine!"
He seized her in his coils, which caused a *ciném-
Athèque* in Athens to explode and nine
Persons to suffer in Constantinople
From heart disease. The snake produced an opal

From his long mouth, which, offering to the rodent
He seemed to love so much, at least to long for
And want to touch, which is an urge prepotent
In all, but snakes especially are strong for
Tactile sensations of their whole belowment,
Which they are willing even to do wrong for,
At least by human lights, he sighed, "I love you.
This whole long season I've been thinking of you."

"No! No!" He squeezed her. "I'm in love with Terence!"
She saw him slumped against the steering wheel
Like someone who is running interference
Caught in a stop-shot. The automobile
Was not much longer graced by her appearance—
The snake had tugged her out. Great waves of steel
Atop a concrete ocean—"It's terrific,"
Said Pemmistrek. Ann said, "Be more specific.

There're parts of modern art which are so difficult
For me and others of us Early Girls.
We usually keep silent, fearing ridicule,
But I think I can ask you why these swirls
Of metal water are at all aesthetical?"
Our scene has changed, it's evident to curls
Of human heads, away from leap- and crawl-ers—
To whom we shall return. Be such the solace

Of all who wish to know what happened next
To frightened Alma and the terrible worm
Who seemed to be so interspecies-sexed
With his great, diamond-studded epiderm,
Who's gazing at her, hoping she'll be hexed
And he can bring his passion to its term
With this small animal, whose doubts we know of.
So Pemmistrek, with one toe from the toe of

One sock protruding—it was glorious spring
Which topped all Stockholm with its towering green
And he had taken his shoes off, like a thing
That anyone would do, but as we've seen
He's childlike, since amnesiac, and a king
Would give his crown I think to have a bean
So full of sweet oblivion and pleasure
As his was, and would add his queen and treasure—

Stood looking at the outdoor show of art
Of modern times and liking it, and Ann was
Puzzling about it, when they heard the start
Of a huge car, of which it seemed the plan was
To run them down. My God! it must be smart
To find a way to be as the first man was,
Adam, I mean, exempt from, in the soft spring,
Attack from others, either strange or offspring!

But not since then, I think, has any managed
To have complete protection. Even Adam
Was by his earthly consort disadvantaged
When she brought him an apple. Thank you, Madam.
Oh well, all right! Then boom! Boom, doom, and damaged,
We have not yet recovered from that datum
(If it is true, which cannot be gone into)
For, ground beneath the wheels of a great Pinto

Gray Stockholm gravel flies in Pemmistrek's face,
And he grabs Ann in one arm and ducks under
The huge car's under part which leaves them place
To go on living while a noise like thunder
Goes past above their heads. God, for a mace!
Cried Pemmistrek, with which to rend asunder
This goddamned car which wants to run us down!
The car sped past them, though, deep into town.

Inside this vehicle was a musician
Named Fine McStrings, a Protestant and Scottish
Who falsely had attained the high position
Of Royal Rabbi, whose main job was Kaddish,
And, needing practice for a new rendition
Of this prayer for the dead—abstractly moddish
As other versions weren't—was multiplying
As best he could, the number of the dying,

Hoping to thus get practice in his service
Before some Royal Family member perished.
Performing before others made him nervous,
And any public things he did he cherished
He had to do until he felt impervious
To his embarrassment. Now with a glare Ist-
Anbul comes into focus, and the hospital
Where a young woman lies, fair as a rose petal—

Not by McStrings run down, but one of those who
Got heart disease when Herman Clover coiled
Himself round Alma. Lucky are the clothes who,
Or which, touch her sweet body, lucky boiled
Eggs that her tongue delects, and lucky No-Shu,
Her Chinese lover, until now unfoiled
By rival—man or malady—now saddened
Up to the point of being completely maddened.

This girl is an important nuclear physicist
And translator of Proust into Icelandic
Named Norma Clune. I wish that she would visit us,
If she gets well, this side of the Atlantic,
For everywhere she goes the nation's business
Improves, and all its men become romantic.
No one's been able to explain this power—
But now she's threatened by her final hour . . .

Which great physicians, flying in from Stockholm,
Nome, and Peru, are striving to prevent.
Her crazy No-Shu wants to run and sock them
Or bash them with a torn-loose tenement.
That man who touches Norma is unwelcome
As far as he's concerned. He had been bent
By horrible experiences when he
Was five years old that caused this jealousy.

His father and his mother had a dog
Named Uncle Patsy, Ki-Wa in Chinese,
Which bumblebees had trapped under a log.
No-Shu, just five, ran out and chased the bees
But then got lost, while going home, in fog
And had a vision of his mother's knees
With someone's hand upon them. Since that time
He had devoted half his life to crime.

He went round killing people in strange ways
Whom he suspected of unfaithful loving.
Be careful! or you, too, one of these days,
May be the victim of a fatal shoving
And be fished up from one of various bays,
Or ground in little bits to be the stuffing
Of the large Christmas turkey that No-Shu
Sends each December to the ONU,

Now that Mao's China's been admitted to it.
Norma, who loves him even though he's crazy,
Had made him go each week to Dr. Bluet,
The psychiatric heir of Piranesi,
Who saw man's mind as a huge, complex cruet
In which he was imprisoned, like a daisy.
He'd worked with No-Shu now for eighteen months,
Who in that period had killed only once.

But now he rages through the hospital's halls
Screaming in horror at his sweetheart's illness.
Doctors propose removing No-Shu's balls
If he does not cooperate more with stillness.
They throw him out. He pounds upon the walls
And plans revenge; and Head Nurse Olga Hilness
Sees Doctor Adam Shrude and feels her heart skip
One tiny beat, and, moored outside, an art ship

Rocks on the Bosporus, filled with many treasures,
Among which a large black and white of Mickey
And Minnie Mouse, a painting, with the pleasures
Great works of art can give, and give them quickly
By power of paint and shape and line. It measures
Six hundred square hectares, which makes it tricky
To get it on the boat and, once aboard it,
To find an angle from which to regard it.

This giant portrait, made by the joint efforts
Of fifty painters in the U.S.A.,
England, and Greece, was to protest the severance
Of Mickey from real life. The painters, they
Felt that a work so huge construed in reference
To this event might touch him where he lay.
By some strange chance it does. In comics sleep
On Sunday papers, he begins to squeak.

This painting's strong effect upon the real
Is not unique, although unusual:
A sculpture of a Minnesota Seal
Once caused the other team to lose the ball;
Motshubi's *Young Girl with Banana Peel*
Caused fifty-five young men to leap, or fall,
From Yomo Bridge; and Titian's *Presentation*
Caused Tintoretto's, and its estimation.

Another case, well known as far as Knossos,
Is how Pissarro, Sisley, and Monet,
By certain kinds of brush and color process,
Made different-colored dots appear all day
On air, clouds, stones, walls, ponds, Parisian *places*,
Cathedrals, sailboats, woods, and stacks of hay.
Mickey, through similar process, leaps to life
And says good morning to his waking wife:

"Minnie! I've had a vision—and a hope!
Of what I ought to do. If I could win
After all, win the race, and somehow grope
My way to Sounion 'mid discordant din
Of gear and crankshaft up the final slope,
Then to the attending world admit my sin
And weep in penance for it, might not that
Be what would be the best? Watch out! a cat!"

Cried Mickey, and, until the tom had passed,
He did not say a word. Meanwhile the island
Of Crete had grown a little bit more vast
Due to the shellfish, which, as always, silent
As to what their intentions were, had massed
Against its very shore, so that a pilot
Flying above it thought it was Australia.
And Terence Rat picked a light pink azalea

For Alma in his dream. And Mickey uttered
His first sound in a while. "I think it's safe.
Now I must try to rise from here," he muttered,
And struggled. "I'll come with you!" She was brave
And loved her mouse when every candle guttered
Of hope for peace and joy. They felt a wave
Of useful force communicated by
The work of art, and rose into the sky,

Leaving the papers torn where they'd been slumbering
Day after day in plain and color comics.
Now over Thessaly they fly, encumbering
The April air, blown higher than the summits
Of Mount Olympus, known to us as numbering
Amongst its gods Athena quick of comments,
Zeus filled with enterprise, and Aphrodite
Most beautiful of girls, whom, in her nightie,

Each girl each night may look like to her love.
Here in these vaults of heaven it was spring
Eternal, and yet changing, like a glove
Or a goodbye, white stairways opening,
And walks that one could not grow tired of.
It was quite obviously the very thing
A human would desire—it was created
By men, in fact, it's said, who abdicated

It to the gods. Now to its summits glided
Mickey and Minnie, the mysterious energy
The artwork gave them having much subsided.
Apollo sees their landing as a prodigy
Of some Divine Good Luck, and they're invited
To stay forever, Mickey to be God of the
Repentant Heart, and Minnie of Fidelity.
Hard to resist is the superior melody

Of these Olympian voices, and the mouse pair,
At last, resist it not. The race abandoned
By them remains, but they can do good elsewhere
By being little gods. And if their fandom
(The artists, chiefly, and those in the house where
There are gross effigies of them in sand and
Clay and cement, in Houston) is not satisfied,
Well, others are. In Athens, where the fat is fried

All day upon the gridiron, Postulakis,
The Cretan cook, whose specialty is octopus,
Known round the whole Aegean, throws a cactus
Into his stew and cries, "Yes, there are lots of us
Who love those mice, and even, yes, the fact is,
Revere them, as if gods, which is half-cocked of us
You may suppose, but now, you see, it's authorized!"
He left the cactus in till it was cauterized

Then plucked it out and poured in what seemed tons
Of olive oil and gristle. And Jose
Jorge Romero, of Iberia's sons
The greatest dancer down Flamenco way,
Cried, "These ees what ees really good, for once,
Zat zees two mice be gods!" And bronzed Earl Grey
Looked up from his tea laboratory stirrings
With appreciative whimperings and purrings—

For Earl Grey was a cat, as few men knew.
It had been hidden from his wife, who rarely
Shared Earl Grey's bed. Then would he, dressed in blue,
Propel a human plastic doll he barely
Could manage to keep moving, to her, who
Would fold it in her arms and love it yarely.
Earl Grey, inside the doll, would meditate
On what had caused him such a curious fate.

Next day, the doll undone, once more he was
Tea Lord of All, and, hearing of the mice,
Even he, a cat and avid for their fuzz,
Expressed his joy for them. I've said that twice,
And now away to Stockholm, where the buzz
Of the King's voice turns someone cold as ice.
King Sven has learned of his false rabbi's murders
And has condemned him to be hung from girders

To be devoured by Swedish ants. "Not that!"
McStrings exclaims, but oh, his fate is sealed.
Next day his skeleton, devoid of fat,
Swings from the Rathaus flagpole, like a shield
Some thoughtless soldier hung there. With no hat
Upon his head, or hers, like one unreeled
From a great spool of gladness, Pemmistrek
With Ann goes by, and does not see that wreck.

Where they will go when they have loved their full
In icy Stockholm, causing curious copies
Of cities to spring up, an Istanbul
With dark guitars, a Rome with yellow poppies
Instead of red, a Bogota *azul*
As summer ocean wherein lies the porpoise,
We soon shall see, but now I'd like to go
To Papend—but cannot quite yet although

I wished it, for Alouette just now arrives
In Stockholm's airport, and this fact demands
Attention. To the cabby as he drives
Her into town she's talking with her hands
Because she knows no Swedish. Then she dives
Out of the taxi, pays her fare, and lands
Inside the swell hotel to which she's driven,
Which caters specially to famous women—

The Stockholmbusgeflossen. Norma Clune
Once rested here, between her Proust translations
And Olla, the first woman on the moon,
And Dr. Anne McFeedbach and the patients
Who traveled with her. This hotel at noon
Gave a great lunch, with generous libations,
And Alouette, now, arrived at the meridian,
Sits down to eat among the gray obsidian

Of the Geflossen's architecture. She thinks
Of Pemmistrek and of the Munster Mooson,
Her own hotel in Asia, as she drinks
A glass of aquavit, which tends to loosen
One's hold upon reality. She sinks
Into a deep, drugged sleep, which is quite gruesome
As far as her projected project goes.
For Pemmistrek is leaving Stockholm! Rose,

An Early Girl whose lover is a captain
In the Stockholm police force, finds him murdered—
His nose and ears cut off and his skull fractured,
What deep hostility was thus asserted
Or disapproval of how he'd been acting.
She did not know, but feared, for she had heard it
Had been because of her, because Yorg Berls
Now knew the secret of the Early Girls.

Berls was a young ecologist. Once knowing
That every time an Early Girl made love
A city came to be, his red blood flowing
Too quickly to his brain made him one of
Those persons who to doctors should be going
To be calmed down with pills. A dark red glove
Of craziness obscured his mind. He wildly
Set out to kill all those who loved so mildly,

So sweetly, and so well these Early Ladies
Who weren't really causing any harm—
The cities they created were like Maybes
From someone who is feeling nice and warm
And whom a later sequence shows with babies
Or smiling through the rafters of a barn—
I.e. they didn't last long. Berls, however,
Killed ignorantly in the soft Stockholm weather.

So that this murder would be Berls's last
It seemed most wise to leave. Crazed Berls himself
Was later killed by No-Shu—but that ghast-
Ly tale must wait for later. Now the shelf
Of the Nord-Sud Express's bathroom passed
The shelf of Igborg Mountain, where the Elf
Igborgo lived, according to the fable.
The train had to be pulled on a big cable,

And in it, eating soup, sat Pemmistrek
And Early Ann and Early Rose, and other
Nearby compartments' windows showed the neck
And face and shoulders of the Captain's brother,
And those of other Early Girls and, check
To see if all of them are there, their lovers.
Alouette, elsewhere, asleep, dreams she's a photon,
Ten billion times too small to leave a note on

Somebody's door to say that you'd come by
To say hello, though you have other reasons,
Just as the cloudblooms have some in the sky
To make it seem like spring at other seasons,
And as the wind to make the pollen fly—
And in this curious dream knew the obeisance
That Matter has to Energy! She woke,
And at her ear a terrible voice spoke:

"You have been given information which
A mortal may not have. Prepare to die.
For you cannot continue in this ditch
Of ordinary living. Now the sky
Invites you to its realms, where there's no hitch.
You will be happy there!" She: "Oh will I?
I don't believe it. Please! I am attached
To what is here, and I would not be snatched

Away from it!" Now the hotel began
To bustle with the sounds of early dinners,
For Alouette's sleep had, like a caravan,
Stretched from high noon to that hour which the Finnish
Call "Eep van artom," time to get a man
Or woman to be with, and while a thinnish
Old waiter turns up glasses, Sol is soldering
The last blue bolts of day, and mouths are watering

For dinner and, once more, for aquavit,
Which Swedish tipplers know as "The Superb."
A man sees Alouette get up from her seat
And walks across to her. "My name is Herb
McFuel. I saw you turn white as a sheet
Of paper which ten sticks of chalk disturb
And wondered if I could be of assistance."
Alouette said, "You'd better keep your distance,

For I'm about to die and be transported
To heavenly realms, and you might be dragged with me
If you're too close." His answer's not recorded
For just that instant a huge jug of whiskey
Was drunk in Texas and a plane was boarded
By someone whom the reader knows from Disney,
Pluto the Pup, who has been working there,
Since leaving Greece, for Papend. Through the air

He flies to Second Venice, where he's handed
An envelope, inside which is a letter
To Aqua Puncture from that man so candid
About desire that none was ever better.
"Oh find her if you can!" And now he's landed,
Pluto, where never terrier, toy, or setter
Had put down paws before—on solid clouds.
"Good heavens!" Huddel cried, "Does this mean crowds

Of people on the Earth know where we are?
Tell us, Sir, how you found us." Pluto smiled,
Or looked that certain way which on our star
We say is a dog smiling. It was mild
And sun-warmed breezy weather. In his car
Apollo rolled about the airs, beguiled,
Himself, at so much beauty. Pluto said,
"I just got this idea in my head

That since Commander Papend could not find you,
With all his messengers, in any country
On earth, that you, perhaps, had put behind you
The earth as someplace alien and bumpy,
Too full of those who menaced and maligned you,
And left it altogether for such sundry
New places as might be—rouge sunrise passes,
Air halls, snowflake pavilions, white cloud masses.

I got myself a little plane and tried
A thousand places till I came to this one.
So no one knows of you." "But," Huddel sighed,
"Who's Papend, who has sent you on this mission?"
"It is all in the letter." He ran wide
Around his plane and fetched it, an efficient
And mostly clever dog, whose sexual preference
Has earlier been the subject of a reference.

"Aqua's out gathering crocodiles," said Huddel—
"What?" Pluto cried—"We'll wait awhile till she
Returns, and then she'll read it." "I'm not subtle
Enough to know what 'crocodiles' might be,"
Said Pluto. "Are there real ones?" A befuddle-
D expression clouds his eyes. "No mystery!"
Laughs Huddel. "They're a certain kind of lettuce
Which Aqua likes and sometimes goes to get us.

It's very good in sky *salade.*" "The name, though,"
The dog persists, "how did it get its name?"
Huddel began to say; then Aqua came, though,
And they abandoned their linguistic game
On seeing her appearing, like a rainbow.
"Hello!" she said to Pluto, and a flame
Danced in her eye. "What's this? A billet-doux?"
Then evening marched across, in darkened blue.

Aqua sits down and reads. Rereads. And she
At last has read the letter Papend sent,
By every method everywhere that he
Could think of, to his sister, whom he meant
To know, at last, and be with. On one knee,
Which like the other's loveliest when bent,
She rests the hand in which the letter flutters
In the night breeze, at which she sometimes shudders

And sometimes not. "Oh best of things and worst!
A brother, a connection with the past
And with the life I did not have at first
And with the world I wandered from at last
To live in love when living was accursed!
O double judgment on my judging passed!"
She sighed, "I feel I must go see my brother."
He said, "Well, you do not have any other—

We ought to go." She cried, relieved. Dog barked.
"Come to my town of Venice for a visit,"
The letter said with which the dog embarked.
"Yes, we can try," said Huddel. "Oh don't miss it!"
The dog said, then round where the plane was parked
He ran awhile, and with this run's assistance
Had a huge appetite, which was diminished
By crocodile *salade* (it tastes like spinach

But it is slightly better, when uncooked)
A short while later, and some sky-blue cheeses.
New feelings now in Aqua were unhooked
And left her unprotected in the breezes
Of early night, at which she sat and looked
Like one whom something pleases and displeases
At the same time. And then she gave up trying
And let herself be overcome by crying.

O brotherhood and sisterhood, how sweet
How very sweet you are, or sweet you can be!
To have small playmates with the same size feet
And hands and head and tastes for the same candy!
To sit together all in the same seat
And be all muddy, slimy, wet, or sandy—
Not having any such in early years
Was what made Aqua now dissolve in tears.

While she sits crying, a tremendous goat
Is walking through that part of Thessaly
In which the rat-pair's car like a docked boat
Is stalled for lack of any energy,
Propulsive, to propel it. We should note
That this is not a goat, in truth, we see
But three Thessalian monks out doing penance
For having wished to visit Second Venice.

Father Propriades, discovering this
In dark and rocky mountaintop confession,
Had bade the lustful holy men to kiss
The Cross and, in a sort of a procession,
Inside a goat's hide which gave emphasis
To just what sort of sin caused this digression
From ordinary monkish life atop
Mount Athos, where the prayers never stop

And where no female creature is permitted—
The opposite of Venice! even Ann
The Ant and Fay the Firefly are excluded,
And viruses themselves must be a man
In order to come in, or else are booted
Like Emperor Hirohito of Japan
Out, he by free elections, virus by
This monkish force that lives quite near the sky,

To walk the roads of Thessaly until
They could prevent an act of lawless lust.
Now, when this goat of men came down the hill
And saw poor Alma pinioned to the dust
It started leaping. Herman gave a shrill,
High cry of snake despair and left in trust
(And haste) his precious rat lass to the churchmen
Who quickly broke the goatskin dry as parchment

And ran to her defense. She needed none,
But only, now, reviving. For she'd fainted.
They gave her smelling salts, a special one
That Tintoretto sniffed each time he painted
Which made his hand go swiftly as a gun
In his delineations of the sainted.
And she revives. They bless her. To the car
She races. And shakes Terence. "Is it far?"

The poor chap asks her. "Darling, you've been sleeping!
We've had an awful time! But those good fellows"—
She waved to where the monks were gladly speaking
To one another of the daylight's yellows
And of the azure air, then did a Greek thing
Of leaping through the air while making bellows
Of pleasure and relief that they had expi-
Ated their bad wishes to be sexy

And now were free to be themselves once more,
Not walk in a dried goatskin—"those good persons
Came to my rescue. Now let's go! Before
That evil snake returns with his excursions
Against my loyalty!" She locked her door,
And Terence gave himself to the exertions
Of starting up the car, but was unable
To make it run. So there upon the table

Of Western Greece's geological furniture
They stay, till they are rescued by a Sodomite
Named Arpel D. McShanes, the famous Senator
From Arkansas who with a keg of dynamite
Blew up Three Rivers Stadium when the manager
Refused to give him tickets, which epitomized
His whole career. He was a violent citizen
In private life and public most unreticent.

He found the rodent pair a short time later
And gave them food and water and a lift
To Thebes, where they could buy a carburetor.
In fact, he gave one to them as a gift,
And wished them luck, then, Senatorial satyr,
Cruised factory workers getting off the shift
At OEDI-PANS, the kitchen factory Thebans
Kept busier than the mind of Wallace Stevens.

This plant had given the first hope of prosperity
To Thebes since ancient times. Its product, kitchenware,
Was made with the same beautiful form and clarity
As Classical Greek jars had been, enriching where
One was accustomed, if not to vulgarity,
At least to plainness. Aristotle Itching Bear,
A Greek American Indian, of the idea
One day in boyhood from his Mother, Clea,

A striking woman ninety-five years old
At present, but at that time twenty-nine—
Sitting cross-legged in the tent, she told
Her pale papoose of Greece's sad decline.
Later, the little boy discovered gold
While playing catch beneath a clinging vine.
Investing it, and saving, he was zealous,
And finally he could make this gift to Hellas:

A mighty factory in which ancient crafts
Were brilliantly and gladly resurrected—
The men who worked there all were taught by staffs
Of the best artists that could be collected.
Outside this plant, McShanes the solon laughs
With somebody with whom he has connected.
They go off arm in arm, his bright green overcoat
Heaving with cheer, as in a storm the Dover boat.

Alma and Terence, then, with the Toyota
In running order, start it up and plunge
Into the Classical landscape, where no motor
Was heard in ancient days, till, like a sponge
Of green in deep green water, the iota
Of what they are has vanished. "I've a hunch,"
Said Papend, "from some curious sounds I've heard,
Which on the Grand Canal has twice occurred,

That some bizarre, unknown event is brewing
In my dear city. What, though, is its nature?"
He stands there in the soft May light, reviewing
A plan to change his city's architecture
By tinting all the matzoh walls with blueing.
"I think I won't," he said. "For in the future
The dye might eat the matzoh meal away
And giant bees of us make holiday."

He turned, in thought. Then a gigantic rattle
Was heard in Second Venice. Papend rushed
From one place to the next, as if in battle,
To find its source so that it could be hushed
But he found nothing, neither in the satell-
Ite isles of the Lagoon, nor in the slushed
Sideways with *aqua alta*. Could it be
An earthquake? an uprising of the sea?

It was in fact that haughty Indian lord,
Son of the Inca, who, preserved in stone,
For several hundred years, did now afford
The day the pleasure of his Royal groan
As he shot up to freedom. Those on board
The vaporetto saw him wildly thrown
Above the Gritti Palace and be caught
Upon the Campanile's upmost spot.

He climbed down to the balcony which goes
Around it and gazed out at the strange city
And closed his eyes and almost kept them closed,
But no—he had escaped from Zacowitti,
He was alive—he touched his cheek, his nose,
Then looked again, then looked back at the Gritti,
Then wept a little. He felt very strange.
Here is the story, in English, of his change

Which he told Papend later. Papend managed
To understand it, mostly. It was curious—
And moving. This young king, half-dead and bandaged,
In secret to disguise him from the furious
And brutal vengeful Spaniards had been sandwiched
Between two slabs of granite, the notorious
Ninety-five edged ones which touristic drinkers
Swear is the greatest thing about the Incas.

Here wedged, he'd lasted, till some odd explosions
Of late (those Papend heard while round about
The Grand Canal on generous excursions)
Had started knocking him so much about
That he regained his senses. Then the Russians
Set off a bomb they told no one about
And he was thrown into the air. "But what
Is all of this?" he cried. So Papend got

A chance to tell him everything, which this
Young man was dazed by. "You know, it's uncanny,
But in the old plan here I'd come to kiss
The prettiest girls—you've never seen so many!
Here on this very mountain top, my bliss
Was raised to such a height that the Great Bunny
Himself could know no more." He spoke of terraces,
Then, too, and made a number of comparisons

Of Macchu Picchu then and Venice now.
"We had no water here except for rain.
The land had trees, with blossoms on the bough.
We thought the earth was hung on a great chain
Which tied around the neck of a huge cow,
Whose name, 'Athpatala,' means 'super brain.'
Your gods are tennis-playing, sensual humans
Whom gold and silver heavenly light illumines.

What a vast difference in point of view!
In style! in everything!" Papend was touched by
This friendship, which, for him, was something new,
Since he had thought, as days and hours rushed by,
Only of getting power. Not many do,
But when somebody wants it, one is struck by
How little else he thinks about. Now, living
Here happily in Venice had been giving

This man the time to think and to consider
Just where his life was leading. It is sure a
Man in his middle years, once a great kidder,
May find himself *in una selva oscura*
And try to run off with the babysitter
Or take up Taoism and tempura
Or of too many cocktails be concocter—
Until at last he's taken to a doctor.

Or, he may simply *think*, till things break clear,
As midst the Muscovites when summer breaks
By force of her persuasive atmosphere
The ice sheets, and the Russian heart awakes,
And, in the Russian wood, the Russian deer,
If there are deer in Russia. In any case,
Papend was one of these, whose intellectual
Powers can meet a change, and be effectual.

The Inca stays. But let us leave that city
To where Alouette sits on the Rathaus lawn
Of Stockholm, wondering why Zacowitti
Has not yet come to take and pass her on
As he had threatened to. She looked so pretty
I don't think I could stand her being gone,
So I am glad that Fate reversed its order.
She stares, then smiles at her red skirt's white border.

"Well, here I am, and, being here'll continue
To do what I was doing, search for Pemmistrek."
He, on the North Pole Train, was going in, you
Could almost tell, a new part of the haversack
Of what was in his mind. "If it had been you,"
He mumbled, in a doze, "why, till the heavens wreck
I'd never leave you, ever." He gave a start.
His memory had come back! This was not smart

Or practical or anything while he
Was trapped in train on mountaintop above
The rocky world which snow gave unity
And he was there with Ann and others of
The Early Girls—he looked around to see
Just who he *was* with. He was filled with love
For Alouette, but all that happened after
Had gone completely, like a rotted rafter.

"Hum . . . who . . . and what—?" I leave him figuring out
What everything he finds around him means.
He looks into one door and gives a shout:
There are strange people reading magazines,
Whose speech and gestures fill his soul with doubt.
He strikes his forehead twice and wildly leans
Out of the window as the train speeds past
A polar bear, who strikes him with one vast

And snowlike, claw-filled paw, and sends him tumbling
Out of the train into the snow, where Ruffie
The bear, who'd thought he was a girl, stands grumbling,
While Pemmistrek leaps up, all fisticuffy—
But the huge bear runs off. Some ice is crumbling
So Pemmistrek, look out! He leaps above the
Crevasse. He's safe. And now he starts descending
As one whose story soon may have an ending.

Meanwhile a transformation comes about
Through a vague impulse animating Minnie
Who feels regret that she once had to shout
Foul words at Clarabelle. And she takes pity
On her. To Samos she had been shipped out
On a kayiki, months before. Now, quickly,
Minnie transforms her to a living girl
With some cowlike effects left, like a curl

That has escaped the coiffeur bent on styling.
She had been *slightly* human, always. Disney
Conceived her so. But now she's so beguiling
That friends expecting me tonight would miss me
If I knew where in real air she was smiling,
Her warm glance sailing to me like a Frisbee.
I don't, however. Would I had a stipend
To resurrect her living from this typing

And be with her, wherever. Lashes large
As shot glasses, she starts to peer in languor
About the shore of Samos, where a barge
Waits, loaded down with works of Margaret Sanger,
Walt Disney, Kipling, Christopher LaFarge,
John Wheelwright, Proust, and Lionel Feuchtwanger—
It is the Library Boat! and on it she
Will pass the first days of her liberty

From almost total cowlikeness. This vessel
She went to, walked aboard—it was all outside—
And stood upon it, reading. Captain Cecil
Castikulokis, with his eyes and mouth wide
Open at the sight, felt moved to wrestle
With feelings that he was insane. Then, "Ouch! I'd
Forgotten I'd grown taller," Clara said—
For on a bargey beam she'd hit her head.

"Oh—Captain—you must be the Library Captain—
Forgive me! I am so unused to being
In my new state. Such crazy things that happen!
In any case, I ran here, upon seeing
These human books—I'm longing to look at them!
Oh could I stay awhile and read?" Agreeing,
As it was easy to, to her request,
He smiled, bewildered. This was the first test

Of Clarabelle's (her less-cow name is Clara,
Which I shall call her henceforth) new-won powers,
Who, more than any cow in Connemara
Or deep Thessalian fields, where, gathering flowers,
Dis gathered Proserpine, herself a fairer
Flower than those she gathered, brought fresh showers
Of joyous perspiration to the forehead
By causing the whole person to grow torrid

Of any man who looked upon her face
And faery form, which now amidst the volumes
Of the library barge has found its place.
These human works will serve her as emollients
To help her flex her mind and fill with grace
Her slightest nods and gestures, which Italians
Someday will call, in thinking of her saga,
Gli atti amorosi della vacca vaga,

For all her gestures had a trace of love in them,
Something, well, indefinably Romantic;
And she stays on the barge, light currents shoving them,
Pursuing bookish pleasures unpedantic.
The Captain, as they pass, points out the Frothingham
Statue to her—she feels a tiny, frantic,
Warm pang of love! and they continue floating
To bring good books to each isle's rocky coating.

Landing on Chios, they behold a sight
Most unexpected: Mickey Mouse returned,
With Minnie, to the Race! Good God, good night!
Clara's embarrassed that her pale cheeks burned
In days long past for that round mouse. It quite
Undoes her. She but poorly has discerned,
However—she was terribly myopic
Since her strange change (an interesting topic—

Some physical changes still being uncompleted
From Cow to Girl). In any case, in fact,
The gala details that her vision greeted
Were part of a Propitiatory Act
To win the favor of the newly seated
Mouse members of Olympus. Wholly blacked
Huge papier-mâché figures, round of ears,
Being pulled past in a car, to thunderous cheers!

The car was even larger than the Packard
The mice had really used. It was enormous
And with red, yellow, white, and blue squares checkered.
Said Cecil, "It is larger than Pontormo's
Saint John Presented to the Virgin Backward,
The most extensive artwork, books inform us,
There ever was." Above it had been strung
Wires on which flowers and bits of cheese were hung.

And songs were ringing out from pink-faced students
From burly fisher-folk and fragile brides,
Lauding the Mouse's conscience and his prudence
And his tremendous driving skills, besides.
Assisting in these great Olympic ludens
Were thousands upon thousands. What divides
From all the rest a faith that's really living
Is just this sort of feeling, is this giving

Of everything, by everyone, to those
Who rule the Universe. And this one island,
The first of Greece to court the mystic rose
In Minnie's hair, led a return most violent
To the Olympians in loose-fitting clothes
Who, since Christ's Western conquests, had been silent
And close to sleep. Now feted, they awake
To passions new. Athena bakes a cake,

Apollo climbs a ladder, Zeus expands
His chest, picks up and hurls a bolt of thunder,
And Aphrodite, looking at her hands,
Decides she is a beauty beyond wonder.
It is the Mice, Olympus understands,
Who made it happen, and they are snowed under
With invitations, eulogies, and thanks,
And make a quick advance in godly ranks.

Mickey becomes the God of Everything,
A power superior to Zeus and Hera
As God is the superior of a king.
His Will determines all that in our era
Has any meaning. When you have a fling
With someone wonderful, or make an error,
Or drive into a cliff with your Mercedes,
It's Mickey who has done it to you, maties,

Or done it for you, as the case may be—
He is the Fief of Fate, the Lord of Luck,
The Duke of Death, and Earl of Amnesty.
His first act is reviving Donald Duck
In a small Cretan graveyard by the sea,
Who, once come back to life, hops on a truck
And speeds into Heraklion for a fitting
At Canard Tailors. Soon he will be sitting

Down for a dish of roasted man with orange
In a Heraklion tavern just for fowl.
Here, with his yellow-white face and beak of orange,
He'll think of Mickey, but without a scowl.
He loved the Mouse—no matter that the orange
Of jealous love had with an angry growl
Squirted him to oblivion! He was back,
Did not know how, but thought, "I have a knack!

There's nothing I can't do! I've lots of energy
And pluck and dynamism. What the hell!
I think I may go into plastic surgery
So I can help to make the shattered well,
Such as that Chinese fellow! It's encouraging
To be alive again and feel the smell
Of Cretan springtime soothing my proboscis
And see these duck girls beautiful as Toscas.

O life, you have been good to me! And, Death,
You too have been okay—since here I am!"
On saying which, he took a giant breath
And was transformed into a calligram—
Words everywhere feathers had been, except
His beak, which stayed the same, like Uncle Sam.
He was a "poetry duck" and not a real one—
Don't bring an orange to him—he can't peel one.

"Pourquoi c'est arrivé à ce canard
De tant changer, en ce qu' Apollinaire
Appelait 'calligramme'?" inquired Bernard
De la Hauteville, a Frenchman who was there
Writing an essay on "The Wingèd Star—
A True Greek Restaurant." Many would share
His curiosity, who saw that bird's
Whole breathy self being shifted into words.

The fact was, Mickey's power, being new,
Was also quite uncertain. Each commandment
Had some ambiguous words in it, like glue
Which stuck to what he said, relayed by cannon
To hilltop temples, then direct to you
And me by gnats and flies. What "like to man" meant
In resurrecting Donald—he had said
"Bring Donald like to man to life from dead"—

Was what remained unclear. Did Mickey mean
"As man would"? Man would do it in some art,
In picture, word, or music, and we've seen
The natural forces carrying out this part
Of what he said, confused, had tried to glean
The maximum effects: first made a smart,
Exacting, happy duck, far from acedia,
Then turned him to a high form of mixed media.

The words which make his feathers up declare,
I think, SOMA PSYKOS SEMA ESTIN,
"The body is the soul's prison." If you care
For intricate deep meanings, this has been
The best part of this story anywhere—
Think how man's language shuts man's meanings in
And is his prison, as his body is!
The French are very interested in this—

Too much, I think, but I confess that I
Am quite impressed by how it happened here.
So Donald moves no more, but now must lie
As art in the mind's inner atmosphere.
Mickey may see his plight, it's true, and try
To do it all again, but it's unclear
Whether he can or not. No need to dread
That Clara too will turn to something read—

She changed while living. Now in balmy weather
Of April, ten a.m., on Chios, Clara
Has slowly come to realize the tether
Of former love that bothered and embarra-
Ssed her need exist no more, for here together
Were not the Mice, but a Divine affair, a
Hail-to-Olympians scene. And now she trod
A stranger earth: "I-I once loved a god—"

She thought, and sighed. It seemed quite natural to her,
For in some books she'd read such things had happened.
It would surprise, though, most of those who knew her,
And it would mystify Commander Papend
That such a lady had felt flames all through her
For something seen most often in a trap end,
And now a god. His Venice had its own
Venetian gods, who loved canal and stone

And were not ever animals, but athletes
Who played Celestial Tennis all year long.
Nor would her story make much sense to Catholics
As they went mildly in to Evensong.
But it made sense to her, although a laugh keeps
Coming to her lips, which she thinks wrong:
How silly Mickey is! or was—who knows now?
And, Cecil bookishly beside, she goes now

In the parade, which is what it's become,
A long procession to the Cave of Egrets
On Chios' rocky top. Recovering from
Bad feelings, she looks forward with some eagerness
To the parade's excitement. Although some
May think that Clara shakes her cloudy ringlets
For Cecil's smile, in Cecil's bed at night,
They're wrong. It's all Platonic, which is right.

And so they walk along. And Pluto watches
Amazing star formations from his cot,
Where he's awake, although the "Buenas noches"
And silence of his hosts show they are not.
"Good God!" he cries, as lights come down in swatches
To cover him and everything he's got
With white, delicious flames. Meanwhile the Butterfly
Five Hundred Sixty-Five has met another fly,

Not butter-, but a beauty, in treed Tuscany,
And they have set up household for the thousands
Of insect babies they will have. What else can be
So pleasant for such creatures? While the mouse hands
Of Mickey turn toward Minnie: "Millions trust in me
And have your and my statue up on mouse stands—
Yet still I feel . . . I'm guilty!" And, then, crying,
"What's power if it is so unsatisfying?

If only Donald could be here!" "He could,"
Cried Minnie. "You have, dear, but to command it!"
He did. Then on a tray of silvery wood
The Donald Calligram to him was handed.
"What's this?" he wailed. He wept. It did no good.
Now turtles have on Mount Olympus landed
With numerous troops, and pistols, flags, and bells
And hostile mottoes painted on their shells.

DOWN WITH OLYMPUS! WHY SHOULD WE ENDURE
AN ALIEN RULE? LET TURTLES REIGN O'ER TURTLES!
AND GODS GO HOME! THE VERY AIR IS PURE
WE TURTLES BREATHE. WE DO NOT NEED THE MYRTLES,
THE OAK, THE BAY, THE SHINING SINECURE!
GIVE US OUR LIVES TO LIVE IN OUR HARD GIRDLES!
And other such. They march toward Mickey's mansion,
A Classical Greek Home without pretension,

Whose simple columns are the purest whiteness
That ever eye beheld and hold a cornice
On which a bas-relief extends its brightness,
To other art as fiveness is to fourness,
A very model of the loving lightness
The best of Greece produced. Secured from soreness
By armor hard, the creatures march ahead
Straight to where Mickey is. "What's this?" he said.

And they presented him their grievance. This
Was, fundamentally, that turtles were
Unfavored by Olympian emphasis,
And, being so, wished to dispassenger
From that transportative theopolis
And find their own. If this did not occur,
To live in an agnostic tortoise freedom.
Mickey with many well-picked words did greet them

Despite his sorrow. He was touched, himself,
By what he felt of kinship with these reptiles
Although he was, by birth, a rodent elf.
True, he had power now, ruled the skies and kept isles
From sinking down below the ocean shelf—
But, when he'd been but mouse? "GODDAMN!" He leapt. "I'll s-
Ee what the gods can do!" But at this second
A billion atoms to each other beckoned

And then a billion more. Infinity
Is hard to think of, but within a basin
Are atoms infinite, and those that be
On Mount Olympus wild at the disgracing
They suffered from a god's profanity
(Mickey's "Goddamn"), suddenly started racing
Together, which explosions threw the Mouse
And his companion out from holy house

And home. Eternal Essence, though, remained
Unharmed, and other gods, who had been visiting
That day in Space. They fell near a two-laned
Hellenic highway, where Divine Necessity
Had thrown them, into a light blue mud-stained
Deserted Chevrolet, whose authenticity
Was shown when Mickey started it. He roared,
Unthinking, down the road, which led him toward

And into Sounion, where he is the Winner
(Crowds cheering) of the Race. He's made a record
In spite of everything, and Dr. Skinner
Of Canada Dry is there to greet him, tuckered
But happy, and invite him to the dinner,
Both him and Minnie, in whose mouse heads flickered
No memory of their fall or of Olympus,
Nor round them shone the trace of any nimbus.

They were two normal Mice again, as previously
They always had been, loving and intemperate
And full of laughter, sometimes acting deviously
And sometimes not, but hardly ever separate.
Mickey, afflate with Saurian wine, inebriately
Starts leaning very close to Sally Everett,
A cub reporter for the Sounion *Nurse,*
And Minnie hits him with her beaded purse

And knocks him to the floor. But they took comfort
In being quite the heroes of each speech
Delivered through the night. They'd hear the one word,
"Courageous," then another, "great," in each
Such praise of what they'd done. How sound they slumbered,
You can imagine, later. With a screech
Trains run together. Pemmistrek's on one of them,
And Alouette's on the other. They make fun of them,

The station men who see them hold each other
And cry and laugh, and cry and laugh and cry,
Move back a little ways, then run together,
Look at the pavement and look at the sky,
And, as if they could really not tell whether
They were alive and really there, they'd try
To stand and stare but then find it impossible
To stay that far apart. It is unguessable

What thing in all of life could move them more!
Is this the True and Culminating Instant
At last? The sea is crashing on the shore,
And new events are moving in a distant
Part of the world we haven't seen before,
But these two feel, and are, perhaps, resistant
To everything, even the wish to know
What's happening now to others. As the snow

Of utmost northern Sweden, like the back
Of someone who's been standing at the window
Bare to the waist all winter long, and crack-
Less ice, like a long, endless prayer of Shinto,
Rush past the train unhushing on its track
One sits inside it seemingly akin to
A statue in a graveyard. Early Ann is
Bereft, alone. Then suddenly Atlantis

Reached up its watery arm to Ingle's height
And snatched the train with all the girls inside it
And all the others, to its hallways bright
With dazzling fish and sponges. The nearsighted
Conductor, Ingar Jensen, said, "We might
Be slightly later than it was decided
We were supposed to be. Something seems blocking
Our forward progress." Far beneath the docking

Of fishing boats, of rowboats, and canoes
The Girls are walking now, amazed and frightened
A little bit, it's true above the ooze
Of ocean bottom, on white stairways heightened
By rose and tulip shades, with some dark blues
And violet yellows which at first they mightn't
Have noticed since what happened was so crazy.
And Pemmistrek in Ann's young mind grew hazy—

She went on loving him but as a dreamer
Loves someone she has never seen in daytime
Sit down across from her and place the creamer
Within her reach, and sing some songs from *Maytime*.
So ended, like the future of the lemur
By further evolution, the great gay time
They'd had together. This quick transformation
By the Atlantic arm was the occasion.

Lonely Atlantides—the place had been
All men till now—had learned of their existence
("The Early Girls"), and, aided by a pin
Which magically did away with distance,
Had found the band of heavenly seraphin
En route to Northern points on pounding pistons
And forced an Ocean arm to go and get them,
And loved them, as they'd hoped, the day they met them.

And so the Early Girls will love again . . .
This time I think it will be, in the silence
Of fabulous Atlantis, once the den
Of porpoise, then of people, city islands
Not simply cities they'll create when men
Care for them there, so far from any highlands.
And, sure enough, it is. Dear palm-tree places
Or little rock isles, which, like masks of faces,

Have one expression always, baby deserts,
And flat low meadowy places which are covered
Sometimes by water, and sometimes by pheasants—
With island urban architecture, buffered
By ocean breezes on their frequent visits.
So Hydras and Deer Islands from the cupboard
Of Non-Existence, soon delight the eyeballs
Of seabirds fond of having nests on high walls.

Terence and Alma, meanwhile, like to those
Who seem to win but do not, still are straying
Across the roads of Greece, and, I suppose,
Will some day come in second. Monks are praying
Atop Mount Athos to the Mystic Rose
To speed them on, and orchestras are playing
At Schweppes's ballrooms that do not yet have
The news that Mickey has had the last laugh

And won the race, although he lost so much.
The Donald Calligramme, forgotten, glows
In a peculiar fashion, and the Dutch
Who hear of it from some newspaper's prose
Come capture it for their museum. Such,
To here, the fate of that bill, beak, or nose
Which once to Hu Ching Po meant such a lot.
Clara comes back to Samos, having not

Read all the books but quite enough, she thinks,
To make her happy for a while. The stars,
Meanwhile, lead Pluto to a silver links
Where he plays golf, and in the Theban bars
McShanes is buying everybody drinks
And rumbling happily. And now the wars
Of night and day resume, this battle won
By rosy dawn, which, festive, has begun

With various cloud formations, among several
One mirroring a white automobile
With pink reflected, in which Richard Feverel
Seems wrestling with a giant Christmas seal,
And in another huge one, light blue Chevrol-
Et-looking, seated at the steering wheel,
Elizabeth Gedall is learning how,
It seems, to drive through heaven. Later, now,

Clara, on Samos, walking (accidentally?),
Bumps hard against the Amos Frothingham statue—
Somehow this shakes him physically and mentally—
Entirely! back to life! He's staring at you,
Not merely standing there. Swifter than Bentley,
He moves, he holds her tightly now. Take that, you
Dull insect Death! And, hearing strange alarms,
He soars straight skyward, with her in his arms.

Noon hits the tops of trees and statues, as
The sun keeps rising, on its best behavior,
Over the White House, Rome, and Alcatraz,
And Second Venice where the light is wavier.
And in the garden they are playing jazz
And bluebirds bolt above the seaside graveyard
Where Donald Duck was, till his re-formation.
And to one reading in the railroad station

It seems, perhaps, that everything has ended
That matters to this story. But—it hasn't.
Strong impulses through the vague cloudbanks wended
And strange new energies became unfastened.
Huddel and Aqua haven't yet descended
To Venice, but prepare to, when a crescent-
Shaped car arrives, to take them to a feast
Where what they know of things will be increased.

They feel they ought to go. It is a plan
That may delay their voyage to the Andes.
It seems beyond the scope of living man
And is in fact the work of Nyog Papendes,
Who rides through heaven in a moving van
And is the Lord of Sad and Happy Endings;
He was afraid his son might not approve
This evidence of his illicit love

And so, before permitting her to travel,
Aqua, to see him, found this stratagem
To meet her at a feast and to unravel
From lacy collar to embroidered hem
The dress of his desire as to how level
With Papend she should be, and straight with him.
At least, such was his first idea. His second
Was to raise Papend, too, and so he beckoned

And had his bugle brought. "I'd best confront them
Here each with each," old Nyog Papendes said,
"Here where they're in the state of mind I want them
The most to be!" And then, attired in red,
He blew his magic bugle, like a huntsman,
Which Papend heard on earth and, as one dead
Escaping human hands outstretched to hold him,
Rose in the air. Canals below him told him

That he was going up and leaving *mondo*
Más delicado for an unknown region,
A place where there were no *gondoles* to run to
Or walk about in furs to shoot a pigeon—
And now the Adriatic seems a pond, though
One knows how large it is upon occasion
When in a vaporetto to Torcello
Going as slowly as a spoon in Jell-O.

And so, away he goes. He leaves behind him
The earth's most lovely women. One may question,
As he does, with this curious rise assigned him
By unknown fates, if his life was the best one
That man could lead on earth. Good-byes remind him
Of all the girls he leaves, and the suggestion
Is planted in his mind that they perhaps
Could have been happier with more numerous chaps,

One man to love each one. He thought, "I'll think of it
When I come back." He had the confidence
And lack of fear of death though on the brink of it
That power gives, like that of innocence—
He knew that he'd come back and I will drink to it
Because my liking for him is immense.
He starts to wonder, too, if his one use
Of women (love) might not be an abuse

Of complex natures for a single tone.
And yet the girls seemed happy. It may be
There was an aspect of Peruvian stone
Which, flaking almost imperceptibly
Changed human nature so that love alone
And such a love as his brought ecstasy
And nothing else came near it. High above
His duplicated city thinking of

These further aspects of his curious life
He wondered, too, about the vasty number
Of girls he wanted. Why not take a wife?
Someone to grow attached to in one's slumber
And be with always, shining like a knife
With faithful passion? Just then a cucumber
Sailed past and almost hit him. He was going
Now through a place where sky legumes were growing,

Not that where Aqua was but quite another—
There are, it's said, six hundred in the sky,
As much alike as sister is to brother,
Though sometimes different colors like a dye
Suffuse them utterly, so that a southern
Celestial garden, such as that one high
Above Morocco near where Zagora
Stamps forth its foot before the la-de-dah

Of the Sahara Desert, where the Blue Men
Ride purposefully back and forth with articles
They wish to barter with some other human,
Seems to be but a mass of purple particles
Though one can see, if gazing with acumen,
The different products growing there. Sabbaticals
Exist for study of such things—but now
He passes through a cloud shaped like a cow,

Then into fading, then more faded, blue,
Until all colors are completely gone
And everything a quite light light-white hue
Like petticoats stretched out upon a lawn
To dry on Easter morning, when the Shoe,
Which children think the Rabbit has put on,
Has left its tracks and also precious eggs
To which the children run on trembling legs

And cry, "Why are there petticoats out here?"
In fact, there aren't. It was the mere appearance
Of petticoats, was frost, which, in the clear-
Er later morning sky is gone, as Terence
Was gone from consciousness, as from the beer
The foam is gone, as from the throne room Clarence.
And Papend goes on sailing through this ether
Where clouds, air, everything he sees, is see-through.

He goes on thinking, which, on such occasions
i.e. when one is in convulsive flight
Away from what one knows and with sensations
That mix the energies of day and night
May bring about the birth of those creations
All kinds of artists treasure, and they're right—
For thought in one particular place has limits,
Like thought specifically men's or women's,

American or Russian, old Chinese
Or Maoist, or, say, eighteenth-century thought
Or rocking chair reflections, thoughts of bees,
Buranian thought. Creators know they ought
To find new thought that is like none of these
Yet where to find it? It cannot be bought.
It can, though, be inspired, which is what changes
Are helpful for, and being among strangers.

He was confused, inspired. And he envisioned
A Venice so much better than his old one
That planet earth would scarcely be sufficient
To be its space—a silver and a gold one,
This Venice, which would be at once commissioned
On his return from Space (doubtless a cold one)—
And he would boat in it with her as cargo
Who was his sister, Aqua, to San Marco.

Now he was sailing through the strangest places
A person could. His mind and heart were shaking
More than the hands of rooters at the races.
I cannot guarantee his state was waking,
But he was wakeful in its dreamy spaces.
He loved the new conceptions that kept raking
The leaves of what he thought and felt, and passed
Clouds like great sails, without a boat or mast.

And elsewhere Huddel holds in firm embracing
Aqua, while space birds flutter on both sides,
As through the higher stratosphere's enlacing
Of cloudy wisp on wisp that couple rides.
The word has come to her that she'll be facing
Her father and her brother, whereat glides
Tear after tear of joyful consternation
Down her delightful nose, which concentration

Can no way keep from wrinkling as she's sobbing.
I wonder if they ever will arrive?
It seems to be much farther than a robin
Has ever flown, or car could ever drive.
Nyog may have made an error, that of dropping
Some zeros from the mileage number. I've
No knowledge of transfinite life-death distance,
So I shall leave them, without more insistence,

En route to where they feel it is they're wanted,
With stars about them now to left and right
And full of secret notions. Someone bunted;
Another threw a curve. It grew more light.
And high above the mountain ranges, stunted
By distance, they all, soaring in their flight,
Are fading fast, or covered by the awning,
Which everyone can see, of early morning.

Impressions of Africa

The back roads, if there are back roads
Have gone to sleep
Daggers have coughs on them
And quoits have cures
And doors have racking heat
The sciences have beds with fevers.

1. MADAGASCAR. SUBCONTINENT

In the Hôtel Colbert, pronounced Coal-Bear
In the bar
I saw a big, pretty girl who looked like Lisa
Behold a magazine a new life of women is about to appear
I sat at my *chocolat* writing
The sea-bird inviting
And the Lisa-looking girl didn't smile or even look
At me but soon she got out of there
And she went walking
Down the sidewalk-colored street not thinking of me
Lisa-looking girl, come back!
Give me or don't give me a little bit of ecstasy
Help me to find the answer
How long does life last?

The Académie Malgache
Is nothing
Wearing my new pink suit
Is nothing
Wishing you were there
Is nothing
But nothing helps me out
It helps me to see the lemurs
In the pre- and post-restaurant air

And in the time before I slide around in fear
On the floor in a nightmare
Which didn't happen in fact
At the Hôtel Colbert.

Change my room!
The fourteen-year-old
Girl still a young
Flower not yet
Into the age
Of her race
And all characteristics
Mops the fields
With her hair
In long tresses are
They women, other, wear
Green and orange dresses
A man holding a rake
Something
To duel with a rice
Paddy? or other field.

Where will it all end?
In the Market, around this bend
As I go down, my feet go down with me
People are sitting lying standing end to end.

To be exploding, like a fiddle, outside of myself
I am thinking on yellow roads of Madagascar
I have been there
Like a bird on a shell
Or like the mountain coming down over that
Sun sea shelf

And like the chair yellow and pink and red
That exists only in the head
At the side of the seashell, in Madagascar

Which is not Africa, some say,
It breaks away from Africa, just in time
To preserve the lemurs
A few hours later
The lions came down
And the apes came down
From a bend at the top of Africa
Rushed there by the climate
Knowing it can't last
Neither did Africa, Madagascar
Left it, storm of red,
Blue, yellow
And rice paddies
And villages with stone tombs left it
With Polynesians coming to it left it
And with the stone booths
And the climatic exchange.

The Earthly Paradise—"Wait till I get there!"
Once in Antananarivo, however, it seemed too far away
(Forty kilometers by sea) and to take too long to get there.
This island, drenched by perfume fragrances, boasts many cabanas,
With paradise—where? A woman in Paris
Told me about it. Ah!
You are going to my country! there you will
Find the paradise—an island
That smells so sweetly
They have the perfume-bearing trees that it is called
Paradise, or Perfume Island.
But in Gaboon, as in Zaire, they said when you get there
Communist-government-ruined, ah you are

Going to Madagascar! I had a fine, confused state
Of mind about this subcontinental island state
An East-Berlin gray broken-up boulevard mist
Ambiance, and *le paradis terrestre*.

Tanarive *centrale*, there is a lake
So choked with waterlilies
That you would not believe
It was not planned to be that way, to take
You by the throat by its sudden beauty—unexpected, boaty,
And plain—but then you can see
It's a little messed up and and goaty
Around the edges, after which it doesn't look the same
When you drive by it on your way to the intersections.

In varied patterns you see them they vary
And they are patterned
Of the crops in the fields
And the clothes of the men
And the women and children
In varying colors, patterns
The automobile running
It used to be a paradise
Flesh but with unusual graces and with a "soul."

Dixebat Julie—*nom correcte? mot juste?*
O Malagasy plumes! In the market so used
Sumptuousness! She said (did) words
Madagascar we feel thrown, we feel the thrown
Stone one out here in the sea (she)
(Didn't) (say it). I thought
It, while she was going around
And around helping me to buy jewelry, it was

Getting dark, in the market. Here is a good stone,
Says she, and a good price, too, I get on this one!

So much closer to me
By big civilization compared
To walkings of Brazza
And even than the poets there!
In a certain sense.
Old hotel—of innocence.
Gare Centrale—mammary of competence.
And nerves under the hat.

Hard to get out of the restaurant
Hard to stand up from the table and pay
Hard to move quickly enough
Through the arbiters gentlemen
Unthreatening who have rather
The mild excitingness which travel
Gives to the un-noteworthy like a gun.

Standing around
The water fountain
Fifteen girls
Or maybe ten
Look at him
Then look away
Nothing happens
On this day
In the village of Ankazobe.

Evenings in Madagascar
It used to be a paradise

According to the French
In a memorial unitary
Naval military
Dotting up of times.

The huge tombstones
Are a traveler's bust—
Finally, Antony's bust is not like Antonina's!
The white cool stones on the path
On the way up to the Queen's hut
Say so again and again and again—
Go out to dinner. Inside, no lights.

The Queen had her own swimming pool. No one else was allowed to use it.
And there was a door of the dead, too, as in Gubbio. And a small, special room
To which only the loyal dead, in their coffins, were ever moved. And this is
     the Royal Door. The whole palace complex was constructed for the Queen
Ramabanabamabanjana by a minor British architect
In the style of a Scottish summer lodge, in eighteen-fifty-four.

The clean way
Up to the palace
And the green way
Down. Down under there's a lot of ground
Where roots and insects stay and all around
The lives of the mild, poor people of Madagascar.

Down there, it's shipping
Up here, it's rice.

Black is the night sky above the central Madagascar
Plateau on which the capital is situated. Here the climate
Is temperate. There below
Are the steamy rivages where all-Black people dwell,
Malagasy-speakers, although resembling the Continental Africans.

The Malagasy all speak Malagasy, she said
They aren't divided up into different tribes
Speaking Tangasy and Longasy and Fugasy
But Malagasy everywhere you walk or drive
Even into the deepest and most remote place.

With its cruel mask of domination taken off
France offers, among the nations, too beautiful a face
Not to have a choice spot
In every free man's heart
Said Jacques Rabemananjara. He drank the rice water.
The French officers drank wine. Are these officers the Presence
France genuinely wants to have in Mad-
Agascar? "The whole problem is there," said Jacques,
The problem of every far-from-the-center action,
Of every far-from-the-center place.

It is a plain faucet
The day goes by
Water! streams out of it
I had thought, A spring, maybe, but
Reality
Has other ideas
Today appearing to me
At Ankazobe with its fifteen girls
Sunset sunrise days go by still
Is there a still center where desire

Is not American enthusiasm, where it is a rushing-
Forward ball of diamond flickers, as
At Ankazobe? Oh, the cloth sleeve on her arm
As she puts it forward to hold a bucket under the swash
Or "gold it under" when the sun comes out,
Of the, for me, as I watch from this distance, soundless water!

Forgetting four months
Going back to a time
When it was powerful
The early morning sun once again picks up
The bare outlines of some straw.

Across the river
First the blacksmith
Then the market. Forging a heel of steelness
He's making horseshoes, he crafts the dullness
Of raw shapeless matter into a thing
That has a ring; he also makes the frame of a bed.

Purple, yellow, and red
Clothes, to make her forget
She is not supposed
To be totally interested in that.
It's just cloth made and dyed and cut
And draped around the human butt
Of Amédie Amenangala
On the way to Amatafy.

Everything naturalizes into on-the-way
Purple and yellow in the eyes' way
Give up!

Whatever you find out traveling you don't know
Whatever you find out moving is used up.

An ambiance slightly rah-rah very unlike that in Brah Zah
Invades, evokes, equips this home in Tah Nah
Where to the Malgache night
We send out words of wisdom slightly flawed—
Find the meaning of what I am doing since Zaire?
Maybe—will she?—or not.

Eheu, Madagascar! Closer to home, what?
Not a part of Africa, really, a hot shot
Among African nations, this subcontinent
Basks in the reflected glory
Of the mappemondo's number-one hot spot, the Queen
Of Continents,
Who graciously grants it this blot
In mid-ocean, not far from the un-concreted shores.

In a constant blither-dither of can't-wait-to-get-out
It gets out, and scintillates, and rises, and fights, and flies,
And careens, and ends up, and was a day, of storms and inclusions.

The crowds of lights
At nine o'clock
In Tanarive
Go out.

Soon I will be back in
The clasping-type shoes of the street
Near the there on the banks of

The Central Lake to be looking at
Anticipatable only after a while
Clapboard houses. The winds take
A ten-hour break. No
Shudder of leaf temples at all.

Vincent RIZERIE Rabehaga the rice
Is still being produced here while at the Chocolaterie
Robert, on the same road,
It is shuttered-up windows, and trees
Edging the closed-down factory, where, in other days,
Came truck and car and wagon to remove
The chocolates over the hills to Tanarive.

And Lake Itasy grows nearer
And nearer, and the city of Tana is passed
And soon we are in the outskirts of Ampefy!
Ampefy is a logging town
And a fishing town. Windows of Ampefy
Open to let the Am air in
And the Pef air out, while Y stays still
In Ampefy, "The Broad-Bosomed."

You are perhaps making too much
Of this little trip to Ampefy
And Lake Itasy, during which
Nothing, or just about as close
To nothing as anything can be, happened.
The ruins (remains) of lake architecture.
The big bee
And the red bird. Above and beyond Itasy and Ampefy.

Holly is the embassy attachée. Other personnel
Darkens. She is the cultural
Attachée. This, too, is a cultural attachment,
What happens today.

A silver-haired calligrapher has stolen my storm window
At night I try to sleep
The air conditioner doesn't work, not really
It doesn't bring in the hilly town and its streets
Or the fields and the air that is with them, so I prepare
To get cool in a non-working shower and go downstairs
To the Colbert Bar, ampersand of my nights and days.

A bird is its own balcony—
And so is Madagascar, an annual rain on its head.

As the sun shines, a man
Is making and selling raffia giraffes
Beside the road.
There are no giraffes here. They moved in
To Africa after Madagascar had moved out.

Not because the bed was hot
Or anyone was married
The road ran on, as far as the outskirts of the city
Then it stopped.
They keep
Giving this government money.
Laurel and Hardy and the elephants
Sleep outside.

Holly of the Consulate
Keeps me in the car. She

Talks a lot. A jar
's for sale in Madagascar.
A woman keeps
Her foot on the tan reach
Of the irrigation ditch going over
To the other, less-deep-blue side.

Disturbing to be on the road
Without a car under you, without a card
To identify you, without a car-nail
With which you could make your name on a stone, if you had to.

On my way!
I sit in the Colbert
And think about Zaire.
The Jillian-looking
Girl reminds me of Kenya.
The dot-dot-looking girl
Reminds me of the Hell
Of certain relationships.
Coffee returns me
But the life in the village goes on.
"The true life," they say in Zaire,
"Is the life of the ancestors.
And the true village
Is the village under the ground."

How far from the true voyage
Is the voyage by car? by air?
I think the one
Who looks like Jillian
May be a whore. She reads
The newspaper. Legs.

The true woman
Is the woman at the bar
As well as the woman she resembles.
The true bar is the one with great umbrellas
Sweeping over seven hundred miles of ground,
Flowing, and bringing no snowflakes down, through Africa.

The thing about Madagascar,
I try to explain, sitting
With no one to
Talk to but myself
While
The "boot" part
Of day escapes—five to
Six-thirty p.m.—is that it seems
More like France, more
Like what I'm used to, thus
I'm more "myself" (I say
To myself) in the
Rather "advanced," mixed-up way
I escaped in the rest of Africa
Because it was so hard.

The capital of Madagascar has streets
One can walk around in at night, although
It does not have many streetlamps. Also there is hardly
Any place public to go. When the French
Were here, the streetways were ignited
With places to eat and drink and dance, and
Possibly, even to find romance, to go from the ball
With someone you have met, into the Malagasy night. Now
Darker, and emptier, it seems country enough so that
In it you don't necessarily forget
The outskirts, with their darker streets

Or the mountains (very high
Hills, anyway) with their trees.

Rice fields are not giving any water
To the gin drinkers seated with some daughters
At the Pousse Café. Besides which, a rice
Shortage is under way. Honk! says Bumbudun of
The Embassy. And the Marines came
At night. I saw them sitting
With their shaved crowns in the way
Of the filigree atop the Bar. And then again at the airport
I saw them, like God's American Swollen Ping-Pong-Ball Heads on
        Holiday. Can you imagine
IMPORTING rice to this country? From this embassy irony a way
's found to the rice water, Malgache specialty, consisting
Of warm water, relatively, in which has been cooked rice.
You drink it, swinging your eyes away to
The field daughters, and others, going home, baskets on heads.

2. SENEGAL. PORT

Keep your courage up
Walk down the street
When the leper comes up to you
Say I am a Moslem
And give him a franc
Soon he will be carted away
By the Department of l'Encombrement Humain.

Go to the Island of the Slaves
On Sunday, said the Black cultural attaché, who speeded me
Down hallways through consular doorways
Then suddenly back out onto the street.
At five o'clock everything closes
Or did he say one o'clock or two or three or four o'clock?
In any case, everything is closed
But I find someone to talk to in a building (mauve)
Past the horse (white).

A young man, tall (high, rather)
And skilled at walking fast
And with his head on high comes past
At an amazing angle and an amazing rate.

Fashions change slowly. And
Books rarely have an influence
Because few people read them. No one speaks about
The pattern of the young men walking
Bisecting and trisecting each other's striding poles
Backwards and frontways hand-arm waving
Beneath palms, on the Place de l'Indépendance.

Don't go to the bars, Jean-Marc said, and try
To talk to the girls. This one is OFF-LIMITS. This one is
OFF-LIMITS. I am ON-LIMITS with my arms. Why that man
Stuck with a tooth stick? The Lebanese
Men go there, with their sisters
They start to fight if you talk to or touch one.

"The Russians in Dakar Harbor are not allowed
To get off their ship for fear that they will
Be seduced by capitalism," he said. "It's the truth!"

In Dakar you are still pretty close to Europe
But three miles out of town you are burning in a pink lake
Unless you get out of it fast with your modicum of salt.
These modicums grown additive on the lake banks
Show white and fair to a far-off who views them but
Up near, they stink. And the salt lake burns you. And, Dad,
I am leaving, you do not say if you are a member of this tribe,
This special tribe of nomads who dredge for salt.

On the boat to Gorée, how cruel
These four Lebanese are, led by this one
Young man who keeps calling to and then laughing at
A Mongoloid (of maybe twenty-five or thirty)—
Laughing at his clumsy gait and at his efforts to please
Them in an absurd and helpless way.

That man on this boat
Looks like Mayakovsky, black—his face
Showing his character and his art,

His violent, virile, and touchingly
Avant-garde, Futurist, lyric poetic art.

Seeds on my head! Sitting under
A baobab. Big, knotty tree—baobab!
You're spreading all over like a Roman or Athenian map!

Everything is wrecked—misery, stoniness, and the color
Of sickness, or dying, is dancing on it all.

Tu as le choc, you have
Ze shock! said Jean-Marc
Aiverybuddy get whan comb to Africa. It goes away.
But it took more than two days going away.
For these two days I hate life, Africa, everything.
Next day, a little better. Three
Weeks later, I am in an enchantment—Kenya!
Madagascar! the sun shock under the place names
Like skin under clothes.

Greater than the shock of the insects of the Congo,
Greater than the clock of Madame N'Zambo's hair.
It's the shock of poor people, desperately poor.
Wanting—everything. Which
In their case is almost nothing. Everything.

The man sweeping the building
After dark is of a higher caste
Than the one who directs the company
And rules it from the topmost floor.
To his air-conditioned office

Suite, comes Eng-al-Baram
And the president bows down.

The slaves were brought in this way
And taken out this way.
Here is where they stood
Waiting for the boat
To take them to America
In chains where they would create
The characters of Darky and Mammy, good slave, bad slave,
Hanged man, mulatto, quadroon, and then would change
To "underprivileged citizens," preachers, doctors—
Violent transformations, while
Africa stayed here all along,
Visited by rainfall and heat spells,
With a different kind of energy and a different kind of change.

The partition of Africa takes place
In eighteenth- and nineteenth-century
Europe, on conference tables. Here is the place
Where one Oolof will wear a beret, and the other a bush hat,
Where one will drink wine, and the other feel lost without his tea.

In Dakar at night
Léopold Sédar Senghor is sitting and thinking
Just as Wallace Stevens might have wanted him to—
But he finds he is not thinking right.
He eats some *moospasla* and goes to sleep.

Blue, brave
Flash of the ocean's
Water, like a screen

Through which I see
The street, the streets,
The teeming, busy,
Commercial, African,
Impoverished, beggar—
Filled, lavish, horrible
Streets of Dakar
The city's been left ajar
Fortunately so that the breeze
Can come in, although Islam
And the rest of Dakar
Don't go out.

Senghor was President.
Poets here are residents, too.
Fleeing from Haiti
Jean Brière (and others) found a free literary haven in Dakar.

Oh the part that's by the ocean that's
Fine, says Jean-Marc. The part that you see.
But in the rest of the country it's horrible—
There's no water, dried out, death to the economy!

I am like a shark at the reef
Said King Behanzu, upon hearing
That the French were debarking at Catarou.
And he delayed them but he could not stay them.
Of King Behanzu's defense there remains a statue
Of King Behanzu as a shark—"At the Reef."

3. GABOON. COAST

As in Gaboon, the white road jumps past the hospital
Up to the sun-
Drenched French bathing suit companies of half-
Naked women who don't ask me along
As if I saw the moon, entirely, one
Body, from an air-conditioned room. The young woman speaks
French, lying on her back, her breasts
Bare, in the hotel pool.

The Malaria doctor. "I implore you!" Steepness.
Millions of pieces of junk on the street,
And dirt. I'll take a walk.
And now it's raining
Again. Jean-Guy takes me
To the "village of sculptors" where
I look at nothing for a while.

Tell me, the young sculptor
Is covered with dust, *Raconte-moi,*
Chef, ce que c'est que la littérature française.
On en parle mais je ne comprends pas. Well, literature, I said,
Is made up of poetry, fiction, and plays. French literature is
        all of that
In the French language. Oh is that it? he said.
C'est cela! Ça alors je ne savais pas!

Dust is flying everywhere
In this half-commercial half-traditional industry
Center, this tiny village, where, I would say,
The heads they make are more half-bad than half-good.
The sculptors have a careful but, finally, a nonchalant

Attitude toward what they are doing. It
Comes out right, it comes out right. No
Question, it seems, of a "break-through,"
Of a new artistic conception of the nature of the human head.

Preféres-tu Senghor ou Césaire? he said. Césaire,
I said. Ah, si. Oui. Moi aussi. He puts down his chisel. Oui, toi tu as raison.

Négritude. A Black world. Black consciousness. What
A splendid idea Aimé Césaire had, for writing poems
And for breaking through the light with something to say,
With days on the calendar, every day an estimate if right
Or wrong the *négritude* and with and when, and a way of talking.
Négritude contre la fièvre du monde blanc, as I take Lanaquil
Contre le paludisme, indigenous to these parks
And valleys that vanish as you sit in them or walk through the mirage
Till Mama Africa becomes *Boum boum boum!*

The horizon's always rounder near the Equator.
O Hotel Rapontchombo elevator
Where I may meet the bare breasts of Gaboon!
But I don't. I rarely leave my room
But sit around and think of "Rapontchombo"
What does it mean in Fang? Jean-Pierre is downstairs.
I bang into the elevator. There's a casino
In this hotel, off-limits to the Gabonese. All the meat
And vegetables come from France. I see an old woman,
She looks likeable—and real. She, too, is probably imported.
It's the sunlight of Gaboon, the horizon-rounding equator
And the rising and sinking pontoon of the hotel elevator!

Difficult, says Jean-Pierre, to meet the *indigènes*. I don't
Manage to do it, except for Jacques Rupombo and Hélène
Desforêts, the only Gabonese novelist, who, when
We appear together on television, shares with me the sweet oxygen
Of the indoors functioning air-conditioning of Gaboon.
Although it is very hot under those lights she says
Kind things. Jacques Rupombo says, "The world has need . . ."
And other lively exaggerations, and I don't know anything
More about the people than I did when I came in-
To the country.

Glamorous she is, in a Gabonese manner,
But she doesn't write well, one of the Frenchmen says—
I couldn't read her novel, my copy of it
Falls a short, sandy, humid distance to the
Floor of Room One Thousand and Sixty-Six
In the Hotel Rapontchombo, from where I pick it up
Later, it may not be her fault that I can't
Read it, there is my sleepiness, my dissatisfaction,
My stomach trouble here in Gaboon! I still
Have read only one sentence of the book and I
Am being picked up in five minutes by Buroombo
To be driven to the airport. What should I do? It's
Heavy, I carry it with me.

Today there is XY of the Embassy and the exorbitant structures
That constitute the Presidential Palace of Bongo, Omar
El Haij, President of Gaboon, whom the little gray French airfield
Is keeping in power. He, being from a very small tribe,
Not one of the big ones, can govern equably
And keep the French language and keep calm the Fang,

Relatively speaking. A little bomb is thrown now
And then, into the miles of avenue lizard shit in this
Sulky "Paris by the sea" as someone described it
To me in Paris, so I thought I would go there, come here,
I'm not sorry I did, but it's confusing,
As Nice would be if it were filled with lizards and all
The food you ate and every thought you had
Were brought in from thousands of miles away.

Madame Ounala's
Breasts in the Rapontchombo Hotel
And her beguiling smile
Madame Ounala, who
Is not half-Christian and half-Jew
But half-French and half-Gabonese
Whose beauty makes my knees
Shiver of the Rapontchombo Hotel
Desk area quiver a white seat
Cushion's inviting
Over there somebody sits
On it gives me the key
To my "deposit box" (*dépot*). Her dress, upper
Dress, moves, as it
Comes only with such swelling breasts
To move—I will never get this woman to my bed.
Perhaps I can manage to have her speak to me
In a somewhat less impersonal way.

A man in a big suit comes to see Madame Ounala
And he must be her husband or her lover with a stolen
Happiness right in the middle of his life
While the sea birds are watching, in Gaboon.

The French in Gaboon, in Saint
Louis, deliberately created
A future native ruling class, as
Follows: the French men married
Gabonese women. The half-
French half-Gabonese children
Were to rule and be happy in Gaboon
But things turned out differently.

At the university, Madame Hua informs me,
It's the country kids who write the best French,
The children from the bush. All of one tribe
In the village, they speak the language of the tribe, and French
Is only for school. In Libreville, however,
Of different tribes, they have to speak French
Or not speak at all, and
It is imperfect, of course, full of errors, and not pure.

The *Mvett's* a Gaboon (Fang) oral epic written down in French
And the best of Gaboon literature, if the very central essence of Gaboon
Is what you're after, it's what I'm after, I read the *Mvett*
Which is full of exclamation, singing, and exaggeration.
The hero sets out to destroy all the iron on the earth
Because iron is the cause of all sorrow—discord, war, and death.

The two members of the "Party," wearing Omar Bongo shirts,
Looked neither humorous nor arty, and that they were flirts
Wasn't something anyone would think of. For them, life's just deserts
It seemed were their ongoing roles in the national Party
Enclosing all beauty, strength, ideas, everything that's best.

They abjure the Gabonese people to work hard each day.
"It is as a bird that is fallen from the mother bird's nest
When one of you does not," says Thin Sad Eye, while Big Fat
Guy spears at his notes, and says: "Each day that you don't
Work for Gaboon it is like a wound that you are giving to your country's
     body."

Light flashes on palm trees
Mosquitoes go around
Toward the casino.
His name was not
Omar until his conversion to
Islam a short time ago.

We live only for our vacations, said the *coopérant*, co-operator,
And four of them said they would phone me in Paris and didn't.
They live at the University,
How end, how start! And there are just no books
Says the Prof. de la Littérature Américaine. He reads to his students out
     loud.
Their favorite American writer is Ambrose Bierce.

"You have made me," the man in the beard said, "vibrate!
I once wrote poems. Then I stopped. To hear
Those poems you read," he said, "though, made me vibrate
Again and I wished to write again, which I may, and vibrate."
Trans.: *Tu m'as fait vibrer.* The driveway stone-white in the tropical flat car
     skimmed
To a stop. Heavy the heat fell over the
Ocean, even. A jar could have held all our thoughts.

I sit what seems forever in this room
Thinking over and over, I am in Gaboon.

The ocean out there is dark.
I feel imprisoned, as in a Noah's Ark
Of which I'm the poetical baboon.

France is still here. Here's their
Military airport. They keep
Bongo in power, I hear,
To prevent the accession of the Fang
Who'd stamp their language on the land of Gaboon
And zap the leaders of the other tribes, and bang!
The French might be out the door, the
French language out the door, but this
Is extraordinarily unlikely
Since there is uranium in Gaboon.

Yes there's a kind of nullness
A superficial supernatural dullness
A nothing no-place-ness of which I am acquiring a sense
Here in Gab-, Gab-, Gab-, Gabon, Gaboon.

Better it should happen here than someplace else
Where everything always meant something:
The shock (renewed) and being sick. Nullness.
Ahead lies the Heart of Africa, and the East
Of Africa, island with animals, and the doubloon
Of the Pacific, Madagascar, the "Sea Eater."

The stirring
Dust makes
Lizards jump a
Wave comes
In from above

Rapont
Chombo place the
Forest is two
Kilometers away
Face there isn't any
Stomach-ache Ptchombo
Rap on, rap on
All the day Tchombo
Engong did away
With the bad parts
Of Ndoumou Obame
His too much power until
At the end a
Swallow flew out of his
Nostril and flew by
The People
In the separate
Villages a great bright
Light engulfed the earth and
No one could see.

There are forty-seven languages in Gaboon!
Or forty-eight. And it was here that Dr. Schweitzer worked in his hospital
On steaming-horrid summer days chasing the microbes none too soon
From the fever-battered bodies of the Fang and other tribes of Gaboon.
His hospital is a long way
From Libreville. Saint Louis
Was the capital before that, and before that,
Before the colonists, there was not even any conception
Of a capital of Gaboon.
People fled from the north and the east, arriving in
The bush, to eat animals, manioc, and each other—the
Fang are cannibals—were. There was only forest then. At Lambaréné,
Where, after, the hospital was, the Effik and Bubu were treated,
And later M'Pongwe and Fang.

4. THE CONGO AND ZAIRE. RIVER

Quoi? said Matila
Sudi (*écrivain congolais*),
You mean to say
There are poets
In the contemporary U.S.?
Pour nous vous étes le pays
De Vietnam, *de* Watergate, *et de la bombe hydrogène.*

The moon seems floating, high, tonight
Above the frames of Brazza-
Ville in which I arrive after a flight
Through the bedtime air over half of Africa.

Henri says
She came to his room
Ambassador of the Ambassador
All the French stay
Put up lamp posts, little enough
Says Jean Jacques
(Embassy driver)
For what they've done
The Chinese on the other hand
Build hospitals
("With those people we get along well")
And live simply
Not in expensive houses.

I thought, Venereal disease, bankrupt,
Father, mother, stymie, stump,
Stunned. This is where the Russians eat
Imperial Café. At night they sleep at the Cosmos.

Take me round Congo
Three hours all day. Goat side
And head. *Merci.* Why Henri
To the white-coated consular eventuality deeply thinkingly costlily friendlily
    frostily (by this time
The pamphlets start arriving, F.A.H. enraged, red
Face from auto emerging) said Zaira Moosa be-a
Freedom offa Congo. Oltremong
Ze hull world eez een trap. So Unmbala Lavinia Black stopped
Shortly front his hotel door. Now, his head's
On around actually, winking and winked at, somewhere else.

More my village sleeping onward
Into the bush it goes. These fragments
On dead rocks, stone. Animals are chased from here
To make the city. Lilies come floating down. Big river.
Big Congo rushing and going and coming—
Said Michel, I'd make ze treep just for that!

Yes, hope
Springs always in our souls
As we cross the Congo
In search of girls.

Bastards! he said. Stupid
Sons of bitches! Jesus!
These fucking people! Christ!
I said,
How did you happen to get
In the diplomatic service?
He said For Christ's sake

Look at those cocksuckers
Standing in the middle of the road
Fuck! Squeal! go the brakes
Meanwhile Henri
Is photographed
For the Brazzaville *Express*
Standing in his white suit with his hand
On Kronemann's *Legal Briefs and Excise*
"When there is no justice in the Congo,"
Says Henri, "there is no justice
For any man or any woman anywhere!"
Shit-heads! said Deak
Of the Embassy. I asked
Why did you
Choose the diplomatic service, anyway?
Henri escaped
The Authorities. The
Black woman stayed in his bed.

I am perhaps foolish
To stand here just looking
And smiling
And saying Bon jour.

All the same in the middle of life
Some white houses in Brazza
Ah, we were all beautiful
Once she said
And cut them and
Gave them to me in my hand
By William Carlos Williams
Look at the view!
Sturdily through the garbage I seek the view.

Jean-Jacques said, Here are the boats.
One woman out in her pirogue
All alone. Later in the day
There are poets to talk to.
My kiss to you (in a letter—"Dear Z.")
Was the main part
Of this three-to-five-part day
I hear Jean-Jacques honking outside
The black and white of bees
N'Zambo's wife, the Congo, confusion extreme
She keeps
Walking down a "street," until—bush!

Funghi, growing under the bridge
Eating the very small orange (tangerine?)
And spitting out the seeds. A bird, in its nightgown,
Goes spinning by. I've got to get out of this hotel.
Whole days stretch in seconds and then into minutes.
I do come out, and then—like water!
Smile of someone—I don't have to eat or drink!

And so are oranges, amnesty-like sweet;
Oysters are absent. And
There is no flirting in the Congo! Deak says,
I noticed that—
These goddamned cocksuckers have nothing!
Oooof! Can you imagine balling one of their women?
I imagined, I balled, I paid the rent.
I am the African, I suffragette, iron hair.

A lack of plan. A plan. Chinese men over there,
Governors of the world—"Governors of Paradise,"

"Governors perhaps of nothing, not
Even of their own souls." When I get up next morning and am advised
About which way to walk
I see the sun, silver-white.

I'd better get out of here—shore
I'll put some wings on—flamingo
I don't want to die—by the river
This way to the television station—come on
You're due there at five o'clock—the apples of Tikastra.

Sur les trottoirs de Brazza
Pays where the Com-
Munist government, like all governments, gets fat
But opens up new territory to the Chinese
Who are building the hospitals, I think
Of that (which is not much), while Jean-Jacques
Goes to get something to eat.

"Some, some, some time!" the birds seem to be singing
While there is a tremendous amount of dirt as we pull up.

O television program celebrating the fortieth birthday of *Pravda* (in
     Brazzaville)
Celebrating it as an organ of freedom, how much the dusty streets
Around the azalea bushes reminded him of Norman, Oklahoma,
And how little she thought of anything in the huge dumb station
That was the building inside which was the program that he was on.
First they read the letters—then this celebration of *Pravda*.
D. H. says, "How did it go?" "It went splendid," I cockneyed,
Hearkening back against lamp posts to frail the dust
Cameos against frock-born ceintures Africa seemed heading for my toe.

It was an absolute waste of time, I added,
While George Bernard Shaw went on being dead, and Wallace Stevens,
    and the author of *Hernani*
In Brazzaville *"la nuit."*

I've got to get out of here! I sat
In a big white chair
In the lobby of the Méridien Hôtel.
The next day
I got out of there
Or one day after that
Of l'Hôtel Méridien.

However, getting out of the Congo is not easy.
You need a pass and transportation and also
"Fucking Bastards" comes along, cursing the natives
But buying me my ticket, finally, so I can get on the boat,
Which is taking me to the "Devil's Disneyland," Kinshasa—the Congo
Becoming very, very wide just here.

The wide Congo
Rushing
Trying to get on the boat
The men crippled by polio
In wheelchairs pushing
They get to carry duty-free
Merchandise to
Brazzaville from Kinshasa!
A gift of the Congo's government
To lifelong victims of this disease.

N'Zambo is his name
He hails from the village of M'Gambutenmhumo

He works for the American Embassy
His wife has rigid wires in her hair.

What a huge river
The Congo is!
But if it were named
"The Wink"—
The Congo, or "The Wink,"
Pushing endlessly down toward the Atlantic.

At the dock, boys,
Men, women, old
Men, old women, even,
Fighting to get at something, or someone,
With the city of Kinshasa behind them,
Ten or fifteen times a day.

Hoongam! says N'Zambo and he takes my briefcase
And leaves it on a shelf where Customs won't throw it away.

In Kinshasa the head
Of the driver. In the village the abdomen and the legs.
In the dog, bark.

The Zairean poets, in Kinshasa, were very good-natured and smart.
Romance seemed to play a relatively small role, I thought, in their art.
To get a book published in Kinshasa, you have to
Publish it privately or have a Catholic or Protestant mission house do
It, but you may have trouble if it is violent, sexy, or if you are a Jew,
The latter not being the case with most poets of Zaire
Who tend to mix Victor Hugo

And African drum-repetition types of sounds and to
Write works that sometimes seem to me aesthetically unclear.

In Kin-
Shasa at the
Cultural at-
Taché's place
I
Said to Su-
Maili of
Zaire: Where
Are your
Older writers? Ha!
He said,
Tomorrow
You are going
To see them
And I did
One (the young-
Est of them)
Was only
Forty-five years
Old. But why are they the old ones? Why
Are they the old ones? Because
Of publishing before *l'Indépendance*.
They are, he said, *les Vieux!*

With a big country around him
And a lot of other writers around him
A life behind him
And a life ahead of him
Odd to talk to, as if we were going slantways
Or sideways
But I like Sumaili of Zaire

Though neither of us may know (ever)
In fact, what our real "subject" is.

If I set out in my pirogue
And you in yours, we're quite the vogue
Floating on the river, yet we notice
Very, very, very little lettuce
Is being grown on either shore
And there's no magic anymore,
At least none that we know of, on the river,
Which doesn't change the strange way we feel, either,
At daybreak, when a gaggle of flamingo
Starts twisting us to shore.

N'Zambo now comes down to check
If one's to get one's baggage back. Not.

With a big packet of zaires (the paper money
Of Zaire, which is worthless
Outside of Zaire) you can pay
For your room for one night.
I take off the rubber band
And look out the window
At the dazzling white cars—mostly Renaults.

It is regrettable
Announces the Kinshasa *Soleil*
That a letter
Mailed from Kinshasa
May not be delivered
For up to four weeks
Or four months
Or a year

To someone who is
Living just kilometers away
(In the bush) and so
This newspaper
Warmed by the morning sun
If mailed, may never get to
A reader in Oon-ga-bu-Dun
Before it is uninterestingly out-of-date.

At the Ambassador's house, the flowers are sitting
In glasses on a table. Tonight he is not the host
But some young woman who is crazy about going into the bush
On a small airplane, landing, and settling local disturbances
That stem from the chaotic ungovernability
Of Zaire, made up of so many tribes, with multifold languages and
Three times as many wives (for each man) and they come down
Over the mountains and
Slaughter each other. "I want to do as much of this as I can
While I'm still young—before I'm thirty-five!"

This is—I forget the name. The
Thing the people eat all the time. Without much food value. Cassava
    (manioc).

You bake there—and never did you fill me with desire
Except when you were young, very young—
Fifteen? sixteen?—and
Your breasts! which that day I hold in my hands, then
Marriage, and a mysteriously useful son.

To fundamental questions
Africa me brought. That's what they all like about it. The excitement
And the illusion of living at the beginning of thought.

Even old Rep told me about it. While I napped
He went out riding on his bicycle, into thought!

Now it is time to go
But I can't mark
The place exactly where a chief took down
A mango from a tree and gave extremely
Small boy deadly smiles to me
To other kinds of look.
That one is all.

A smokiness is rising from the fire flakes
Old woman crouching there a hand shakes
As I go by. *"Veloum!"*

You can tell which house is the chief's said Will
There is the chief knocking down a mango from his tree
Before becoming Protestant he wore the antelope mask
To the puberty ceremonies, a screaming and a thumping hid the ground.

The elephants came
They were easily overpowered
The dogs came
And barked. The more fertile parts of the ground area flowered.
It was dark. Zaire
Means River. Mobutu
Is King. This means nothing
To the grass. But to the people who pass
This way, it means something. Hip bone

Thigh bone and chest bone, it may come to pass,
Pass into subservience under a moon
That shines equally on Paris and on Gaboon.
The hill wears the mask of a traitor. Will
Drives around and then up and down this hill.

Being here
Gave him a sense of his "destiny," I think,
In a way that
Being in Chicago would not—being
In these dried places, with no place ever to go,
To arrive at, to drive to.

The air
Is faded
Has faded
Is fading
Away
From the river
You see
Dissociated houses
Also very rich Belgian rush
Residences but not
As from the other side (Brazza)
Do you have the Congo right there
To walk up to
And the woman in the boat and the grass.

"They appeared on the scene immediately.
I was handcuffed and knocked about.
They carried me away;
I was not even allowed to walk.
From the prison to the truck

They tossed me about like a stick of wood.
I was taken to the airfield
And immediately thrown into an airplane.
They twisted my neck.
I was badly mistreated.
I arrived in Elizabethville
And came out of the airplane
Like a common bandit—"

Independence brought a lot of death with it.
It brought Lumumba with it and threw him away.

"There are no more tribes in the Congo
There are no more Bakongos or Bangalas
There are no more Wagenias
We have only one free people—"
Tshombe, on the other hand,
Refused, even, to let Lumumba's remains
Be sent to his family.

The insects!
The insects of the Congo and of Zaire
Some known, some still being studied, some
Probably still unknown, are terrifying—
Landing, biting, and leaving, like a traveling death zone.

I cannot deem the rough of this hotel!
The speaking into a welled tube at night.
The grouch of linen. *Movimento di* windows. Outerness
Wearing masks
The mask of a maiden with a pointy chin
And narrowed but widening eyes, a thin
Fragile smile. The elevator

Takes me up instead of down! *Il faut
Partir!* Valery Larbaud's *Journal
de A. O. Barnabooth*, and, as well,
Henri Michaux's *Ecuador*,
I fling into my bag.

N'Zambo says, I don't carry baggage.
His wife carries the baggage.
I do not carry the baggage. I am no and have no wife.
And I have a bad back. Into the
Cool air, in an orange cotton dress, goes N'Zambo's wife
With one suitcase under her arm
And another in her other hand.

Everybody will read these
Verses in Zaire. Everybody will talk about
The statements they hold dear. But
What about Bird Africa? what about Luck Africa?
Angle Africa? Eat Africa? and Sunk Africa?

N'Zambo has arrived at the airport,
The airport of *bella* Kinshasa. Here, as the night heaves
And coughs gropingly, fifty-five persons
Are fighting at the same place
To get tickets at a hornets'-nest-like window.

Here, you wait here, says N'Zambo. His wife
Waits here. And I wait here. Jillian
Is standing in the middle of the vast
Airport hall.

Burundi, Upper Volta, Côte d'Ivoire, and Nigeria
Are places you can't go to from here
Because of political conditions, explains N'Zembi.
However, here, look at this ticket. Your
Plane should be coming in anytime now—in three or four hours.
To the balcony (airport terrace) we rise
Shined on by the warm night eyes
Of Zairian stars. Jillian has her own "security group,"
A man from the Peace Corps to help her get on the plane.

The Colonials came
With disorientation
With exploitation
With aggression
With contempt
With no caring
With thinking
They were the people
They were the earth
They were the men
And theirs was the space
And the time

And, often, the Africans let them
Drooping in the sun
Not knowing what
They were up to

And by Colonial standards
The Africans were terrible
By African standards
The Europeans, as magic, existed.

But the Blacks weren't part of a magic world
For the oil-spattered-pants-scattered Belgians,
Germans, French (and English). They were "gooks,"
They were part of a White nightmare, they could be put to use.

Meanwhile these Europeans
Educated some Africans
Built up cities
Brought them a language
And a universal religion—
No more thunder in the cheekbones
No more crocodile knees.

Proffering, too,
A cash-crop economy
They fucked-up the old village-
Self-sufficiency economy, ploughed
Young men into the cities
And, finally, granted Independence

After the other life was almost gone—
The tribe, three wives, old man,
Manioc, dancing in the straw, saying
Gandara saloum to make the crops grow—
Almost, but not completely—

Civil courts still hand down convictions
For witchcraft. Leaders do monstrous
Things, unable to rule if they're not devils.
Christianity affects the lives, as
Do politics, and the city, but it is
Hard to tell where anything really is
Or where it is going.

One thing Africa has, it's plenty
Of that kind of thing! is help,

Extremely interested help from every Left and Right party
Of the European, Asian, and American world,
Each of them wanting its minerals, its land, and its support,
Its "voice" in UN assemblies
Before the final war—
Those four over there, in blue
Suits, heading for the Cosmos—*ce sont les russes!*

Nel servizio diplomatico
Esiste una categoria
Chiamata "hardship." You get extra dollars
Hundreds of thousands of additional zaires
For living and working in Kinshasa
Or other Zairian cities or its bush.

"What you get is the naked, raw thing in Africa—
Life without sheets, or blankets. You see it in the market
In Kinshasa, where everything is cheap.
People are lying around and walking around. They are
Squatting and begging around. (We sleep in the street.
Under us, the street sleeps.) In the village each family has a hut.
This city is their one big hut. And the city is the scene
Of behavior of the kind you find in village and hut." Jillian comes to my
    hotel
Because she doesn't have any place to stay. She
Opens the window and won't close
The shutters. A hot, wet
Heat shine comes in. What
Happened to her Black boyfriend? "He was at the University,"
She says, "and, well, Mobutu closed it down
And sent all the students back to their villages—he is
Hundreds of miles in the bush now, no way to come back
To Kinshasa, and to me. . . . Well,
The part I really like, I lived

344

On this courtyard, it was actually a sort of market,
Everybody always talking,
And always lying around—African, really African," she said.

We didn't bring our wives because they weren't invited,
Confided N'Jombe. And, besides, we poets don't
Marry literary girls. Those girls, they are other
Ones, who like the writings. We prefer
A woman who takes care of the home, at least those
Are the ones we have married—not the literary
Roses who come serving me the dangerous prose of
Food and drink at the Zairian Club des
Écrivains, girls, not married, and in the
City, and doing all right—calm, like
Everyone else, in an ambiance, all the same, of physical excitement.

5. KENYA. SAVANNA

In the great, bracing air of Kenya
The lion runs. Seeing a lion
And two lionesses together,
The Italian woman said,
"*È il leone,*
La sua moglie, e la sua madre"—
Id est, the wife's mother,
A sort of chaperone
To the lion and to his wife.

The lion's muscles
Are amazing. The air
Is filled with lions' grace.
Viewed without any
Human component around,
The lion is sensational
Simply of and in himself.

Luciano on the other hand,
Returned from a "Montale Conference,"
The first one, celebrating
The first anniversary of Montale's death,
Says he is "exhausted,"
Says it in Italian
And turning, neither
Like a lion nor a roebuck
Nor any other of the lion's prey,
Those ones who are always
On tiptoe sniffing for the lion,
Into the elevator goes, in America, up to his apartment.

Power in the forefoot and power in the back
The sleek musculature doubling up all over,
Or seeming to, before leaping to attack—
I spent ten dollars on a book
That would have cost two dollars anyplace else
Just to have something to read—anything—
About the lions. A lion is sleeping.
Another lion, a lioness, a "girl," is almost sleeping at his side.

Being depressed is middle class
Said Cornelia's mother
But this is not enough.
The lion is not depressed, it's true,
But neither does he have a social class.
The lion is not upper class
He is dirty
He lets things fall all over him
He is uncouth
He lies around with the lioness asleep all day.

Yes, you left me to run around
Without you and by myself.
At least you didn't leave me out there
On the savanna, subject to the appetites of the lions!

The lion stands up
With a great deal of assurance.
He is not a romantic sort.
The lioness is there and he is there.
Together, they form smaller lion animals.
These run, jump, play, and attack.
Any one of them could give me, if I saw him
Alone, a heart attack.

The lion is admirable
In one way
But in another
He just fills up his stomach
And then sleeps
Until he's hungry again
Then does the same.
Doing this, he
Is powerful.
People
Who live this way
Become fat—and uninteresting.
The lion, however, knows
When he is hungry.
When he is old
It is hard for him to hunt.
The lion becomes mangy
And weak.
Sometimes, just for a second,
His old grandeur shows through—
He evokes the fear of death
In some young giraffe, or antelope,
Or wildebeeste, at the close of day.

The Anglo-Saxon poet characteristically
Presents himself as a good lover, wrote Arthur Waley;
The Chinese poet, as a good friend. The African poet
Often writes poems to his mother (sometimes the mother is Africa).
He presents himself not as a son
Who is there, to work, and to help to keep away the lions,
But as a son who, gone far away, still thinks with passion
Of the warmth and other attractions of his first home.

Is the lion awake? What
Roaring Americans
At the windows of my motel! No,
It's not the Americans.
It's not a lion either. It's
Some elephants
Making a ferocious racket breaking all
The limbs (both live and dead branches) from the trees.

In the Maasai village,
Flies, attacking
Nose, mouth, eyes
You can hardly see
Much less breathe
The Maasai's air.

Maasai drink
Steers' blood from a leather-and-bone vessel,
A kind of long, thin cup that is being held out to me
Next to a thousands-of-flies-thick hut
In their cattle-compound home.

The young woman pilot (English)
Says, when I ask about Maasai
Religion (we are passing
Over "agglomerations of their huts"),
"They don't have any!" Amazing!
"They're simply savages!" And on she flies.
Later she confides to me,
"This place was beautiful once,
Before Independence!" The Maasai, meanwhile,

Do nothing that's not determined by religion.
If you eat a wild animal, the lions will kill your cows.

I read, in
An essay by Kenyatta,
About the Gikuyu—
They would apparently look right through you
If you talked about being sonless in that tribe.
You have to have a son, for, without one,
You never can come back, after death,
To what is best in life: being alive,
Or knowing you are, or feeling you are alive
In the warmth and in the bosom of the clan.

Lighting fires for you
A son!
A son's son, a son's son's son—
He brings you back in.

Twins have to be killed.
This is wasteful
And cruel, but of
Each two one is a demon
And both must be killed.

I feel so far away from this,
As far away as I do from the life of the zebra—
I feel far from Luciano, too, and the Montale Conference,
From the Zion of Ancient Rome, and from the village under the ground of
        the ancestors.

However, this idea of ancestors
Is quite prevalent.
Anyone who dies, or whom you kill,
Immediately becomes an ancestor.

When a wife becomes a mother
Her husband takes another wife
To make love to him and work for him. The other
Gives all her time to the child.

Polygamy, a crime
In many countries, thought of
As a good time in others,
Is a practical matter here—

No lost or unfortunate women
In the village. No prostitutes.
Your brother dies, you marry your brother's wife.
Everyone is taken care of, and connected
To each other, and to the ancestors
In the village under the ground.

The stones
Didn't move
When the birds
Flew so fast
You would think
It would move
Even the stones
Suddenly leaving
Red, violet
And almost totally
Not plain.

The elephant lifts
The big sheet
Of plastic stuck to his trunk
And tries smashing it
Against the ground. He
Stamps it with his left foot,
Raises it and stamps on it again
And again, slowly, for a long time
On the hot, gray-green savanna.

The drive empty for two hours!
We had to get up at
Five and a quarter hours
To see Kilimanjaro
Covered by mist
And now no animals
A zebra gives two nickels a
Lion eighteen the rhi-
Noceros is the jackpot!
Then we see the rhino
Mother and her child
Bathing (?) (eating? drinking?)
In a little pool
One-fifth cool kilometer in the distance
She is dangerous says N'Gambo
Think, then some
Time later say I, Let's
Get out of here! The Kil-
Imanjaro now has
The sun. Well,
It's a great sight, I suppose
(A bit boxed after the rhinoceros),
Seeing the snow
Way up high, when
It's so infernally hot down here.

The vultures and the jackals
Approach the carcass
In a kind of ecstasy (mixed
With fear) of eating and
Approaching and backing up and eating and
Approaching and getting and backing,
Or flying, a little bit, up, and
Eating and then coming back down.

The hippopotamuses don't like the climate,
Everyone said.
And that's why they spend all day in the river.
I thought this was stupid and bound to be wrong
But apparently it isn't. Either the climate
Of East Africa changed, or they migrated. Probably
They migrated. But why did they come?
What ghastly necessity obliged hippos
To run in great masses, against their
Common interests, away from a climate they
Loved, to the scaling, baking dryness of a horrible (for them)
Area and then resign themselves
(Intelligently?) to rivers? Who was the hippo who led them
Away from the danger? And what leader found them the rivers?
Or were they led by many? Did some, not finding rivers, die?
At night they go up on the banks and feed on the grass.

In the hotel there are civilization conditions.
A hundred yards outside it, nothing obeys anyone.

As attractive as a wild condition is, I just don't have the teeth
Or the paws with claws or the power in my back and legs to do it.

I didn't even when I was young. I'd have lasted,
Perhaps, five or six minutes—
If I were lucky a few days, a few
Hours. Impossible!

Of course I wouldn't have been surrounded
By (near me) two hundred or so
Members of my tribe (species), each one
Alert, on the tip of his toes, his tail
(Or her tail) swishing, head, even when browsing,
Turned slightly aside
To sniff out, or spot, the presence of a lion,
The burny, unmistakable smell, some top flicker of the grass.

I thought so, looking at the zebras
For a while.
Zebras are young and strong
And race, with style.
They are styled in black and white, zebras.
Their ambition is not to be eaten
By the lion or the cheetah.
As they move about, you see them gazing to the side
And ahead and back, as they lawn-mow and,
Toward evening, seem to glow, and they grow
And multiply in the wild savanna.

"The hippopotamuses
Are all Communists,"
I wrote when I got to bed,
Extremely tired, exhausted,
Thinking of
The way they looked at me
With suspicion, perhaps

Even a glint of hostility
Just eyes and nose above the stream.

The tsetse flies
Are unsung heroes of Africa.
Over enormous areas
They dominate everything.
Elephants, Maasai, lions, flamingos, everyone, everything
Runs away from them. They carry
Sleeping sickness surprise.

I am glad I wasn't turned into an ancestor,
While strolling aimlessly around on the Serengeti,
By the bite of a tsetse fly.

The shots! the shots! are nothing
Compared to one tiny tswish of a tsetse fly.

With a subtle change of the light—it's not so subtle!
It is night on the savanna, and those animals are in trouble
That the lion hunts.
Then dawn comes, with a slighting wave
Of a hand of wisp of smoke and cloud, the bones stay
There but the flesh is gone, to be part
Of other flesh. The lion goes lightsome now
Whether waking or sleeping, thanks to his eating.

The Rift is a huge dominatingness of non-presence
Dividing, which will cut you one half
Of Kenya and make you another. It is a rift
Dividing Maasai from other Maasai. It makes
A difference in the climate. Geology looks at it

With scholarly and mercenary eye. The dawn goes to sleep in it.
Here, you can tell what Africa was like
Hundreds of thousands of years ago, geologically.

Now rain blow, storm lines, Rift-caused, then showering
Sunlight past accolades of drift.

Returned from the Maasai Mara
The lions and the savanna, and back
From Amboseli, as well,
Kilimanjaro and its rhinoceros
And last night
In Nairobi with its guns
In the hands of soldiers
I sit at the hotel (Serena) and drink coffee
At the yellow wedge of this table by
The purple wedge of this pool, while a hedge
Of tourists passing through
Are dividing themselves up into a car.

At Maasai Mara
There were buffalo first, then
A jackal, a carcass,
And a vulture—then a lion
And then impala, wary of the lion.

Elephant mothers do not decree
The lion to be present chiefly
Because for lions an elephant baby (a calf)
Is a manageable thing to kill and eat.
Not so a big elephant. With big elephants around
Like swinging, wavy, shipwrecked, cargoed scenes
In a friendship series, calf is safe and sound
Protected from the lion in the thwack and whack and bumping of the trees.

One of which (elephants) nearly killed us,
A female, charging for our "bus"
Whereupon Julius vavoomed us fifteen more feet away
Toward some other pious-looking elephants at the bay
Of some serpentine now falling-apart trees. Hey
Julius I said what if she had gotten us, knocked
Over the bus. Oh said he, then we just
Raff as heard as we con. And at our laughter
(Mine, Julius's, that of one French couple, three Japanese
And Margaret of Australia whose camera caused the scene)
The heavy, tusked, wide-eyed symbiotic elephant would back away
Justly terrified. What? Laugh? No,
Julius said, *Raff, rafv* the engine!

Later, the next night,
Margaret is deemed a danger
To the UNESCO conferees
Invisibly (i.e. unknown to me) being
In the Serena for several days.

No—hand on my shoulder—no
Dat—grapefruit juice, with
Ice—No dat
Lady in dis hotel. Where
Go you, sir? And gently are we expunged

Into the Kenyan night. You go
Find dis everyplace Nairobi
Tonight, says the
Taxicab driver
Whose back is becoming visible at the lights.

The animal scene
Is a scene and a set, a
Theatre inside a country. Kenya
Profits from it, lives
By it, but isn't it. Banded men in Nairobi
And standard men in Nairobi and granted women
And an estaminet of money white and green
Set off another, central human scene. And then
In the middle, there is Julius, for
Example, whose grandfather was a hunter, he
(Julius) is a Protestant, with just
One wife, enjoying the benefits
Of *something*—comparatively Kenya
Is "doing all right." La Côte d'Ivoire, says everyone,
Is prosperous as well.

When the Rift came down through Africa
From Egypt to Kenya and Uganda,
It did not fill with water
And become a Congo—there was nothing,
No boat, anything, before airplanes,
That could cross it, but, by that time, everyone
Was used to being on one side
Or the other, and not to crossing over.

Don't go to Mombasa. It
Is *remplie* with German tourists
And they romp the beach. Just a swimming hole
For *Tedeschi*, said the brown-olive-fair Italian
Woman I'd have given anything for of to have had the house
Keys. The lips of her turned bronze as she turned away
And I didn't see the promontory of the bird saints, either,

Or the woman's keys, nor the oily fair rumps of Mombasa
The City by the Sea, Kenya's industrial mermaid domino.

Termites in Kenya
Have big, really tremendous
Houses of their own. Termite control
Would mean destroying both termites and house.

In downtown Nairobi
Modern it is and dark. I take a path
(Turn) onto the Avenue Moi
Formerly Avenue Kenyatta—
One kilometer further
And I'm home—
The Hotel Serena. It is
(Its lot is) littered with cabs.

On the Edge

Sleeping one day beside the Zuyder Zee
Dan was awakened by a noise of honks—
A situation quite unknown to me:
I spent my childhood in a sort of Bronx—
I placed a goldfish bowl upon my knee—
Angelica was packed inside my trunks.
At Harvard I wrote home "I'm coming back!"
And did, and through the country like a crack

The train sped home. Dan took a blossom down
From off the blossoming tree. I slept all night
Then spent the next day walking through the town.
Angelica woke up to Roland, light
And bright and fair. Dan sighed and looked around.
He couldn't see Roberta anywhere.

As in—Crete, near the ditch—old grave spot (gray spot) as
By the Greece's Acropolis's invisible waters—Parthenon—
Agh, what vents!—and you too, monopolistic
Bypath-or-street-ways, little Merkaton
Of old Athens plus light blue shimmers from the cliffs
In other places and I couldn't explain
What I felt at Heraklion, I'm sorry, or with
My nose pressed to the train—everything else stubbing
And stumping. I'd planned—but wanted to know. Reading,
In the day, complaining, stormed, red and blue lights
Until traffic, I think, is right here in the chains
Of what's holding all these chairs, this
Stuff together—up in the air, I think.
Zett calls, and now I have a drink.
Cold is the kitchen sink.

Forms to feel it out
Quietness to bring it in
As someone "felt friendly" Stendhal pushed the door
Egg was inside, time Easter Egg of Monsieur Montelfior

Who made the wind his messenger
Outside, in the penniless air
Of the warm white sidewalk and the street, thinking
Whether I am in the cloth with her or not
Then suddenly to think

Finger in the beehive
Harry says Watch out!
A drove of French novels
Particularity of stone-dead windowpane, without charity
Or trump—esthetico indeed! why, I'll
And so you—one minute—are falling, it is orchids

Paris, C.'s apartment
Claudio on the phone, the receiver
Tucked between his chin and his shoulder

A panther has escaped
From Nankra's Zoo! I lay confidently
Embedded in the light green grass of the Bosco
While A. A. de Celestin smoothed out her thanks
Blouse sleeping softly and mandarinly toward me
No sensations but in commands, you too
Storm and confusion. Roberta? Angling—whom?

She lifts a shoe. Where is the other one?
Jean-Claude came to dinner, etc. Sitting here, it's a café

Summery Sunday, Notre Dame des Champs,
Noël and Joanne come to take us both
Out riding to the forest. You have *gants*,
Being *frileuse* as I am not. We wear coats
Because it's, after all, the winter *temps*
And no one's in the Bois in little boats.
Ecstasis perigrensis. Première acte.
Mutatis mutandis. Life in love lungs locked.

364

The scene is—writing—but remembering the buffering strums
Memories of a de-cupola'd Hôtel de Fleurus
Triggered with leaves sidewalks a fluttering
I say something as red clouds and you said
I remember the name—going forward

Now I want to. Forces! yelled Jim Dine, and
Fairfield Porter, surprised, "Maybe! Let's just go and see."
These extreme persons of the time
And the forward and back—
To café! a cold university

Thanks for your criticism
I am thinking
Feeling my way across the yard
B-Zunk doesn't write me I figure she's
Having a love affair with Arc
Having had not much going but making love to each other
Our relationship soon fell apart

Dan is a hero of a different nature
The Colossus of America, England, and France
He is of an ordinary stature
Remarks someone at a dance
Dan dances with her and then he goes away.

The mountain of roses and the dog. What is that ripple?
Happiness, a street vine, and the nude
Weather forecaster, now dressed and out, it's day
For this monument, as if life
Depended on it, lilac, that scent, so many times!

The water fills with flowers—hibiscus, waterlilies. Ventur-
Ing then when Jan and I got in the boat
My parents objected, Haven't you got to the wrong hot spot
Of water if what you're really going after is adventure?

Adventure of the third kind
Desire driven from the mind
To the Greek statue arm muscle
We floated and then
Five years later it's of a doctoral order
Board walls of a house
And flowers tacked onto it. Hey, shining.
And Bart said You're not a scholar but a jeweler
And Schlumberger said Keep talking—until guns fired.
She hangs the wash on hooks, outside.

"What's the matter, anyway?" I say
To my friend
Toujours plus pessimiste
A quality I find *assez adorable*
I thought if he could just
Now we are racing toward the dust
Quality of a friend with the trace of a suit on it
Blue-brown, a necktie, red, yellow, compromising
Avec ze style of ze time, so Wallace Stevens said
"You should keep the same style," this little guy
Said A. W. jokingly, partly, has done more
For the philosophy of—Jesus! If we had time—The green ledge
Walking sideways on it without
But full of, interest, by being purely
Physical, Leger, at the age of thirty-three, a finite hem
Explaining things to me
As another always interpreted. I don't,
I said snobbishly, like it much, but

Well, you know, and everything
He liked Spring, the sweet spring
Then backing down the water (alley) with a blot
With friendship talked a lot
And was indifferent
However, there he is!

And other Elizabethan literature
I said: It's great!

Oh, it's great
        all right,
                said he
But would you read this? I'm so
Depressed!
        What?
                We—after death
And his passing—but
                also ours

Reading what I was reading, like the girth
Of that building—from the *Four Quartets*
To the *Macchu Picchu* of Neruda, neither
There nor in between was there to answer
The inevitable brio of light
Not surreal, not fragmentary or anything but
A white sidewalk—do you think?

If I had known then, in nineteen-fifty . . .
There was one introductory class at the university
And others at various places and times. The *u* was difficult.
The noses of cars kept dodging on the street
With knowledgeable humans inside them—
Not simply having experiences and growing up
And trying to judge the various stages of joy
And ecstasy and how do I get published? but
Actually participating in the crescent
And crossed edge of Being—I thought.
Sometimes, eating with you, I'd drop my plate
Or glass. You said, They are infinite. However
Just this morning I see the old man, presumably a worker
With shellfish, I don't know!
What I did the chairs were bunched

In each café. "Get out of the way." Ovvero, climb with me, the play *Truck*
Is being presented. So many girls then
Sidewalk hitting with its cement
The fabulous others who gradually fade into myself
Like the Epidaurus Theatre, starring Acts One and Three—
Act Two is your own revolution.

To deal with frost-bites
Into the old earth, on the surface of which all
Societies lived: French bourgeois society
Bon soir, Tante Adélie, ed entra la cugina Karamazov
On the edge
Of the cup,
Of the street,
Of reading Mallarmé
The door opens on the same spaces again.
Bird news was strafing past the window
Full feather time. I opened it and went out
Into the car.

And then last night (198?) the a.m. air was sharp
Outside the bar, Place de la Contrescarpe
And I walked home alone, not wishing to
Get in the car, since Hugues was drunk. I thought
Being alone quite the best thing to do—
And with my small red guidebook's help I brought
Myself to where I lived, *cette jolie rue.*

Our modern—fragmentary—Dan stands up—it's about time—reason
Sunrise—he is going to start
White sleeves
But day puts its finger in his eye
Eyes. The white vagary temple is starting up
Aislewards—
The waves were coming home! against a tree
They wash. Fifteen

Years it lasts, and no end in sight, and no
Beginning. A topic is pink white pink stripes.
Drunk. On gin, lemonade, and fizz
White as the cover of the book and of the pages inside.
Fifteen years, or is it ten or twenty that it lasts. Sexual forces,
Greek logic, Aphrodite, in statue form, born Irish girls, smiling
And removing a blouse, beginning
To snow in here, writing out notes
And flying down the street, noble as far as
Bed could be commanded by what's outside.

Or he was writing, sitting amidst the unpacked trunks
In a state of composition, while the trunks, then, are in a state of
Saturday afternoon position, as at the Mayor's house

What she was then—what a beautiful bloom!
And people sitting round their desk for hour
After hour could only exclaim, "Well, fine, boom, to hell with it,
Let's go to Tahiti, anywhere,
Out of this worm-eaten building!" At last
You wonder about the filtering down of consciousness
Till even the moth, so sensitive to light,
Is stepped on, on the stairs. The band plays
Full out—

Sometimes the feeling was so strong it came out
Sometimes was dancing or "rage" (being mad)
Biting and sleeping and then in the beautiful morn-
Ing, when to be young was very heaven,
The yellows, light on buildings' separate heaven
Of warm apartments, not too warm, now, open
A light-bulb light—
The limping man and the doctor—complements
The drink and the thirsty girl—oxygen

In questo momento scrivevo poesie
Al soggetto di un grande industriale

The subject is not in the world—the subject's
A limitation of the world. Thus, no true subject.
The Hôtel de Fleurus was of the world
Now vanished, literally said Bob
It's turned into a private house, of many apartments
No more the door unopenable from inside
It wasn't a "subject," however. The nature
Of hotels is a subject—whose thigh?

Red bird, white bird, jumping around the house. "When you're not
Inspired, when you feel 'dry' just write anything!" False
Scholarship, false Solomon's Seal
Am I the height of Heaven or is blue the thrust
Of some addlepating ecstasy that's flooding me? Cancel
Your bills, believe in me. Proud to be Representative
Of Frock-White-Flowering Day appeared on doorstep
With Russian Moods and Count Weight. If only someone had told me,
Some intelligent man, said Stendhal,
To write two hours every day, whether
"Inspired" or not, I would have saved ten years of my life.

Sitting in a tiny café I read Mallarmé's *Le Livre*
I don't know whether or not this is something I want
I wasn't happy but I was absorbed and I was curious
I felt on the brink of something,
I kept reading, and in the book there was nothing doing
It may have been all just a laundry list but something was taking place
       in me
Did I have a mistress? Maybe. Had we been to bed? Well, not quite.

Thursday, three in the afternoon. Learning
Dutch. . . . Five minutes
Sandwiches . . . the fury in the hall ninety-nine francs
Don't like Like it Madame
Dantonville return four chemises front

Window alive serenities festive
Remember call BO 6-2279 Magyars
A visit in the sea . . . cruet . . . vast availability . . . five sleds—shirts
And then a tremendous space
Then space   space   space
Following: a list
Of debts?

Tears to remember again
One-fourth or one-sixth part of it

So I went dancing out into those streets
But on knees and on my knees it was the day
Lying catalyzed, a book. I'm not a roof if also if you mean that!

He actually made a mistake said John. It's wrong.
"Gyrene" but we continued. But Mallarmé
Fippery ovoid subject but I didn't pay
Attention. Loaf. Lilac book.

Martin McScrumbold who controlled the sedge
For fifteen companies of marble fusions
Clambered aboard the high financial towers
To make himself the toast of sanctity,
Seeming to be more holy than he was
By manufacturing gimmicks propped galore
Against the definite walls which adversaries
Totalled between themselves and him in vain.
Sunday he smashed the sleep. . . .

Summer on the folding step
And somewhere on the other.
A side step. Sunlight. Perhaps it would phone me
To be so ablution inseparable
Twenty-five years
Before nineteen-eighty. And bright

Flocks of automobiles go past
Green flight
Of centimeters, one, and up and down.
In the morning to look for
Blisters in the sidewalk Egypt of Their Time

The Journal of I forget
Virgil's *Eclogues* how they connect to the life
The show-business falseness is carrying on.
The bed is stored over where the light
Was, with futile and inconsistent flight. O "scatalogue" that gives me
Rushing around from feuding hours of the night
To spirited activation of the doll
Speaking in the morning
Huge halls. Not nearly buffered very long.

An ideal book for me was also that
I wanted to have and give up every subject
And I suspected it would end in about two seconds
So many painters were cracking their plates in the seminary
Of other persons' kindness while a large snowflake,
Faintly and intolerably slowly, falls. Flirting and courting heartbreak.
The Greeks—A brick blockade
Is knocked down. If I'm to be a painter, help me with your tears!
He said. Then I sat down.
Is it this—a historical
Meaning—out of your control
I crossed the wave
Of pink cement
Dawn! and study not far away!
With Eleanor, containing the football
Its footfalls, its stories of cinema'd scorn.

Bear—
Alone I think
It's

A laundry list
But still happy

Here are a few phone numbers, too

Ulla said Don't came to visit me in Sveden
Badly I threw myself as if from out of a
Bucket onto the train. Hallo good-bye said she
My boyfriend is here. I will not see you. But her flat face
In Paris, with the light hair in her eyes, her capacious
Be-loving-me sexitude, hunh, what's happened
To that? The Stockholm railway station loomed
With mounds of produce in a bag
Of each it held

Writing
Saving ten years

A blouse (blue)
Came in the entryway, drama
To perception
Instantaneously and in light
Of the moving seconds
I'm sitting and talking
Or else, exhausted, glad and sorry
Dog straining forward
Hating the seemingly automatic activity
Either language or either brain does on its their own
Wrong with so much fucking literature
French boredom bong
But as I romp around
Blonde bang bomb
Scowling
Event, climatic, and strong
How if we all came over
Or you come to my place—

Why not throw this, said Jim,
Into the fulminating fireplace? Giggled, savagely aft
While maturity stole a scarf and took her place
Beside Janice who was dreaming of a plan
For a whole season. Stanley: We displace
So many phantoms. Jean: Garage.

The ecstatic muddle does, didn't it, take place
February seventeenth nineteen-fifty Samothrace Tuesday immense

Dan walks around. He waves
His hands above his head.
Upon his tombstone it shall be engraved
He did what no one else could do instead.
He was a morning slasher. He engraved,
Summarily, upon a day of red,
The melancholy taxi of a kiss
Upon a sidewalk edge, for emphasis.

We walk out
And at a desk
On a bridge
Popular leafy upstairs
A form oh to go
Pink and white
Rose "oceanness"

I'm sympathetic to animals and all that, said.
Rescuing the fly flew into
Above water splat. Sit looking at
Specific gravity on its wings.

Crossing my sleeves with hers
Nineteen-fifty
Prepare
The quilts, mattress, bed-covers

Circa nineteen-fifty-four
Larry says Why don't you stay there
Another bluish bit
Of sidewalk and her hair
Human feather

Window, diamonds flashing
A. hard at work
Extemporaneous fingers
American Claw is reading about Van Gock (Go)
Pages of Keats (*Endymion*) This side of the cluck
Is belted with sunshine, G. Entwery
Also is recommending movie junk
And class ("I don't know why de Mourneville
Doesn't get off his ass and make more films. . . .")
All the witty things we know are wasting
That used to be the center of the world.

Harry walks with me through the show of roses.
We talk about Maxine. Elizabeth
Is dancy at my side, as she supposes
I like her. I am somewhat out of breath.
With Jean I walk along and the place closes.
We dance beside the Marne. I love my desk.
As a drowning man to a spar I hold on to my desk (F. Kafka)
Hydrangeas bloom, seen from beyond the desk (Flutsworth)

And friends call Janice sits on the bed Frank calls
The momentary euphoria of understanding
Dan, much preoccupied, steps to the landing
Doesn't free me from these feelings after all
After all she was like a bird, flown off
Seems more than I could do when I mistook
Shadowing for boxing, evening for no lights in the hall
But now a fine mercurochrome like the dog's complacent ball
Into these fire vicinities. Frank said it was like it al-

Ways was, except that we were broaching entire infinities
This time, and, if I drink any more coffee I'm going to ride
Into the sky! Janice at nine in the city, cold are celebrities.
The fire plugs are cold. While they are alive
The whistle is metal, was not foot—needing—awfully—years before.

Avenue du Maine, with that wall with the posters on it
Everywhere saying it's forbidden to have posters on it,
Where I lived in the time I was a drink student
And a clink student of all flourishing Proust-things and I went out
Into the fulminating gravel of that damp sleep. That never came out
How civilized you are! we are! I was! It is, cow in and then out.
I went "to bed" with the two Swedish girls, Ana and Svenita, I don't
        remember,
In fact, their names—
You have frightened me into these staminas
Where the different associations they come running!
The bloom of helio-plaster, "medicine of the sun,"
Will absolutely cure your solar system, clean it out
So there'll be summer everywhere and always. Huh?
I loved the following women: BLANK
Out of discretion—But . . .

Alleyed-to-interview maze. I pleaded
Guilty, saying, I'm glad you're that,
Big, thin, notable, heart-
Shaped, sweet, irregular,
Smiling, quiet, tanned,
Around. Whereupon a ticket machine goes thumping
"Air raid! O climbing ceilings!
Birds that didn't add to visiting things!"

Paris
        And nineteen-fifty-two
    Fresh air

Clean warm spring morning
And I am in love with you
            Answers!
There were more answers than there were questions
Almost—questions I had to make up—

What is a "stair person"?
Do you know what a "bid minor" means?
Do scows have ears?
How many charge accounts can fit into a building?
And so, in love with you,
I walk the streets
Pretty littered asphalt, hut to roots,
Walking, talking

One shoe
Is that October or is that March
Summery day
God says, "Don't take that drink!"
What portion is two? what sidewalk?

Accidentally
Running into her. The wave
(One second). Hello. Admired Miranda!
O wild West Wind, thou breath of Autumn's
Being! Getting into Harvard (half a minute).
The log head and the pavement, stone hotel.
Dear K., I am
Leaving (three times). Why, though?

Vanishing into the Nile this comes only once

Dan was waking up,
Finding the world, some fluff from blossoms landing on him
A short breeze ruffling his
Clothes, summering sleeves, a little sun

Greatening in the white to be a big one
And that fresh air so invigorating
That he jumped up
Feeling where he wanted to go
He turns, then, sees

Thousands—need for food—all the critics say
Almost all—leaning on a railing
And looking out far—nails in the shoes—riverbank
And the motory smell
A white horse comes up
In a non-animal civilization—
The established ruins (products of four hundred years)
While the dream of the day
Is in the arms, later
Darling wronged
Sweetheart
I bray
Like a donkey (five seconds)
And the music is then of laughs (one
Second *et demie*). K. K. finds a cat and feeds it
And its kittens (seven days)
This moment and then coming
Completely up-to-date (almost), like a bat,
Seeing a cloud and thinking "It's Cleopatra!" Two seconds.
Knowing she'll take off her clothes (instantaneous).
Realizing I can't stay in the apartment
Cold, breezy nights
A collaboration (eight years, though
For the time spent working
Actually about two hours). Percentage of days
Counting the days (one,
Approximately). Times I had to work
Instead of doing what I thought
I wanted to do, some. But times I did work

And didn't do what my "life-boast," "life-bomb," or
"Shoulders-o'-stone" wanted done—
Flowers in every window of the street
Music playing behind. Friends come around. That's an excuse
(One dog). And the times, the times
Asleep, trying to sleep, making love, drunk

I notice the sunrise—it's quite something, the day!
My desire—Eleven a.m. too
And five-thirty, just before dark

Mathilda Roberts bumped against a window
Seeing a sheep, but Dan came through the day
Walking, his white coat hanging over his arm,
Left arm, and what could she (La Roberts) say
"I have been falling asleep," he said,
"In rocky different places. Beside a peak in Gstaad
Once, and by the Ceremonial Summer Beak in Tchad
As well as of course beside the well-tamed
Sea of Zuyder
Jusqu'au plus soif. The wind is very strong!"

Another day guilt is all I'm feeling
The gloves go on and off in simple whiteness
Weather is moving, and personality
Which seems just over the horizon, Greek, and homeless
I walked around
To the back of the car—sunflowers—an April evening
Living (awhile) but not living very long. Totals
Of time spent merely in the society
Of other people without improving anything
Learning anything or really
Doing anything (enormous). Time
Music was of the essence (unknown).

A leg moves
To another section of the bed
I am up
Newsily bemused and musing
On what has just happened instead
Of carrying on with it. Proust wrote the book and he was dead
On the bed table, evidence! that suddenly they become
Business men and business women
As the delicate white gloves of the sun
(So *dixit* Svana)
I got to get up. The gun
Of a new day is pounding got to get
On my jacket's got to get
New translating job jobs at the embassy go to
Get ready for bar tonight, get
Going, up—everything

Bathing and raving—
Classic symphony, outdoor beers. Blue awning. Capes. Stone. The flashing
    substance
Of sleeves and neck and collar and the subtle
Shade of pink in cheek and slight resistance
And then surrender! Lipstick in the puddle
At the umbrella'd table close to Customs!
I—I—you—skirt—it's my—flags—in battle—
Your—by—sleeves—listen—I'm—wait—sperm—ova—
Interest—bud—easy—luck—Vita Nuova—

Never again that Sunday in the Peugeot
Spinning to Fontainebleau! I take a hairpin
And bend it sharply till it is a bow
For a minute it seemed to be there
Small white flag
Of hard dress unburdened
As the poets say
By "time" whose neck

A sheep, buttons
Of a capacious (big, roomy)
Wedge, and then

Used at breakfast to sashay me until
Sitting, somewhat sprawled, in a chair
Reading Lautréamont. Oh for God's sake
Let's group out of here. Lieutenant,
Cross over the glass porcelain men!
Wake up said Janice dear. I was walking
In nineteen-seventy-two, when suddenly
E. L. was nineteen years old, A. R. was twenty-three
And I was almost fifty, *cinquante ans*—

Now it is later I have just come back
From Africa, to which for the excitement
I went, and Noël still is on his track
Of pneumonology. His wedding statement
However's changed, and Z. is gone, a fact
Suggesting their first choice as not the right one.
Both middle-aged and changed by that fantastic
Chimie du temps in almost every aspect

Split seconds of a chair in a café
Time the note on a glass window
Says they are coming Change
To sarabande attire, ice of the Sixties
When to be Decemberish was the soul of claim
To interest and enticement of the muse of flame,
Forties of the gnarled How-to, Fifties of consentment
To split and tower and ropes weather, islands of the
Damned insane Eighties hues cupped in flame
And no car because the secret to get out of, caught in history's game
Scattered about like furniture, too wise to be the main
Movers of things, already too dead?

Reading "Yellow violet"

Appointment with nnn hayerdresser, she says. We are to meet (met)
Later, I don't like to eavesdrop. Soap.

What pompous! what ruckus! and what creates!
The whole women of Proust! the pavanes and the flowing carriages!
The doctors on horseback, their patients behind them in stalls
In Middle Ages weeping, "Cure us, or give us our money back!"
I run and put on my ducking—
Why am I wearing ducking to this place? Whose mirror is that above the
    piano?
It is Ferdinand de Lesseps' or Fernand Léger's! *Qu'en sais-je?* I may not
    have Stendhal's talent, after all,
To get down what actually took place.

The adornments of these clavicles, says Rodeson
(Panoscopic visions in a multifactored box)
Presuppose an Aegean civilization. You're right! What? I love! (Mayakovsky)

Do you suppose? he said. Oh, I don't know, I—
Well, that's a thought! I'd better use the tele-
Phone! The sails seemed white forever.
It clatters down the stairs. You have a fever
But stand and walk around.

Elizabeth is glad—it isn't raining
Or snowing, but the sun's out. She has just
Become nineteen. She notices
A plan, coming off the wall. That's a MAP,
Old Chinese restaurant, with a small
Waist, back-breaking task,
While sunshine rolls around

Take me with you. You don't love me. Scowl
Blank. Go.

"The secret," Harry said, "is that eternal
Fluctuations make us workers here
On this great hill of art, where on a clear
And not-too-populous day one notes the vernal
Intemperance of carnival—we cheer
The musing flowers on their slapping way."

And Bukaku hadn't yet met him so had not yet intro-
Duced me to him I was reading, voraciously, Guido Gozzano

The pink air was guzzly a little and fashionable

Harry, in any case, now in appearance, says
"Call up!" The eternity of messengers was behind us
Scattered all over, the roses of the Bois de Boulogne.
It's very convenient to be there, the earth is a phone
So, Worm, you can call anyone—Whose are the fragrant cashews of this
    spring
Of Roman-Indian fragrance, out into that "cool gray dock"—of "advance"

"If only we had done something, really,
Like inventing the steam
Engine. When we do (invent something), though, it instantly dwarfs us."
I thought Rilke must be standing in that zoo,
Said Dan, so I went up to him, I
Thought, but it was von Spitz, inventor of the atomic stream.

A fiery bracelet. Dishes pile up later.
Don't criticize me so much
I couldn't—I will—I don't think anyone will
Remember my sensations. Sometimes it seemed
All I was doing was going to sleep
Or trying not to. Did the smokestack throw
Less fire because of hell me?
In any Etruscan I found it was all there.

If they're not actual—I mean, outside!
I don't care—or think they could be outside,
They are, I can get to them! I plan to speak
To someone—the first breasts of the sky—shush!—Go to sleep!

The house on Hydra when we lived there once
Was a small house whose whiteness was its wall.
We actually stayed there just two months
Of wide, hot summer scrambling into fall.
The waves against the stones made noise like punts
While walk along and Katherine says Good-ball
Good-bye. Goats as from a frieze
Make blunt the room.

So did my white shirt-cuffs—cow path,
Jessica stays at loops, Mycene December
And French autumn, Christmas, blackness, risky
Flower arrangements, so that above the prow
Emeritus mummies appear, clement to wake us up—
The elegant white-pink of an eggshell dusked
By damask in the magician's petrified cloth—

On the side of the sparkling
Glass sliver—something—peace
In its light-red-blue reflection.
Dan puts it to some use

This earliestness has wings, like Fra Angelicos, in cars

The bed was white
Its sheets were
The moon (or what- who-ever was there) was waiting
In the morning
I bent, leaning
From one to another place

Vision of Machu Picchu, God what heights! (one minute)
Botticelli's Venus—two seconds—
Three minutes, eight minutes,
Planning to go there, being there, *che splendida giovane!*

Do you remember the storms, the depressions, the unbelievable
Disasters? and when you think of them, can you sleep
And eat? I thought my life was going to be a scrapbook,
It turned out, instead, to be a heap.
A heap of what? Noël said, laughing. Joanne was laughing,
Her skirt was on a spot
Slightly blue-colored on her right leg, white skirt
Now her gray eyes peer at Speed across the tabletop
Speed! tell me, when are you seeing Dan?
As in a Yeats triptych cognitized in a dream
Skittering, warm summer morning. A day of the orange
Expense account of fragile invested sunlight
But I said Which? Orin was switching the lights
I didn't want to think about or forget
The mesh, of the subway, the powder on the table
Is blowing somewhere else.
Irganian Eskimos asked him for his life
In bondage in the snow, to which he savantly replied
Yes and no, sleeping my way out
Focusing on the pale night
Driven into the streets
Desire to find out
Dripping and edged with green and orange paint
What institutions connected to what sensations?
Law to nudity?

Bread without thought.

Advancing to the typewriter (sheep), and unboxedly looking at the sky
    (weak), the
Bones of the climate and the poles, one week

The stems in the throats of those conversations!
The strong young woman emerging—Venus, not
Music playing behind.
At other times, stunned time, time being stunned, stunned
Intervals and times of anxiety's careering like a body
Inside the regular body, with nerves
All that seem in between

In Paris there was no one. It was cold out there
But it was something. Inside you was a baby.
Inside Thomas Hardy was *Jude*. I thought
What is in me? A day of secret stuttering doors is in me

"Elle craque, tu sais, elle absolument craque!" syzygy
And blankets of stars which would put even Dan out on a limb
Of "Unusual groceries!" whereas, touching his chin—Loves, good-bye!
However, my hat doesn't ever get away from them
Keeping so busy I had no time to go out
When anything was open or anybody wanted to go with
Me—You're lucky! said Jim. Do
Come in, said rafafafa of daisies
But necessary be welcome to this town
And sit and read

He is very encouraging, usually, in particular
For whatever you propose. Going to drink coffee
Listen! My head is going to blow off if I do
But yes, let's go, quickly! Aspects of a job
That can only be done magnetically. You've got it!
Laughing and coughing in a brightly lighted street
Or a dull gray one, away from
The bright sun I saw him—the funeral
Men and women glaring at their sleeves unhinged

Do you remember the "real writers" of nineteen-fifty?
Do you remember the pretension of that spot?

Lake Sholem Aleichem was produced off-Broadway in nineteen-fifty-seven—
Dogwoods, meant for the next year, was never done.
Do you remember the bad faggots and the crackpots?
The masses of mouldy customers and the crumps? the grumps
The unsatisfied? Do you recall the Eliot Divide?
The bad, sad, and second-rate, our souls unsatisfied?
Painters shifting a place there with the paintbrush
Ain't doin nothin, nothin that counts! And it
Was true, too—
Apartment-wall-side proposed to a flame
And kept the villains inside
Who wanted to come veering out (melodies) while
Cracking a whip above the dances (waltzes) and
Wouldn't let the moon inside
The paintings! Outside on the side-
Walk side, where time was the clout of all their canvasses,
Men walk by. Sighs
Over Garbo and Dietrich, jumping excitement over Coleman
(Ornette)? Do you remember the cordite starring in *Diaspora*? Good, and
    bad!
What dark red afternoon did Otto Luenig
Afford my snobbery vis-à-vis Stefan Wolpe as Frank crushed
Dissension by seeing the bright in everything? It's cold in here

And it was a dawn
In nineteen-fifty-eight, firing pin on the levees.
A flood is coming! Over the hill
Dan kept moving. Reading Stendhal
La Vie de Henri Brulard in nineteen-eighty
I said my goal be that!

The celebrated "inside-outside" feelings
X wrote Y when he was only twenty-one
A cherry tree (sneeze) of precocity
Annual mump
I wonder about the fig tree

On Island Ump—Hydra
Your red silk is freezing
On this sand-of-me-beep-through-the-car day.
Why a car should talk
(Seemingly) and a head
Be blinded (for a moment) I don't know.
Why am I not a tropical man?
If I can look at all these things and not be blinded, what do I think
I think at one moment and at the next moment I don't
I am blinded
Think
I see the plate
I live in this civilization
Dumbbell

All the same, though, this sad night seemed lost
And others right then, too
Nonetheless blathering hoop-la absconding frequently
Filled my days and creepings with such abundance of regardings
And suddenly (it seemed so) glad fixations on
The non-parliamentary procedures sun
Shining to plate, I said, Dearest when all this is done
When are we going to get anywhere or know anything
Slate, faculty, and pocketbook. Bust, she regarded
The soon-maidened day. Well, we will! she said.

An upward look, which is depenetrated
Southernly, by a stretch of Freud. Oh look at the complexes
The dust road is wet
Clouds' days are climbing all around.

They roll
The top
To show
The lot
How climbed

And clean
The hill was.

But well a day
It stops to say
(The air)
My clouds
Are pillows!

So run, run!
This is not
Herrick nor John Donne
But some modern
Inky fellow's
Prized Armageddon
De syllabes.

And on one opaque filled-with-joy daylight-blue-and-pink-and-white-faced
    morning
She kissed him on the cheek
Whereupon

For five hours of which the first fifty-five
Minutes are the most intense. Joanne, stopping
And with letters

They always do find them, said Dan.
He took the manacles off Schiavona's wrists.
And went home talking about *The Alchemist*
The good the bad acting the dubious kind of direction
The musty smell of the theater and the rest.
D'you like it—them, replied.
This lunchtime. Oh, how—
Bearing secondary (or supernumerary) parts. I am on the ledge
Later the doctored-up paintings and
Alone, cold

Sitting in the bundled coats and thinking Well
It's over. The lamp went out.

The car, *quel tas de* junk
And U. was at the wheel, ridiculously drunk
And divided between about five girlfriends
I was so much older I should have been in the trunk
But I was there, am, now, however, edging my shoulder
Past C-Jump I could see that with every act
I was hoping and she was singling some quality out
To arrive at later with better but could not afford now
To be the one I buttoned on clothes with; still, there she was
Radiating fullness in the car,
Once home, no chill, relief, cabbage in the dawning
No those are light green cloudlets coming up the trees
So then I go to bed, it's as in the car—snore,
Raffle, awake, then back to slump, and sleep—

The wavy secretary speaks at the bend
Of the desk office, now I am met by the head
Agent. I stand up, the secretary's gone. Good-bye.

Beautiful figure
Of everything! Then
Suddenly down the sidewalk
Comes the truth
In the form of a girl
Into 35 rue Notre Dame des Champs
Hey, is this the closest place
To where I want to be? Noël says
A joke is a joke. Come on, take
The box out. We don't
Quarrel, actually. B-17,
Farewell.

Two girls
Ana and Svenita
One of them
Is studying Arabic
What do I care?
The water glass is on
The Frigidaire
An American patent
A big heavy white bird
Flown from America
To here in France
I place my
Hand on Svenita's
Shoulder—
And the white flag
Of seasonal peripheries
Is scuttering everybody
To dunk back into the beds
Whereupon suddenly
All the same

It is a force (Yeats)
A catastrophe (Quevedo)
A chase (Montgomery)
A flower (Keats)
And beauty with a graveled mace has done
I see her at the airplane counter—South

Outstretched—North-wind rubberband?
Is it religous
To dream of the Southern Cross?
The band is playing, the Riviera has walks—
Whiteness today is our special, I mean of the sun—

In Nice upon the Walk attired in whitest
Silks and linens men and women went
Forwards and backwards in what seemed the brightest
Light to earth the sun had ever sent
Baking the sidewalks white, with an excitement
Felt only insofar as it was meant
To be the belt of paradise around one,
When, striped with thirst, one stops beside a fountain

The white roadway shines ahead it is
A sidewalk! In front
Beyond the windows' cou-cou-cou. I grow up
Into these shades, white and referenced
Of slender wood, somebody being always nervous about the time

Tremulous and capsizing fresh stone in the hall
On which you stumble—I catch you—
Today is seeming, in truth, a beautiful day
"You use that word too much" is a seeming
Indifferent, well maybe not so much, distinction
And the restaurant of the animals, door, is hay
Which to them smells "beautiful" and I am out my door "beautiful"
Day, sitting on the speech stump and worrying about the door—

Comatose *amidon*
Hand held and then released
Stairways
Always on the edge of
Seeming to want
The book opened and then the book

What is outside—cars, windows
Abroad what is inside—aimlessness, scarves,
Or, in another view, thoughts,
First smell of cattle over the evening
The burning (hot was used as an ashtray) shell

Later evenings—it was already summer
Reflections of the outside
Taking the inside's form and making it follow

A grassiness is bursting in the light
That makes it seem more than autonomous.
A good trick, then, to be phoning. My (our) "nerves."
Visiting, it's vicious, it's long-gone time.
I walk down this sidewalk it's *frappant* it takes where you are

Blossomingness—and she says, You have a car, yes
We hot car have legs, shine cross, then, there
High nothingness elevator my clock "re-spaced"
Tables away, plates away, gavels away, the nothing
And something in a yellow dress while
Someone in a blue and white shirt bends over
Something made of wood with four legs. I hadn't read
Marcabru yet. Oh an
Old friend's poem, encased in a letter,
Smelling of soap,
January morning, while a truck goes past.
A word decelerated from a window. Type
Evaporated
From a newspaper. *Daily Cross.* Done
Nineteen forgotten
Centuries
Of progress, red
Shoes, white linen
The Russians are doing an experiment
In painting. Summer
Collapsed on summer like a clothes-
Pin snap on a piece of clothes.

He asked her to dance.
So Larry and I go to look at the picture
Of Z. Z. de A. pinching the nipple of Bambambomba

Dominique Celestin *qu'en sais-je* with the little briny street
The painters lived on, whiter than a mule of hay
And vigorous in a blank unquestioning manner

It was sixty-five degrees
Out. Perfect ("perfect") weather.

All right, let's get married. Will you marry me?
This marriage is done. I want you back.
You never had me. Bringing the suitcases around.
Bringing them back. Sitting in the Hotel de Fleurus.
This floor is sandy. With you,
The best way is to separate today

I couldn't then—Oliver says Think it over!
But lost for that holiday. It stings, it
The Greek art collection, walking
Sideways, it was hard to keep up. The greatest person ever to come in
This restaurant. Her fine-boned person
And rouge et le lipstick all around
For all anyone ever understood
About it, really

John said The hula hoop identity
Of all these straw persons interests me
Then finally he was promoted
To laugh at the bar of heaven We poets are the Jews of Literature
Scamping around at me—Especially you!

I can't believe you're doing this—not insured
Not protected by anything, I felt her hand, wristbone, of my own
The Danilova equivalent, a starring baggage—then chair
Being have brought out upon the sidewalk
The bed that Dan raved about checks in with and this suit

Printed in gray letters, on the top of the fire escape,
Look at it Guillevic said, look, look at it!
Proof that we live forever, or at least in a magazine!
For example, and we look at it. Place it
On top near the coffee, well, that's all right

Going out into the flawed light meter
Of a desky October day
Cutting it so closely as she did with the card
Then off cut a little bit of her hair top too with the names
I don't know where to put the import actually
Outside or in

Listen, I'm up—electric hand
Go to my shoe and bind it to those feet
That walked around the wings
I was unwrapping
Profit from it smiling what where is it

Hidden underneath South winds tabletop
Centered on
Each of us, face gone
To wondering silently about
A day and its intimate whether
I should have been in the storm with her or not

Alone without shoes she is bending half the time
Morning comes but safely takes away its wild go-out-
To-get-me-something spared by the future Palatine
Formed which the weeds shout. Two girls, one acting lazy
And the other hooking around, then S. X. comes to the door
The ballet is grazing, across that marble floor
In such time we sectioned off a daisy—I said
On time, but admit today's a failure
Because of its electricity

Drunk in my white suit at Noël Lee's house
Taking a shower I thought
Essences, never seeing anything at all
So wrapped around me as collectedness
And then (she) going to sleep, bearing me goes up
To future sky, post-Cubism, nineteen sailing nought
To cure all that
Dashing, but it won't work. Summer *französisch*. Your love.
Gunshot. These partings from some
Time

Flowers umphing around
And scratch to this to that for
I and the skirt the body sums
Keeping and smiling up
To walk

It's in the goat
And in the footnote.
It lamps what is not to come
As well as what is, a bannister of bones and a hat.
It felt like forever.
It feels "interrogating flat." It feels shown.
Vanning about and straggling. Why is it so unknown?
Getting out of the car and going back.

Seasons on Earth

There is a way of thinking about happiness
As being at one's side, so that one has but
To bend or turn to get to it; and this
For years I thought was true. Or that a basket
Of sensual sensations brings a bliss
That makes one as the winner is at Ascot.
With *Ko* I had the first idea; the second
(Some first one, too) went with the story of Papend.

With strong opinions and with ignorance,
And with indifference and with aggression,
With my own odd idea of what made sense
And being happy some sort of an obsession,
Ignoring most contrary elements
By going outside, or changing the discussion,
I used to live for it, like cows for clover—
By my hot, happy sense of things bowled over.

In spite of the real suffering around me,
And poverty, and spite, I had the sense
That there was something else. Each midday found me
Ecstatically in the present tense,
Writing. And you would have to come and pound me
Quite hard to drag me from my innocence.
That sense that now seems almost unbelievable—
I love it, loved it—is it irretrievable?

Well, now, at sixty—please, some frankness, Muse!
I think about it less. It's an accompaniment
Of doing what I ought to do; and news
Affects it, and the vagaries of my temperament,
To some degree unchanging. I find clues
In books, in actions done and statements somebody meant
To be the truth, in love, with its crescendos,
And traveling, sometimes, looking out the windows.

There's no way now I can be quite believing
All feeling will take shape and I'll go walking
Up to that place where light blue air is weaving
A cloud supply for birds to fly through, squawking,
And that each exquisite sensuous day or evening
Is an announcement of a door unlocking
Inviting me to enter. Oh, my narratives,
That kept me thinking of such kinds of paradise!

I had the thought while I was writing *Ko*
To get into the poem every pleasure
I'd ever had. The Ortopedico
Was down the hill and, up the hill, the treasure
Of arms and legs that Michelangelo
Gave to his *David* white and huge of measure.
Janice and Katherine, like a Perugino
Mary and Child, shared with me the *villino*.

I was at that time thirty-one or thirty-
Two, even then glad I had lived so long,
Long enough to influence history's verdict
(I still believed in that) by my big song
Of baseball, youth, and love. No way the Arctic
Of death, disease, or pain had bent the strong
Support floor of my being: happiness,
I thought, was what life came to, more or less.

White days above the Orthopedic Hospital!
That patients came to from all over Florence—
Some young, some not so far from a centennial,
Though few from Rome, and none, I think, from Corinth.
Three miles away, about, the railway terminal
Next to the church where the Uccellos aren't—
They're *in restauro*—gave out toots and whistles
To friends and lovers kissing near its trestles.

Down the hill this side streetcar tracks connecting,
And the Piazza, and the via Forlini
Gave someone who old Florence was expecting
A slight shock, being plain as boiled zucchini.
White hat white coat policemen though, directing
Us cross the bridge guide us to what has meaning
Historically, aesthetically, emotionally—
Statues and Giottos known here almost socially!

We spent long minutes waiting for the bus that
Went up our hill, the M, pronounced the Emmay—
A wait it would be very hard to fuss at,
Rather the kind to put in mind an M. A.
Thesis on the Sublime, or wait till dusk at
Until its beauties vanished like a mermaid
On one side into walls, on one to sloping
Of hills around. Who could be there not hoping

That that white some-such in the air betokened
A happy state convincing as an iron is
Pressed on a shirt whose collar has been opened,
Or sight of dogwoods in the Carolinas?
Inside our house we had someone to cook and
Help care for Katherine, who was two years minus
Some months, and make our sweaters bright with Woolite
While Janice read Gozzano on her Fulbright.

We'd come there in the winter. February
Already brought warm sunlight to the shoulders
Of Perseus, and to the Virgin Mary
In Convento San Marco, as to boulders
On the long walks we took; and on one airy
Young day, while gazing at some yellow folders,
I wrote three stanzas that made me feel dizzy with
Delight, as if I wrote for Queen Elizabeth—
In fact it was an Ariostic azimuth
I tried to trace, of all things on earth vis-à-vis.

Such happiness, it seems to me, that went
Into my stanzas, paradisal octaves!
My mind from death and heart from hell were bent
Each day as I pursued the same objectives:
The getting all that *primavera* meant
Into my work. I heard Divine directives:
Those poets write of bones, but truth is elsewhere.
Keep at it till you get to the elixir!

It was the time, it was the nineteen-fifties,
When Eisenhower was President, I think,
And the Cold War, like *Samson Agonistes,*
Went roughly on, and we were at the brink.
No time for Whitsuntides or Corpus Christis—
Dread drafted all with its atomic clink.
The Waste Land gave the time's most accurate data,
It seemed, and Eliot was the Great Dictator
Of literature. One hardly dared to wink
Or fool around in any way in poems,
And Critics poured out awful jereboams
To *irony, ambiguity,* and *tension*—
And other things I do not wish to mention.

All this fell sideways past our Florence windows—
That is, it had not much attention paid to it.
Dry, stultifying words, they were horrendous,
Inspiring in the breast a jolly hatred—
And then new lines arose, like snakes to Hindus,
That for *depressed* spelled out *exhilarated.*
O metaphors! Compelling satisfactions!
The truth might be in the right mix of actions—
Like snow in spring with lilac's blue reflections:

You can call me on Saturday she said.
The hippopotamus walked in the room
And then, with a blue towel around its head,
Ran straight to the sky-mirroring lagoon,
Sank to its knees, rolled over, and played dead.
Meanwhile, Ceylon experienced a monsoon—
Such sequences, perhaps, if gotten right,
Might find the truth, as flowers find the light.

Outside the house, azaleas in a clump
Where I pick Katherine up and set her "walking,"
With hopes that she may reach yon mossy stump—
Jan, *in cucina, con* Erzilia talking—
All this to whirl in one poetic lump
To make a shape of with a heart knock-knocking.
Domestic trials, quiets, and disturbances,
Tourism, friendship, love and its observances.

Other days, I took some days off, some pesky
Insect or sound might drive me out, I'd stare at
The Foundling Hospital of Brunelleschi
That in my Blue Guide was one-starred for merit,
Or was it two? It very much impressed me—
Early straight Tuscan columns that a parrot
Could fly among and find no place for resting.
And in its laboratories there was testing.

Confusing and mysterious places, clinics
With stars in guidebooks, landmarks, like the Hôpital
Saint Louis in Paris, art and its gimmicks
In serious places, as if in *Das Kapital*
Marx had included flowery script and comics!
Dark streets and light all part of my occipital
Amazement, and where Dante, pre-*Inferno*,
Stood and saw Beatrice on the Lungarno.

Writing my lines, I felt them close as skin-tight:
What I did in the shiny afternoon,
When I was walking round, was part of insight,
And when I ate, or looked at a cartoon.
Whatever happened fell in place. I'd think I'd
Run out of lines, but then I'd see the moon
Running across sky's Arno like a searchlight
To shine for me some thought upon a churchside.

My life was in the poem and just outside it.
Nothing was written as it "really happened"
But all took place as rhyme and chance decided.
My typewriter was there, my pencils sharpened.
Ko pitched and made the team and was delighted
And threw so hard the grandstand beams were opened;
Exit the old ex-catcher. I spent hours
Walking around in the all-kinds-of flowers

That gracious grasped the hillslopes with their sweetly
Beguiling selfness. Doris looked at Andrews
And knew now she could love someone completely.
April then May came fluttering through the branches
Of peach and pear tree all around the neatly
Landscaped young villa two miles from the campers.
You, six months pregnant, lost the baby; it was
The saddest thing that ever happened to us.

You almost died. They tried to give you oxygen
In the wrong way, in the bare-beamed Municipal
Hospital. I helped save you. They were lax again
With blood. Good God! All life became peripheral,
A mess, a nightmare, until you were back again.
My poem had not a trace of these things medical;
But it was full of dyings and revivings
And strange events, that went past plain connivings—

Such as the thrust of Asia to the east
And men turned into statues. There was also
My whole past that came fizzing up like yeast—
Joy in the fact that Ko could throw a ball so
And Pemmistrek a hog. Good health increased.
I wrote some things for *Poetry* Chicago.
Alouette went to Asia, doing well
With an enormous, new resort hotel.

Life in the work? It is as if two orchestras
Played separately and sometimes simultaneously—
One from inside, deep down, where García Lorca says
Duende dwells, which sometimes intravenously
Gets fed by that outside—thus, metamorphosis!
Lamp into day. Or else a drumbeat famously
Heartlike inside turns snowflakes on the windowsills
To sounds like cries, and then abstracter syllables.

Should one be ignorant? Did I have knowledge
Instinctively I don't have now? Is knowing,
The kind one gets from every kind of college,
The opposite of the ecstatic showing
Of what life is in the amazing sandwich
Of art? Is wisdom sun? Or is it snowing?
And how much of one's life and where it's going
Gets in the work? How is it filtered? altered?
What paths through clouds rise from the chocolate malted
One drinks on a hot day and feels exalted?

Is that truth truth still now that all is older—
I, Tuscany, our language, Katherine, *tutto*?
Truth now that I come to experience colder
Than ever I did then, less *absoluto*,
With more "good sense," with decades in my folder
Of proofs that quite a lot of things are futile—
What's left? what lasts? Does it make sense to bring out
Old poems again? O bells that ring ding ding out

There in the air and do not have this problem!
Give me advice; or you, convulsive air!
You, hill; you, field; you, tree, great candelabrum!
New, nature still exists, but what is *there*—
There, I mean, in the words I wrote while Katherine
Was sleeping and her mother stitched her bear?
Then some years later when all strong sensations
I had I hurled into *The Duplications*?

The Duplications! Hardly is that word out
When a vast image out of Spiritus Mundi
Reminds me of what it was all about:
Life as a violent wild event-packed Sunday
That makes the people scream and makes them shout
And ply the sky as if in search of funding—
Venice and Samos, Stockholm and Peru,
London and Athens, gardens in the blue.

There was no Florence anymore, however,
And no sweet feeling of a Quattrocento
Harmonious mix of you, me, and the weather—
No Poliziano and *Io mi rammento*,
No *tutte cose* coming all together
And intimacy springlike as Sorrento—
The street was gray and modern; and our marriage
Was more than I could mend with my then courage.

My writing now was more investigation,
Or, better yet, a sort of archaeology
Set out to find the great civilization
That once existed, maybe; an apology,
Also, for what I couldn't do. Sensation
Was what it rode on, action its theology—
Away from all that troubled you and me so,
In a sort of poetic *paradiso*.

That *Ko*-like bliss—I had grown so attached to it,
Could use it writing, it was even practical—
Made me think bliss could be mine with no catch to it,
No fear, no fret, no nothing but sabbatical,
As if it were my, not I its, constituent.
Anxiety, any strain, seemed unaesthetical:
Not now, I felt, I thought, Don't pain, don't tire me!
I'm in a state, and that may disinspire me.

Now fifteen more years later, looking at them,
These poems, of different times and different systems
Of using life as if one had a patent
On its effects without regard to wisdom,
I feel sometimes delight—and sometimes flattened.
What is there, that I am at sixty, in them?
How can I ever hope to get in synch with
What they're about? What do I have to think with?

What's here if I'm not that same sensual Kenneth
Of years ago, nuts for exhilaration
And always willing to convene the Senate
Of nudes and nights and nerve-ends of the nation
For one great further push through the impenet-
Rable Castello del Realization,
To its high hall where, on the gods' advice,
Is painted the true face of Paradise?

What is, I want to know, the truth if there is
Truth in the view of things I had, and what is
The source, if it's mistaken, of its errors?
Do we come into life with minds and bodies
Ready to live in some ecstatic Paris
Or is the limit of our lives more modest?
Is there a seed in us? are we the pod? Is
The blossom pleasure, and the fruit the goddess?
Did you too ever feel it, like a promise,
That there could be a perfect lifetime, Janice?

I don't know. Don't know any of this. My decades
Six now, with the beginning of a seventh,
Counsel me, sure, to dance to slower records
But I'm still trumped and bumped by glimpsed-up heavens
And think they may be true—but just for seconds.
Two words, one word, it used to be a sentence.
Nothing has come of this except my wonder
What it's about, before I'm shoveled under.

Is its being vaguer, harder to put trust in
At sixty odd, proof that it's false? or that I,
Its register, am wearing down or rusting?
Is it not, some may say so, slightly batty
To dote upon this carnival combustion
Amidst so many things that really matter?
And what about the threat to all this fluction
And fragrant life, the goddamned bomb's destruction?

They're right. You're right. I'm right. I'm wrong. I have no
Answer except the one that poets often
Sport occupationally like an Afro,
That what we give is what we have been given,
And hope we are of use that way, as Svevo
Has helped me live since I was thirty-seven.
I've been concerned with various things, and active,
But this one makes me radiantly reflective.

The question stays, for me, and in my reading
These poems again, and stays outside such study;
If I'm a house, I feel that house is leaning
And soon may fall. I want to ask somebody
What it's all been about, but not believing
I'll find the answer my young years made ready.
With things another way, might one come stumbling
To the sweet sill of truth—and get to something?
Is there a City? Was there? And a Woman
To go through death with, even, like Tutankhamen?

O sun! exhilaration! and regret!
Am I advance, or am I cataclysm?
Do I believe this anymore? Has it
Gone down, away, oh have I lost my vision?
It may be here, for I'm still hit hit hit
By what seem its surprises more than wisdom.
But—what here's mine if I'm no more that wit
To whom the academic world was poison
And every modern critic full of shit
(And all their works a spilled-out shaving kit)
And wished most poets would by dogs get bit
And was content with one good friend to sit
Or with another, in the fading glit
Of twilight, happy as a catcher's mitt
And full of futuration? In such status
How could we, I, dream of time's splintering lattice

Which would take Frank away, and Janice later,
Turn John into an Eminence—though now
We get along all right, our verbal Seder
Reconstitutes, but not those times, O Cow,
O Holy Hathor, Egypt's Cultivator,
Not those delicious moments on the brow
Of Tuscan hill, when, happy as gardenias,
We gave our souls up to the evening's genius!

It's nineteen-eighty-six, or eighty-seven,
Depending if you're reading this in holograph
Or in the book. The past, that seems quite often
To be false, or fantastic, like a hippogriff,
Or to be a huge book we have been given
Of which we've hardly time to read a paragraph,
Is in these poems, I hope, some way, at random—
Story and past as if they were in tandem—

All in these stanzas that remind to clumsiness
By needing rhymes that interrupt one's quietly
Attending to one's intellectual business;
Demanding, make one feel one can't entirely
Say what one wants, and profit from this funniness
By mixing things that in states of sobriety
One would not mix, and give the proper airiness
To what is neither chance nor arbitrariness—

Stanzas still here! how strange it is you're present!
Stanzas I wrote upon the via Susini
Where Ottavino, saying "I'm a peasant,"
Io sono contadino, pressed the greeny
Latch of the gateway, smiling as he entered.
That was fifteen years after Mussolini—
A long time past. Now, as I read you over,
There's something new I'm trying to discover.

Here it is May again. And the wisteria
Smells sweet, and there's still tape splat on my window
From last year's storm. I've planted a huge area
Of wildflowers, perennials, with no end to
Their coming back, it says. What fond hysteria
Our writing, our remembering! Where to send to
To find out what's the truth, when living tramples
Down everything it gives us as examples!

It's gone but in the head it stays and sizzles,
It's gone but in the heart it stays and sings.
It's gone, sometimes, like boomeranging missiles
And it comes back, and makes, and breaks up things.
It's past. You cannot find it. Yells and whistles
Help not at all. But when the spray first springs,
Watch out! you've got it in your pectoral muscles
And in those colors first eye-closing brings.
Is this the past? Or life's sure force, in purity,
Without the mask of memory or futurity?

Some years ago when I went back to Florence
Up past the Ortopedico to where
We'd been, I found it cluttered with deterrence—
New buildings, not quite a suburban smear,
And filled with smiling children and their parents.
Sad, I let all my sadness disappear
Going back over where we'd walked, then driving
To a new town while thinking of arriving.

O bed and base and breakfast of these times!
To work, love, and good actions the cadenzas!
O possibility, sweet chance that there is
A wholeness only hinted by the stanzas
(Struggling into existence like raspberries
Or, in the Caribbean mold, garbanzos!)—
Do you remember, Janice, the sweet Jerez
We drank ten thousand years ago in Spain when
We picnicked far from Barcelona's pavement
And you were pregnant, wearing your pink raincoat
(Which Spanish men found puzzling or hilarious,
Your being so big and garbed in such a color)
And we walked uphill talking to each other?

I want to dedicate to you these rhymes.
I know it now, it's not made of sensations,
Happiness, nor of Florence and its treasures—
Can there be something greater than all pleasures?
And true? Oh, was it ever yours and mine?

A NOTE ABOUT THE AUTHOR

Kenneth Koch published many volumes of poetry. His shorter poems have been brought together in the recently published *The Collected Poems of Kenneth Koch*, and his longer ones here, in *On the Edge*. His short plays, many of them produced off- and off-off-Broadway, are collected in *The Gold Standard: A Book of Plays* and *One Thousand Avant-Garde Plays*. He also wrote several books about poetry, including *Wishes, Lies and Dreams; Rose, Where Did You Get That Red?;* and *Making Your Own Days: The Pleasure of Reading and Writing Poetry*. His fiction appears in *Collected Fiction*. He was the winner of the Bollingen Prize (1995) and the Bobbitt National Prize for Poetry (1996), a finalist for the Pulitzer Prize (1995) and the National Book Award (2000), and winner of the first annual Phi Beta Kappa Poetry Award (2001). He was named Chevalier dans l'Ordre des Arts et des Lettres by the French government in 1999. Kenneth Koch lived in New York City and taught at Columbia University.

A NOTE ON THE TYPE

This book was set in Janson, a typeface long thought to have been made by the Dutchman Anton Janson, who was a practicing typefounder in Leipzig during the years 1668–1687. However, it has been conclusively demonstrated that these types are actually the work of Nicholas Kis (1650–1702), a Hungarian, who most probably learned his trade from the master Dutch typefounder Dirk Voskens. The type is an excellent example of the influential and sturdy Dutch types that prevailed in England up to the time William Caslon (1692–1766) developed his own incomparable designs from them.

Composed by Creative Graphics,
Allentown, Pennsylvania

Printed and bound by Berryville Graphics,
Berryville, Virginia

Designed by Soonyoung Kwon